AF333448

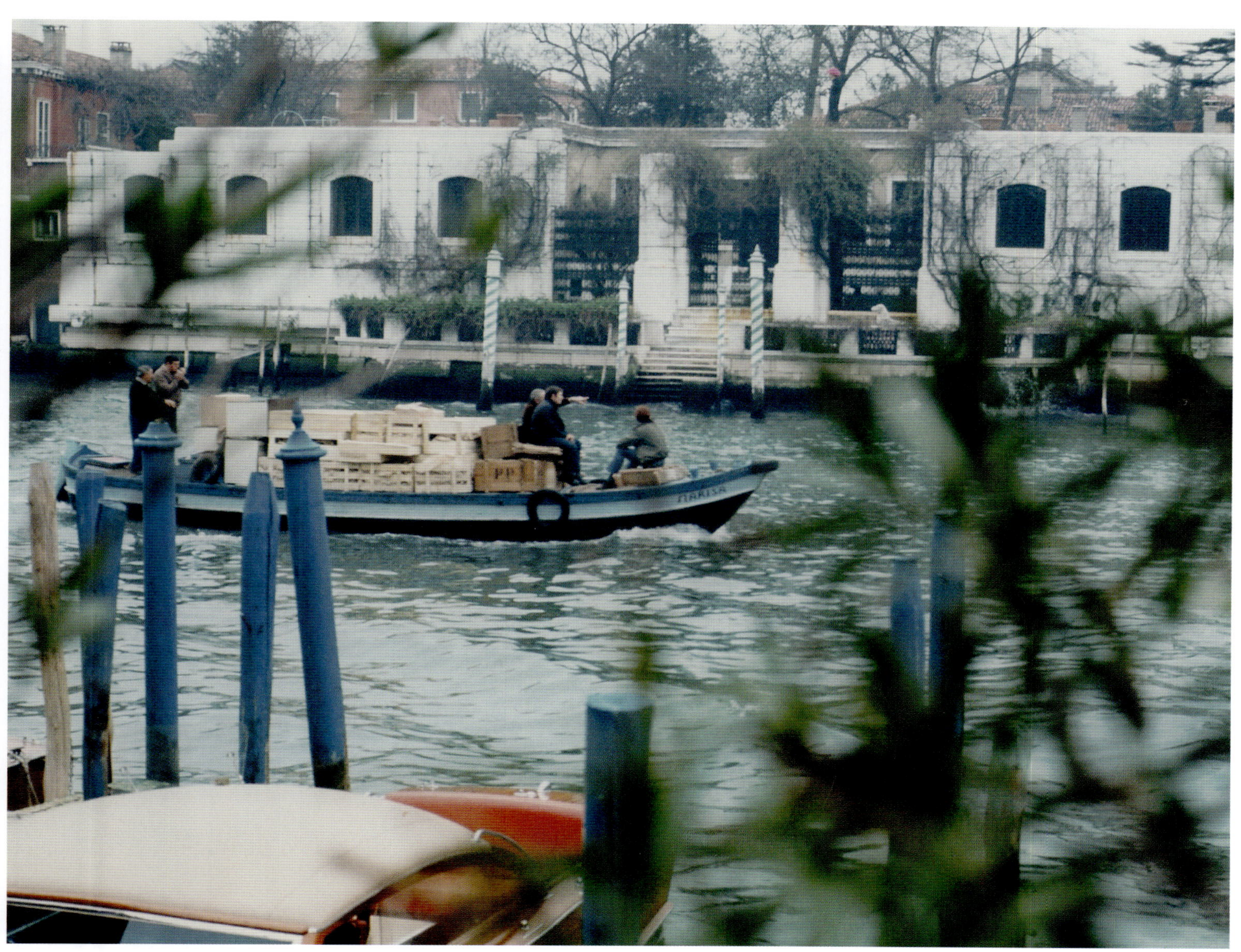

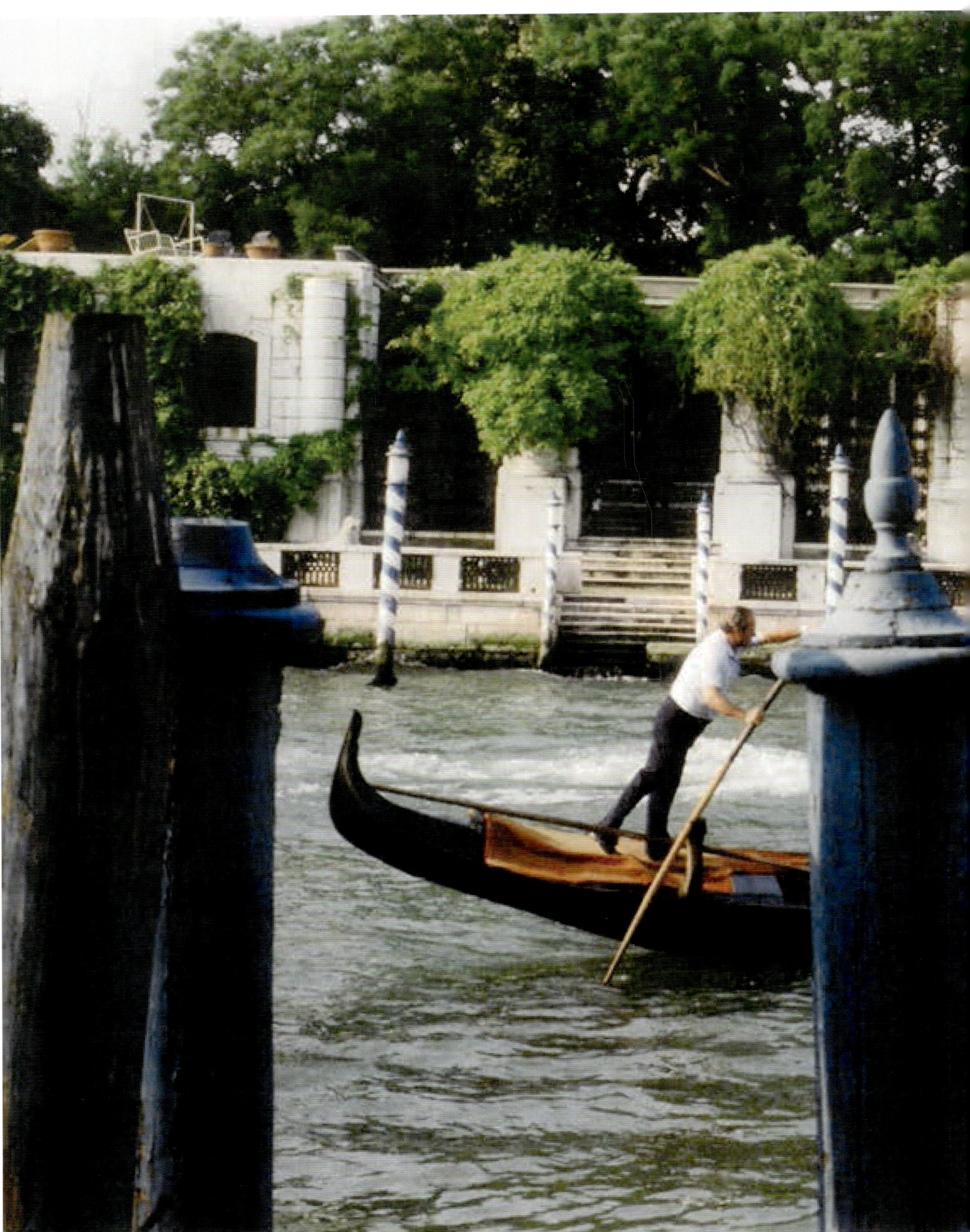

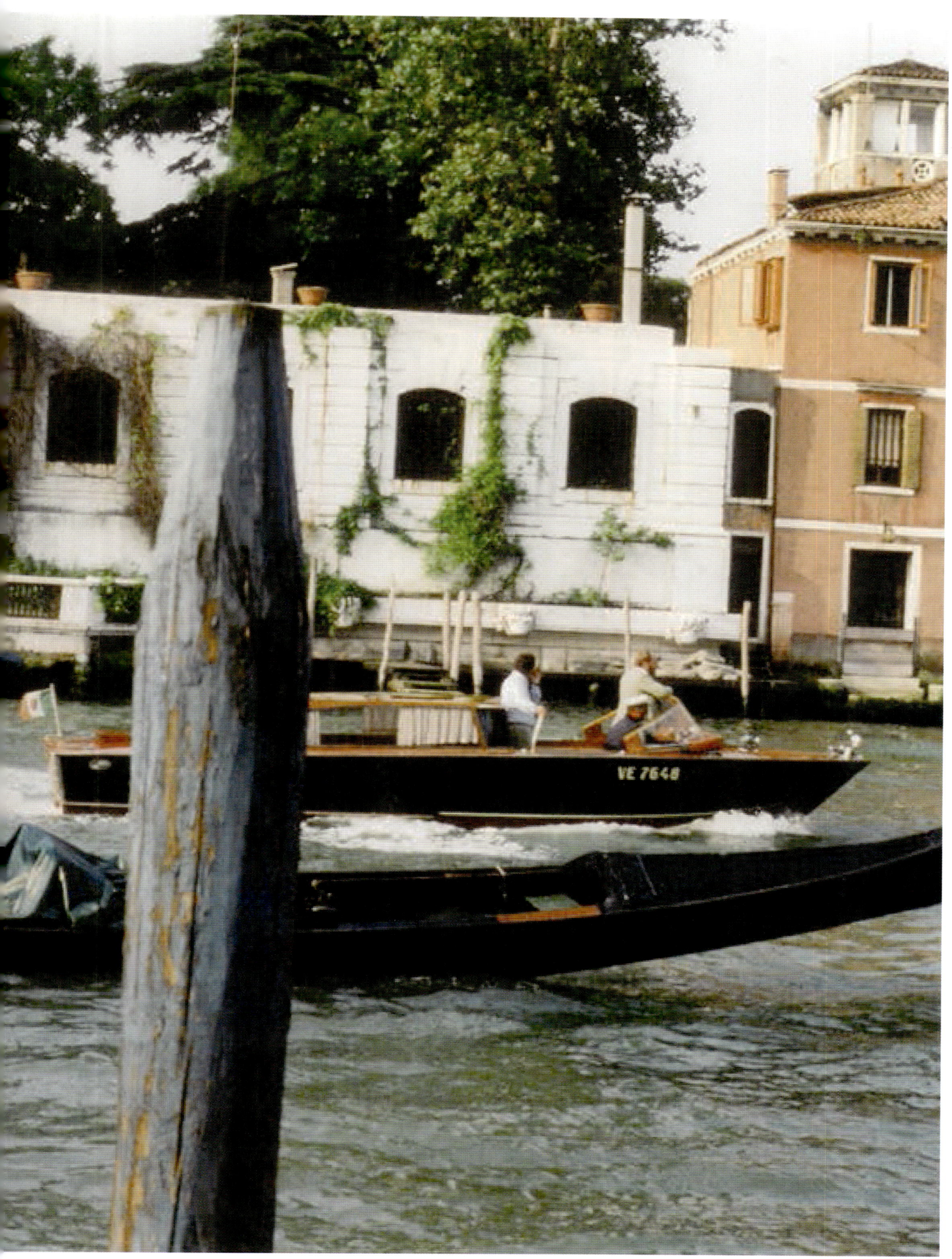

VE 7648

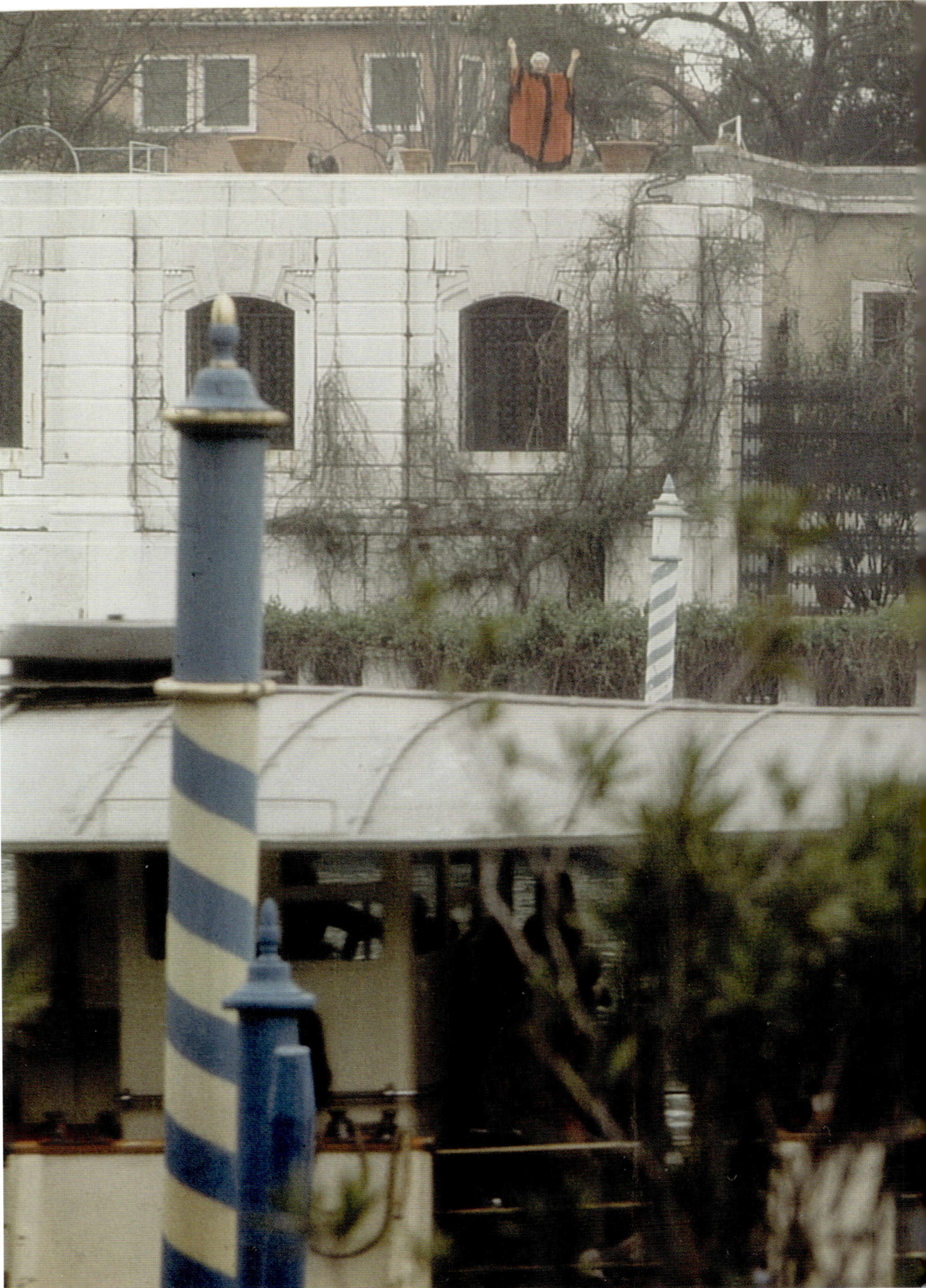

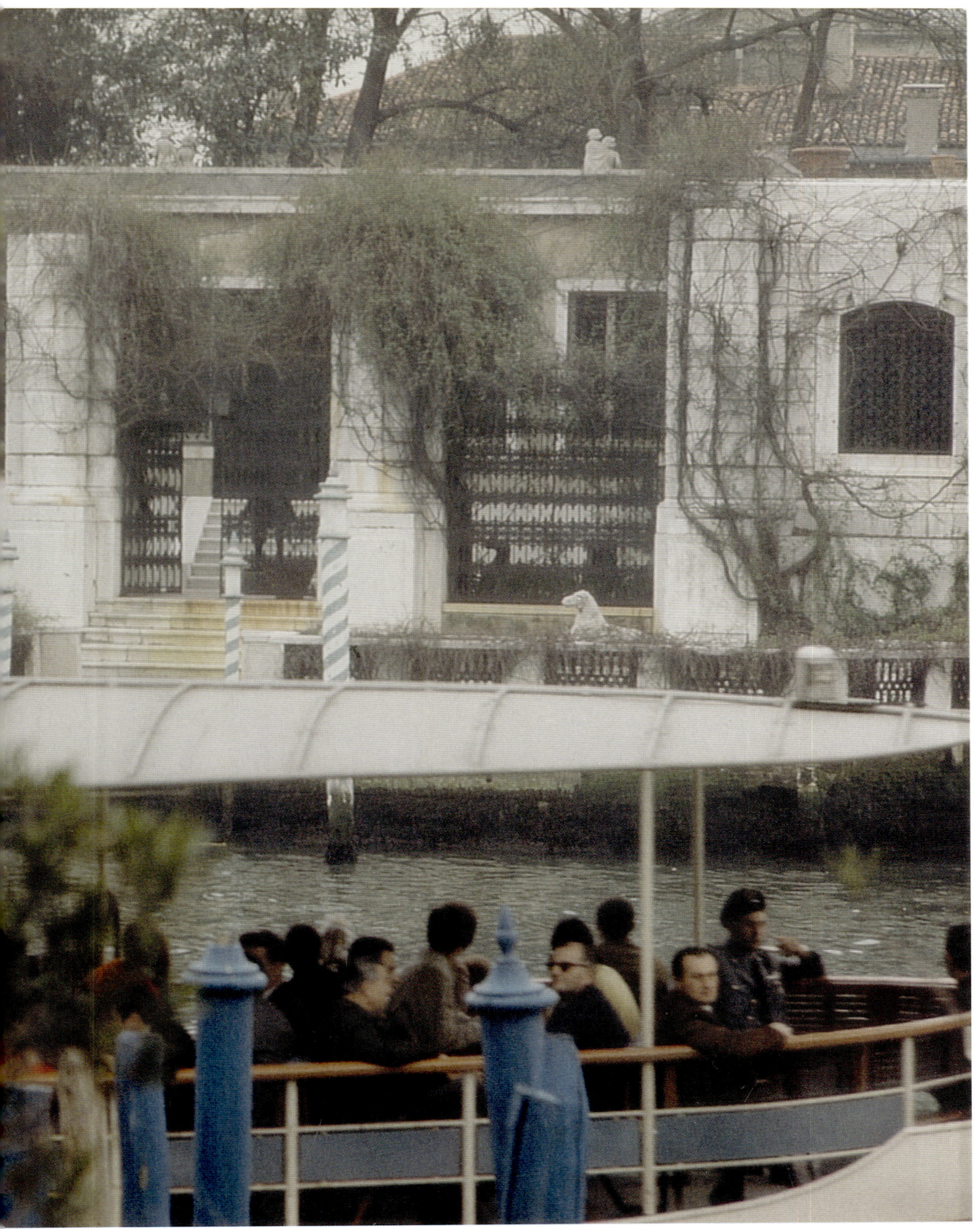

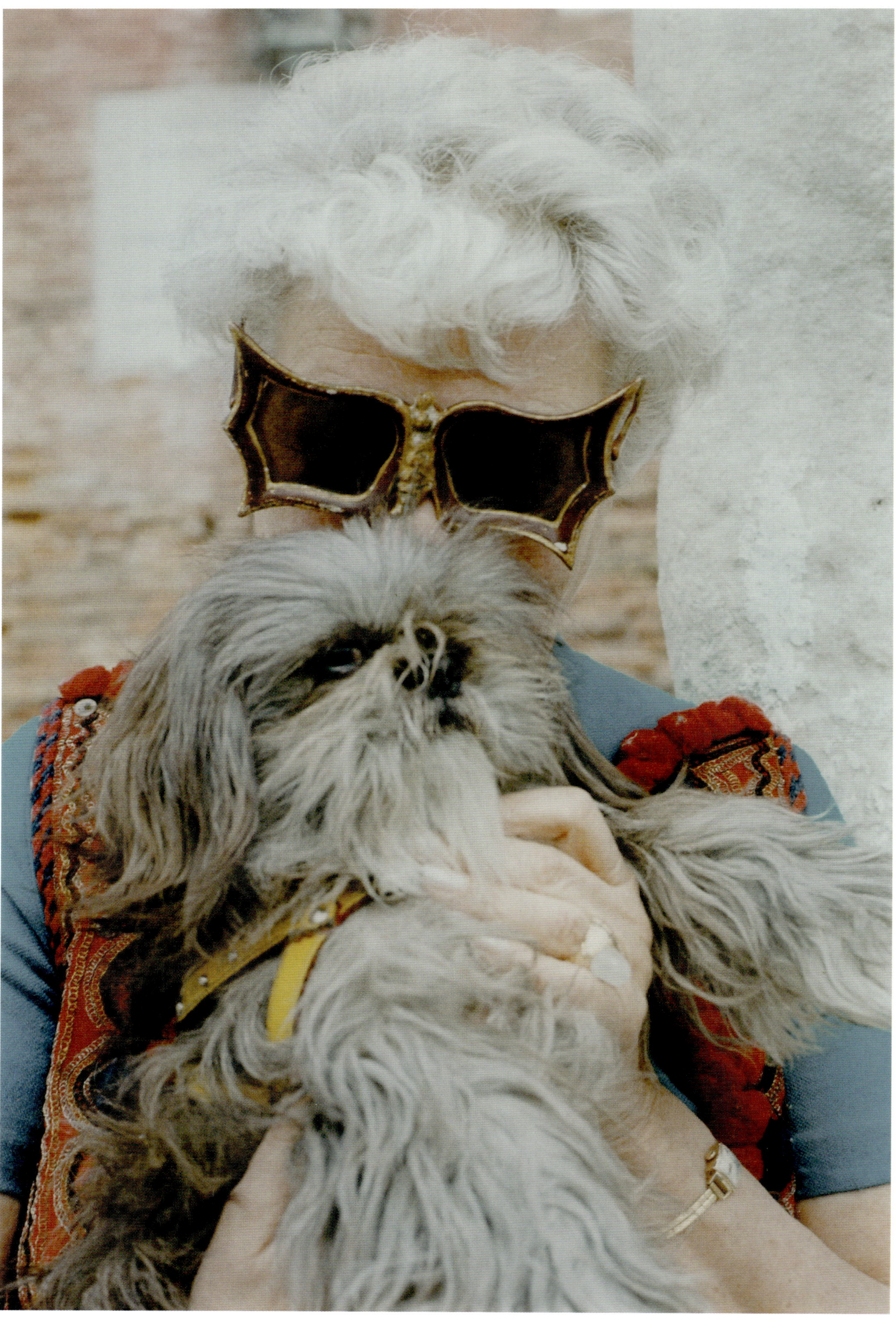

# stefan moses

## ENCOUNTERS WITH

# PEGGY GUGGENHEIM

Preface

Philip Rylands

Text

Thomas Elsen

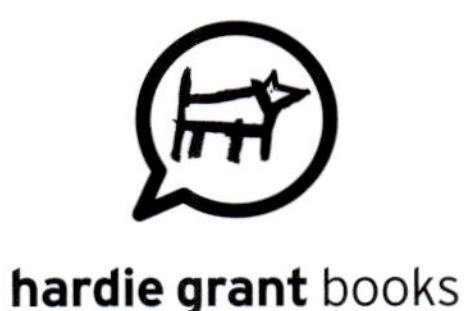

hardie grant books

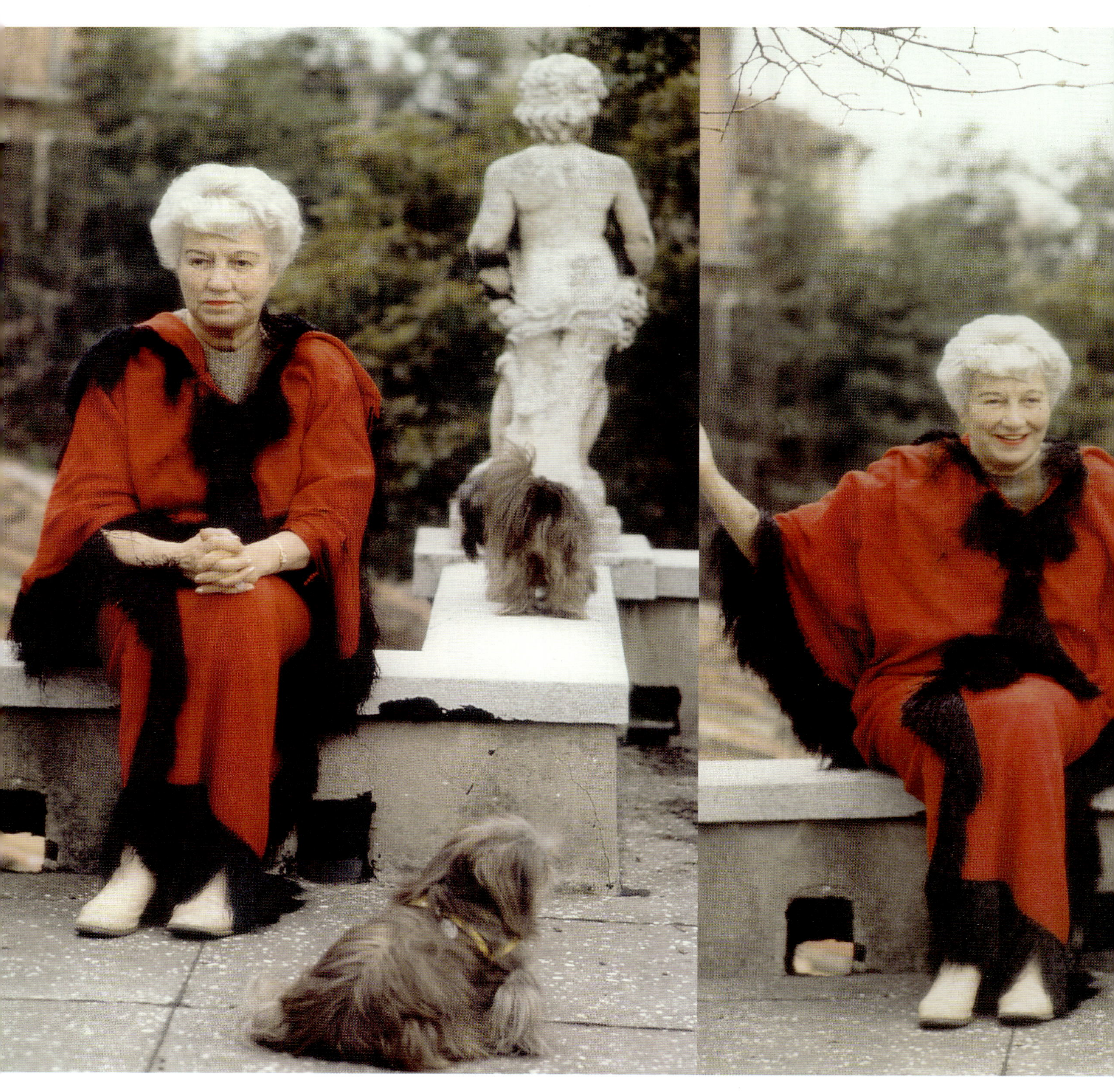

Peggy and her beloved Lhasa Apsos on the
roof terrace of Palazzo Venier dei Leoni

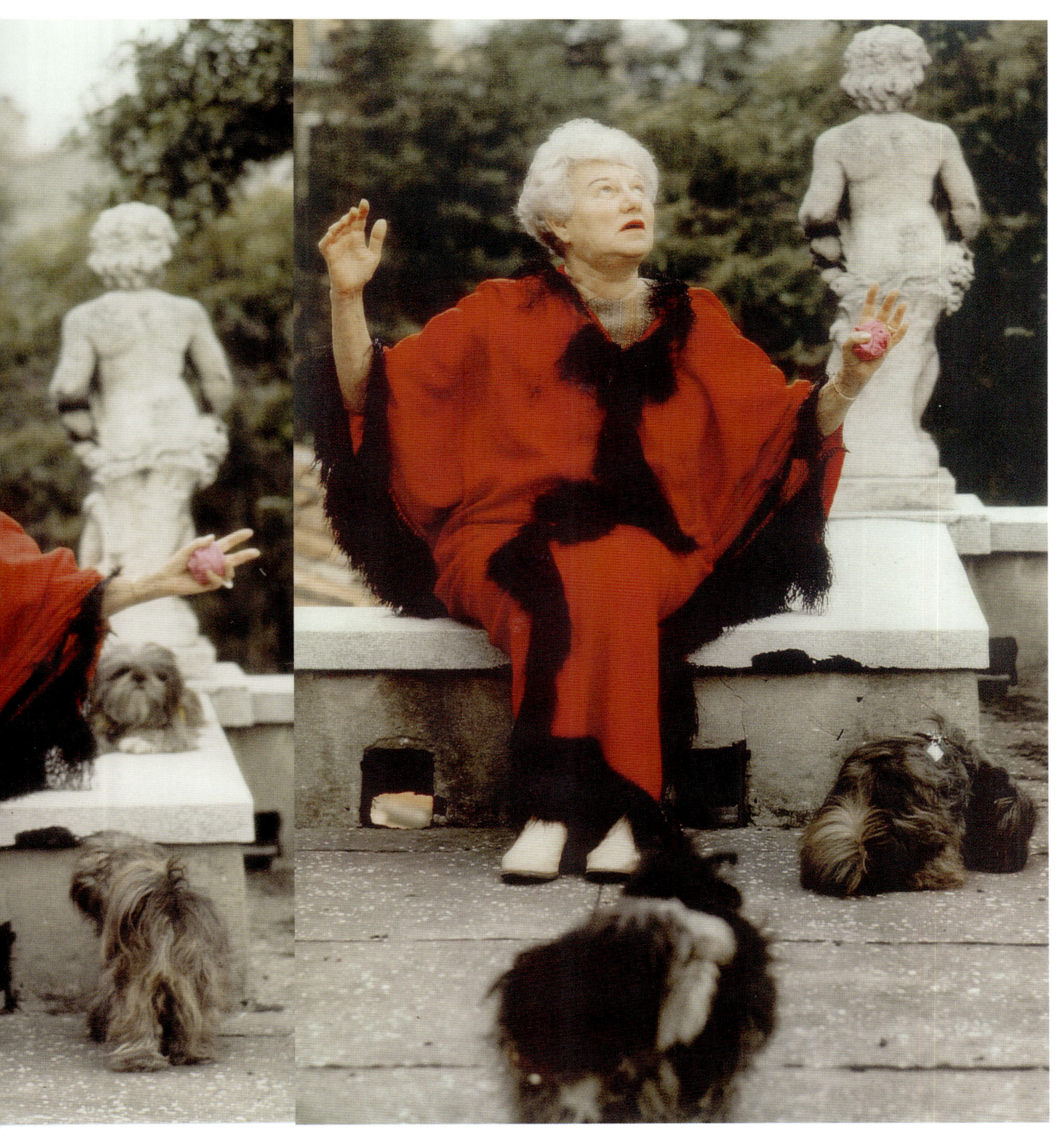

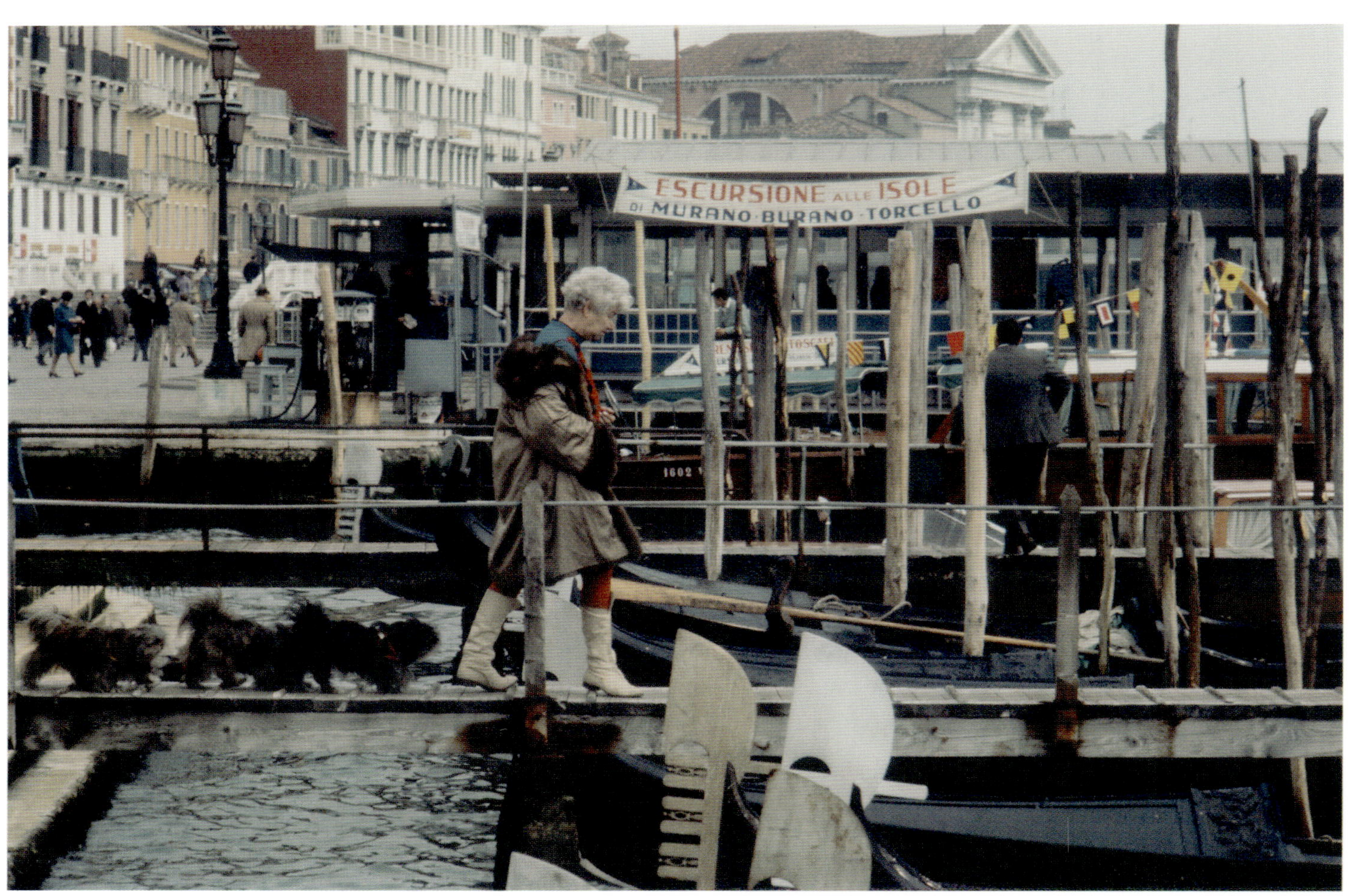

ESCURSIONE ALLE ISOLE
DI MURANO · BURANO · TORCELLO

A historian remembers for us that which will otherwise be forgotten. The photographer is a historian, and Stefan Moses is a historian: his photographs of Peggy Guggenheim record for us that which would otherwise have vanished into darkness, like the void of a never-exposed sensitised photographic plate. 'Flesh perishes, I live on, / Projecting trait and trace / Through time to times anon, / And leaping from place to place / Over oblivion.' (Thomas Hardy.)

Moses photographed the albums that Peggy kept with photographs by others: other people's snapshots, or some of Peggy's celebrated posed portraits, by Man Ray, Ida Kar or Berenice Abbott, assembled in bound books that already betray an affinity to a volume of written history. Moses was surely prompted by the intuition that the photograph is the servant of memory, as if rendering homage to the photographer's profession. Each photo was a story, of friendship, of places, of maternal love, snapshots of Peggy in that society of intellectuals – writers and artists – in which she thrived from the time that she volunteered for the Sunwise Turn bookshop in New York in 1920 to her retirement to her Venetian palazzo in 1949.

It is always said that a painted portrait can look deeper into the soul of a sitter than a photograph. Henry Kissinger looked at Titian's Portrait of Charles V, painted in Augsburg in 1548, now in the Alte Pinakothek in Munich, home of Stefan Moses, and projected onto Charles's aging features his sorrowful inability to forge a hegemonic government of Europe. Yet the photographer has the advantage of spontaneity (the sitter photographed unawares), and of multiplicity (the sitter photographed in different moods and attitudes). We see Peggy at rest and at play, a passeggio in Venice, chatting to children near the Renaissance portal of the Arsenal, where we sense the comedy of her irreverent Lhasa Apso dogs circling the pompous marble lions. We see her somewhat oppressed by her friend Giuseppe Santomaso as they inspect a painting of his, still today in her collection. We catch her surrounded by works of art, constantly moving them from one place to another. She sits on a Quattrocento cassapanca while making a telephone call, a Munich-period Kandinsky at her shoulders.

An old master painter can pull 'attributes' into his or her composition – objects and emblems that comment on the sitter. But so can a photographer. Moses had the wit to suggest that Peggy should momentarily hang a portrait of herself as a child, one of Franz von Lenbach's last efforts, while he photograph her before it. The symbolism of childhood and age – of innocence and experience – is vivid and touching,

*Philip Rylands, Venice, February 2017*
*Director of Peggy Guggenheim Collection, Venice*

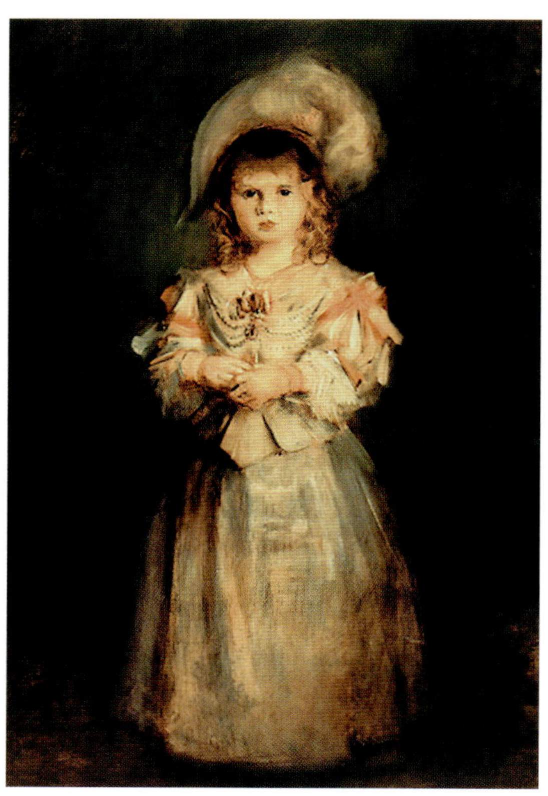

Franz von Lenbach, Portrait of Peggy Guggenheim.
Oil on wood, c. 1903

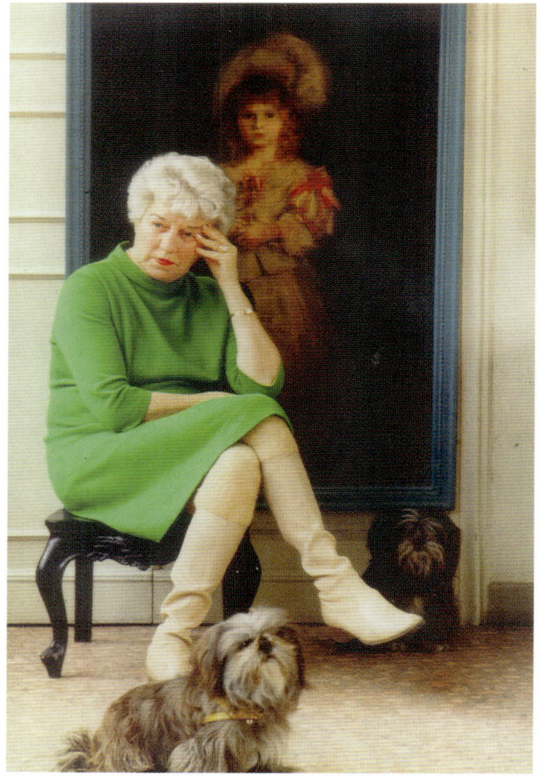

Stefan Moses, Peggy Guggenheim in front of her portrait as a child.
Photograph, 1969

# ENCOUNTERS

## THOMAS ELSEN

In April 1969 Stefan Moses met Peggy Guggenheim for the first time. Together with the author Uli Weyland, he visited her in Venice at her private residence, the Palazzo Venier dei Leoni on the Grand Canal. A second visit, this time with the journalist and returned emigrant Franz Spelman, took place in November 1974. Examples of Moses' extensive series of photographs arising from these two encounters were published in *ZEIT-Magazin* in 1971 and in the German daily *Kölner Stadt-Anzeiger* in 1974.[1]

Conceived as reportage images in colour, Stefan Moses' Peggy Guggenheim series deals with subjects outside the main themes of this major twentieth-century photographer – the artistic documentation of and reflection on German post-war society. Set against the familiar nature of the rest of his oeuvre, these images seem unexpected. Indeed, the series of photographs that Moses created right from the very start of his career – the exhibition catalogues and the monographs document this work – attest to his black and white photography as an authoritative, pioneering vocabulary. They alone encapsulate his work – establishing and developing his photographic style. The process started in 1967 with *Manuel*, a 'photographic era-defining book' (Christoph Stölzl) that was innovative within its genre. It was an extremely personal homage to his then five-year-old son, dedicated to him and to childhood. It continued with *Transsibirische Eisenbahn* [Trans-Siberian Railway] (1979), and with all those trailblazing photography books that, together with the numerous and impressive exhibition projects, were at the root of the subsequent reception and understanding of Stefan Moses' photography: *Deutsche* [Germans] (1980), *Abschied und Anfang* [Parting and Beginning] (1991), *Das Tier und sein Mensch* [The Animal and its Human] (1997), *Stefan Moses fotografiert Ernst Bloch* [Stefan Moses Photographs Ernst Bloch] (2001), *Ilse Aichinger* (2006) and *Deutschlands Emigranten* [Germany's Emigrants] (2013) – not to mention the collected work, *Die Monographie* [The Monograph] of 2002. All of these, plus further examples, form the recognised canon of photographic images by and about Moses. The Peggy Guggenheim colour series, ignored in the discussion of Moses' photographic oeuvre, remains excluded from this canon.

In the year 1969, Peggy Guggenheim received the invitation to exhibit her collection at the Solomon R. Guggenheim Museum in New York. That year, probably not least as a result of this project, she also decided to assign the collection, along with the Venetian property that was housing it, to the Solomon R. Guggenheim Foundation as a gift. The gift was on the condition that the Foundation maintain it and leave it in its habitual location in Venice. Here in the lagoon city of Venice, Peggy Guggenheim's great vision of establishing her own museum became a reality. This was a vision that had started in Paris with her first gallery, 'Guggenheim Jeune', continued in the shape of short-lived plans for a Museum of Contemporary Art in London under the intended directorship of Herbert Read, then from 1942 to 1947 saw an avant garde development in New York in the form of her all the more successful gallery 'Art of This Century',[2] and had now arrived in Venice in a setting as if made for her. The enormous resonance experienced by her and her collection here was the confirmation that in Venice she had found the ideal location.[3]

The year 1969, when Stefan Moses met Peggy Guggenheim for the first time, was therefore an extremely significant one for her. If you once again examine the 1971 *ZEIT-Magazin* from a modern-day perspective, on the basis of the selection of images presented, to a certain extent an impression of reportage-like levity might initially be confirmed. The magazine's reduced and purposeful selection creates a picture totally at odds with the comprehensive overall view of an artist who thinks in sequences. Furthermore, the accompanying text seeks to draw on the images to illustrate its purpose, hardly referring to the photographs and instead alluding exclusively to Peggy Guggenheim herself. Nearly half a century after their creation, the jovial and playful curiosity and the intelligent photographic allure one immediately detects in Moses' images become all the more evident as, for the first time, they are presented in their entirety throughout this book. It becomes clear that the camera not only photographs what is there but also visualises Moses' continued pictorial thought process. It is a photographic narrative that he presents before the eyes of the amazed observer in his assemblage of 123 pictures. The panorama of a city and a time – one might almost say a time parallel to the pace that in Moses' photographic output is otherwise as strict as it is clear. Absurd theatre and a magical flow – the city as a stage at the centre of which Peggy Guggenheim acts as a moody and charismatic star and bird of paradise. One moment she is knowingly and stereotypically caught between doves and a tourist photographer on the Piazza San Marco, and the next moment she is strolling incognito along the Riva degli Schiavoni by the Grand Canal. She is to be seen together with children at play and accompanied by her Lhasa Apsos before the gate of the Arsenale di Venezia, or positioned between her dogs on the red wooden seat of a motoscafo, exotically bespectacled.[4] And we now see her resting in her home, immersed in her own history and surrounded by the treasures of her magnificent collection, which encircle her like a multitude of patron saints.

In around 1903 Franz von Lenbach painted a portrait of Peggy Guggenheim as a little girl in Munich. Her father Benjamin Guggenheim had taken her with him on a European trip, and had commissioned the master from southern Germany to create a likeness of his daughter. The impressively sized oil painting on wood is not part of the collection brought together by Peggy Guggenheim herself, and so as a personally evocative object it is all the more important. It is an example of a painted biography and a precursor to her later collecting activity, which focused exclusively on the artistic avant garde of the period. Moses succeeds not only in shooting Peggy Guggenheim in front of and together with her painted likeness but also in making Lenbach's image a natural component of his own spontaneous artistic production – together with the heroes of modern art from her collection and in the hostess's living quarters. Right in front of the painted portrait one merely sees a red handbag on the floor, representing the collector herself (the very bag she also has with her in front of the lion sculpture on the Piazza San Marco, with children at play at the Arsenale di Venezia and on the terrace of her house). This, too, is almost unique for Stefan Moses: a portrait without a person.

He gets even closer to her where her face appears immediately in front of the canvas of the Lenbach painting, contemplatively pondering and gazing into the distance, with a detached and questioning look. The five-year-old Peggy here looks over the shoulder of the older Peggy – for the photographer, the core of a pictorial concept that Moses creates in front of and with his camera.

In another sequence, significantly more relaxed than before and seemingly little aware of the camera, as if there were no one else in the room, Peggy is lounging on a white sofa in the living room of her home. Before her stands a gentleman, offering up art. He is her neighbour, the painter Giuseppe Santomaso, who is at that moment visiting to present her with his work *Vita Segreta* (Secret Life), which she has acquired for her collection. The Venetian artist Santomaso – a multiple Biennale participant who at the time was already an internationally successful artist and was represented at the first three Documenta exhibitions in Kassel – is presenting the back of his picture to the collector and the front to the photographer.[5] Stefan Moses is here very clearly more interested in the complexity – indeed the bizarreness – of the situation than in the actions of the individuals per se. His photos tell the inconsequential tale of the meeting of the people they show. Another subtle component, lying on the hostess's smoking table, is Moses' photographic book *Manuel*, which he had previously brought with him as a gift, as he recalls.[6] Once he has noticed it, it is included time and again in other photographs in the series. The fact that he succeeds in coaxing the fêted celebrity into the realm of the self-evident and the way he does so, creating the maximum proximity within the image, yet not divesting her of her unique essence, aura and dignity, are testament not only to his virtuosity as a portraitist but also once again to the intuitive clarity and sensitivity of pictorial storytelling.

Stefan Moses has time and again showcased the significance of the preservation of childhood, in the very same way as his symbolic comparison of himself with a cat. Bearing this in mind, everything that drives him and has ever driven him as an artist is nothing but a human game – always being wide awake, hungry, curious, eager for knowledge and enquiring. To this end, Moses' camera – *his*, not just *any* camera – serves him as the appropriate tool.[7]

The silver bedstead in Peggy Guggenheim's bedroom, that was created for her by Alexander Calder during 1945–1946, is shot by Moses in exactly the same way as other works from her collection, including sculptures. The latter include Marino Marini's bronze sculpture *L'Angelo della Città*, a still provocative equestrian statue that lives up to its name and immediately and spectacularly seeks to draw the attention of visitors coming in from the Grand Canal. Further such sculptures include Constantin Brâncusi's *Maiastra*, a highly polished bronze sculpture alongside which Peggy Guggenheim appears in a picture as her own likeness, with one arm leaning on the plinth, and Germaine Richier's fantastic and surreal sculpture *Tauromachie* [Bullfighting], which now appears more relevant than ever before. Moses of course shoots the collector amidst a simply overwhelming forest of pictures hanging on the walls, spread out over the floor or leaning against the collector's items from New Guinea. Peggy Guggenheim is shown here as a true 'Self in pictorial form'. A symbolic and actual visualisation of her personality at the point of arrival at the Palazzo Venier dei Leoni, characterised by an existential passion for collecting – a personality for whom 'from the beginning of the Venetian period of her life … collecting [became] the predominant concept in Peggy's cosmos'.[8] Stefan Moses, too, was always and is a collector by nature. Ever since he can remember he has loved being surrounded by images. In Venice his interests and those of Peggy Guggenheim meet in an absolutely direct and previously unplannable way. All of this is integrated into one of the short pictorial narratives that are so characteristic of the photographer, with Peggy Guggenheim's facial expression transformed from a self-conscious pose with raised head into a relaxed smile – close up and genuine in a way rarely seen in photographs of her. In the magazine selection printed in 1971 only one of these photographs is seen. This book includes three, as a short sequence or mini narrative, in the process providing an exemplary demonstration of Stefan Moses' unique vision, his constantly active eye and his communication with the subject of the portrait.[9]

Together with him, Moses allows us to accompany Peggy Guggenheim further. We see her looking cheerily, indeed joyfully, into the photographer's lens, through the crowds of visitors to her home. We observe her between her grandson Nicolas Hélion and his wife in animated conversation on a bench. She is to be seen at an extremely private lunch at home, seated at a small and simple wooden table (incidentally the very same one that serves as a table for catalogues sales when the building is open to the public, and at which the hostess has at times also sold catalogues herself[10]), with fish, wine and ketchup being served by a liveried waiter. We see her from the opposite side of the Grand Canal, captured on film on the roof terrace of her house, whilst beneath her the visitors bustle around in her collection. Stefan Moses' photos from Venice tell us all this and much more in cheery, extremely lively and animated short episodes. In them concept and real-life photography congenially merge to form an individual pictorial language – a unique artistic design.

Moses' photos seem like a casual walk on a carefree day. As an artistic diary, they are like a photographic excursion drawing on his own output – a capriccio that, dipping into the pool of work that has already been long in the making, nourishes itself just as unquestioningly as from the cheerful spontaneity and the immersion in a new and different terrain. 'Colour is evanescent – black & white persists,' he once said.[11] He himself delivers an astoundingly plausible explanation of why, in this instance, the rule presents its own exception: 'I did in fact actually want to photograph the images [in colour], and that's why I had so many colour films with me.'[12]

With his approach Moses in no way changes his own perspective. Rather, with great delight and nonchalance, he undertakes a photographic endeavour that is as light as a feather. In the process, effortlessly, he seemingly breaks through the pure doctrine of all previous responses to him, without actually overriding it. Venice is the ideal terrain for this. Seeing the city as a stage, Peggy Guggenheim's collection and her eccentric persona in a single overall view is what facilitates this. The transfer of this apparent paradox – black and white versus colour, concept versus life – to this unique book, monographing his work once again, demonstrates how the intelligent humour of the picture maker Stefan Moses takes effect. The process is farreachingly self-evident, inventive and characterised by nothing other than a spirit of absolute artistic independence. With respectful humour, he also encounters in the series Peggy Guggenheim's horde of deceased Lhasa Apsos, ranging from 'Cappucino' [sic] (1949–1953) to 'Sir Herbert' (1952–1965), their names carved in stone by a wall in the garden of her house; to this day they are appropriately appreciated.

A number of prominent photographers had already shot Peggy Guggenheim in her earlier years,[13] amongst them Man Ray (c. 1924), André Kertész (1945), Gisèle Freund (1939) and Berenice Abbott (1942). The collector promoted and financially supported them back when they were still promising yet unknown young talents. Despite the original artistic style of these pictures and the mastery involved, their status remains that of succinct but always statue-like staged single portraits of a conventional classical nature.

By contrast, the photo series Stefan Moses made of Peggy Guggenheim in 1969 and 1974 demand to be viewed in their totality as series. Their character is that of pictorial narratives, and every single photo in them is a miniature chapter in its own right. The winks Moses sends down the lens, without any loss of seriousness, are reciprocated by Peggy Guggenheim. Sometimes she appears more neutral, but never really distanced. It is a game full of free emotional dramaturgy that develops from image to image. Without any kind of set strategy, but with a secure instinct and feeling for development, Moses allows his images to speak for themselves. If you 'read' them in their totality, a personal dialogue between portrait creator and portrait subject very slowly begins to be reflected in them. On occasions, it is also a kind of ironic dual between photographer and model that was hardly plannable in this form and that becomes apparent from the energy exhibited over brief periods of time. The pictures Moses takes of Peggy Guggenheim show her in

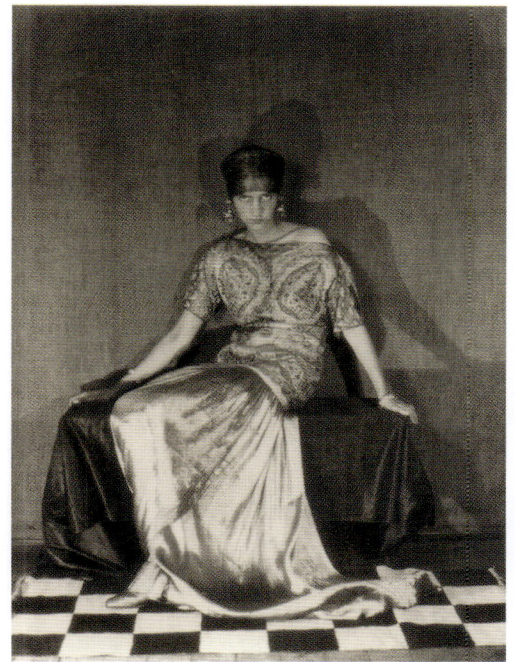

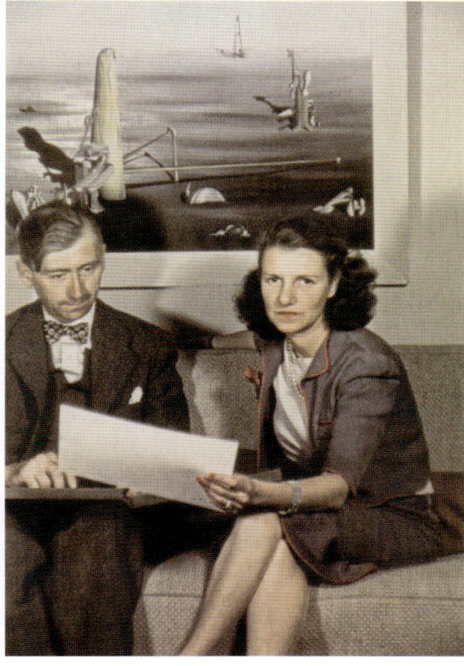

Left: Peggy Guggenheim, Paris, c. 1924.
Photo: Man Ray

Right: Herbert Read and Peggy Guggenheim, London 1939
Photo: Gisèle Freund

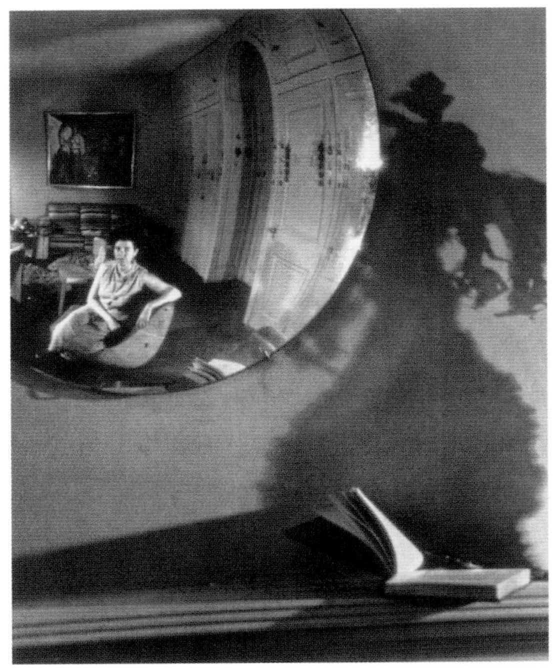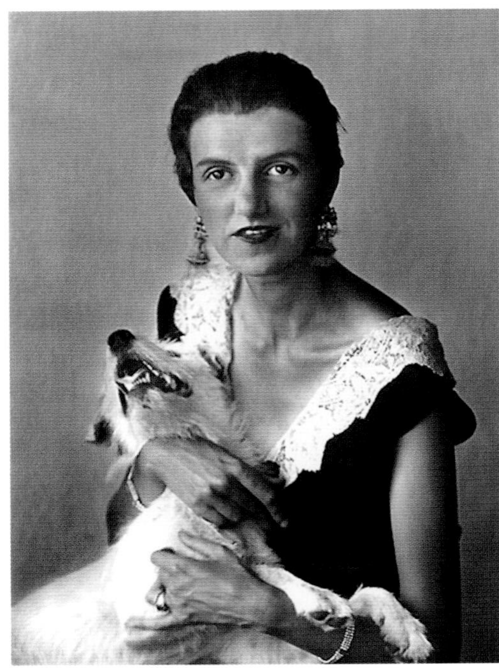

Left: Peggy Guggenheim,
New York, c. 1945.
Photo: André Kertész

Right: Peggy Guggenheim,
Pramousquier, France,
c. 1926.
Photo: Berenice Abbott

many circumstances, from provocative poise and complete relaxation through to concentration on the part of a woman who is at all times aware of the presence of the photographer and the situation of being photographed.

With Moses the principle of working sequentially was already significant at an early stage, not only as a stylistic element but also as a philosophical thought that sought not the one 'magical' moment but the transient – and thus the awareness of time as a continuum.[14] The awareness of this permeates Stefan Moses' entire output with great consistency – formally detectable above all in the triptychs he presented back in the early 1960s, and most recently almost formulaically in *Le Moment fugitif*, a poetic photographic book project together with Alexander Kluge.[15] As is so often the case, here we once again see small narratives – narratives that never just depict a specific moment but essentially always show the facets the photographer is capable of realising. In terms of his ability and his desire to illustrate this, Moses is equally a selective artist with the camera – someone who combines the ability to create a unique singular portrait with the ability to simultaneously see this image, be it only for a very short period of time, as a sequence and to photographically think ahead.

In response to the question as to how he himself sees the Peggy Guggenheim series within his own output, in spring 2017 Moses said in a downright cheerfully relaxed way: 'My life and times was twentieth-century Europe. Photography is of assistance in the reality research into German societies.' And he continued: 'All the world's a stage, and we all act with one another, from the great elders to the indignant flower children of the late 60s. And the not particularly welcome returning emigrants Thomas and Heinrich Mann, Fritz Bauer, Hans Sahl, Herrmann Kesten, Josef and Anni Albers, Ellen Auerbach, Sascha and Ludwig Marcuse – the unredeemed societies of East and West.'[16] But getting straight back to Peggy Guggenheim again: 'The albums are eminently important. In them are gathered people from a life – her life.'[17]

The albums Stefan Moses is referring to are Peggy Guggenheim's private photograph albums documenting her personal social environment, of which he became aware whilst at her house. They contain photos of family members, friends and artists, as well as a number of not immediately identifiable persons and situations. Moses did not just photograph the collector skimming through these albums. He quickly directed his attention to the albums themselves. Page by page he photographed the black boxes with the multitude of photos stuck in them. Driven by artistic curiosity he thus embarked on a visual and cultural voyage of discovery into the world of Peggy Guggenheim. This cultural lust for discovery is perhaps one of the main keys to the visual development of his Peggy Guggenheim portrait series. A treasure reveals itself here in her albums, the viewing of which is tantamount to dipping into its owner's personal memory. What Moses practises is photographic archaeology in search of records of memory – a visual excavation in the field of her personal history. He is extremely interested in the visible and invisible relationships of the people appearing in the albums, in the sense of a human chain that can help provide information on the development of a person's nature, and ultimately on where everything comes from.

Not only is the classification of the photos in the albums curiously reminiscent of the pictorial *Mnemosyne Atlas* conceived by Aby Warburg in the early 20th century, whose black and white photographs of cultural records arranged on black panels were intended to lead to new content-related references. Moses' handling of the albums is also related to the concept of the pictorial atlas. With the images of her world combined not only chronologically but also associatively, Peggy Guggenheim created meanings and references that were obviously important to her – highly personal overall pictures that were primarily intended for herself and were to remain recognisable. Moses photographs the individual pages as vertical panels – as a private atlas of the universe documenting the encounters between people and experienced events.

Peggy Guggenheim brought together numerous portrait photos and personal passport photos on a dedicated page of one of these albums. Stefan Moses has formed a collage by adding his own photographs, thereby creating a new arrangement of his own, though this process is barely recognisable if you are not aware of it. This is fundamentally the same process as the one he had already used in the photos in which Peggy Guggenheim's red handbag is to be seen in front of images of her collection, or in which she herself, sitting in the middle of the Palazzo Venier dei Leoni, gathers her pictures around her for the photographer. In all these instances Stefan Moses experiments with new combinations in order to seek and discover meanings through his own changed arrangements. And should the essence of essayism consist in the mode of searching,[18] as suggested by Wolfgang Ullrich, then Stefan Moses is an essayist in the best sense of the word.

With his two series of 1969 and 1974, Moses created in two stages not only the most comprehensive but also perhaps the only existing photographic narrative concerning Peggy Guggenheim, beyond the numerous individual pictures taken by others. In Moses' images, which never stylise, beautify or exaggerate, you see and feel an inner self-encounter – a dialogue between the photographer and the subject at eye level. It is not private views, receptions, studio sessions or other official occasions that are the focus but simply a poise that conveys proximity – a sense of normality within the extraordinary that is above all posturing. You feel in Moses' photos that Peggy Guggenheim has arrived.

As an artistic searcher for traces and a protector of the path of recent German society, just as throughout his life as a photographer he has tracked its – 'our' – mentality, closely observed it and cheerfully given it a helping hand, he did the same in Venice, as a diviner with a camera. And why should the German European Moses have done things any differently?

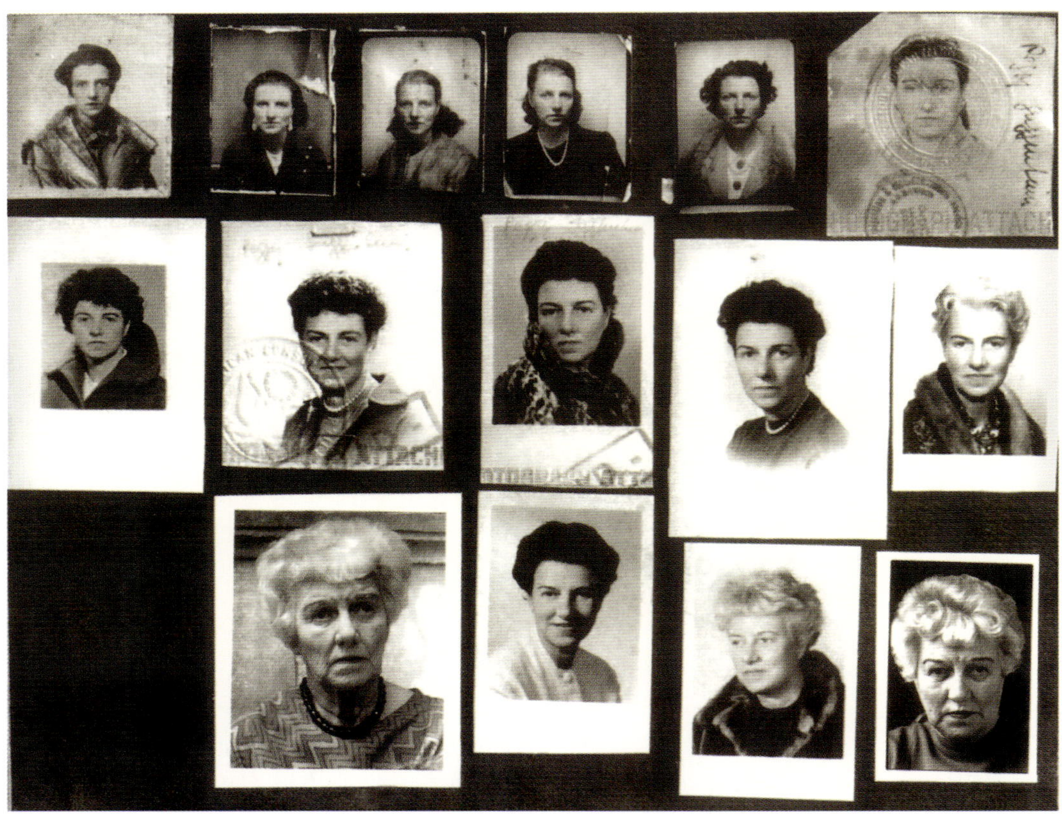

Collage, Stefan Moses: Passport photos, Peggy Guggenheim, 1920–1974

**Comments**

[1] 'Besuch bei der alten Dame' [Visit to the old lady]. A report by Uli Weyland (text) and Stefan Moses (photos)', in: *ZEITMagazin* No. 35, 27th August 1971, pp 12-17. 'Ein Leben für die Kunst' [A life for art], in: *Kölner Stadtanzeiger* ('Bunte Blätter' supplement), 16th/17th November 1974, p. 1; and: Margret Kämpf, 'Ihr Schlafzimmer ist eine Raritätenkammer' [Her bedroom is a chamber of curiosities], in: *Kölner Stadtanzeiger*, loc. cit., pp 4-5. In March 2015, in a special issue (No. 854) dedicated to Peggy Guggenheim, the cultural magazine *Du* once again included eleven of Stefan Moses' photos.

[2] 'The influence exerted by Art of This Century and Peggy Guggenheim on the New York scene was so great that her collection has assumed the status of a historic document. She is to be deemed a part of history that firstly gave us a picture of events in New York during the years 1942 to 1947 and secondly considerably influenced actual current events.' Philip Rylands, 'Die Geschichte der Sammlung Peggy Guggenheim' [The history of the Peggy Guggenheim Collection], in: *Sammlung Peggy Guggenheim. Ausstellungsführer Venedig* [Peggy Guggenheim Collection. Exhibition guide Venice], 8th edition 2009, p. 16. Further evidence of Peggy Guggenheim's position in the New York of this period is her initial promotion of Jackson Pollock. In addition to her own purchases, she also organised his first solo exhibition.

[3] In 1949, two years after returning to Europe from the USA, Peggy Guggenheim had acquired a property as a residence and a public museum for her collection. This property was a palace near the church Santa Maria della Salute, the building of which had started in the mid-18th century but was never completed. The year before that – in 1948 – she had already shown her collection at the Venice Biennale, with great success.

[4] The motif of Peggy Guggenheim as a taxi-boat passenger, sporting eccentric sunglasses created by the US designer Edward Melcarth, was recorded by Stefan Moses in variations on a sequence. As a black and white motif it was published many times, including back in 1979 in *Transsibirische Eisenbahn* [TransSiberian Railway].

[5] At Santomaso's suggestion and through his agency, Peggy Guggenheim was in 1948 able to display her collection in the then empty Greek pavilion of the Venice Biennale.

[6] Stefan Moses in discussion with the author in Munich on 7th March 2017.

[7] "Much of what Stefan Moses later incorporated into his educational canon derives from this area of tension between the fabulous and the jocular that he had surveyed since childhood. Everything had its place then, and the biggest contrasts had an effect that was not destructive but stimulating," said Christoph Stölzl on the occasion of the presentation of the 2014 Lovis Corinth Prize to Stefan Moses: see 'Begegnungszauber' [Magic of encounters], in: *Ausstellungskatalog Regensburg, Kunstforum Ostdeutsche Galerie* [Exhibition catalogue Regensburg, Kunstforum Ostdeutsche Galerie]. Heidelberg (Kehrer Verlag) 2015, p. 21.

[8] Anette Seemann, 'Peggy Guggenheim. Ich bin eine befreite Frau' [Peggy Guggenheim. I am a liberated woman]. Berlin (List Verlag), 6th edition 2006, p. 267. Her book is the most detailed German language biography of Peggy Guggenheim hitherto.

[9] In another context Moses once said on this topic: "In photography there has to be a connecting spark; I have to like the person in question, or I quickly stop. Photographing someone is analysis: you communicate with each other. Taking photographs and talking to each other does after all constitute a kind of therapy. Taking photographs and being photographed together is an analytical process … photography is permanent memory work. My work is capturing people before they are lost to us." Stefan Moses in discussion with Simone Dattenberger in: Münchner Merkur, 5th December 2002.

[10] Franz Spelman says: 'When, in order to prepare the images for the photographer Stefan Moses, we routinely asked her for a catalogue she gave us this one, but then asked the following day "Would you mind paying me the 5,000 Lire for the catalogue?"' From an undated, unpublished manuscript belonging to Spelman.

[11] Stefan Moses in: *Kunst aktuell*, No. 12/1 1998/99, pp 10-11.

[12] Stefan Moses in discussion with the author in Munich on 7th March 2017.

[13] For an overview see most recently: 'Peggy Guggenheim in Photographs', curated by Ziva Kraus. Ausstellungskatalog Venedig [Exhibition catalogue Venice] (Ikona Gallery) 2016.

[14] "There's no such thing as Cartier-Bresson's *moment décisif*. This decades-old myth has become the major error in the contemporary philosophy of photography." Stefan Moses in discussion with Felix Hoffmann and Ulrich Pohlmann, in: *Die Monographie* [The monograph]. Munich (Schirmer/Mosel) 2002, p. 283.

[15] 'Le Moment fugitif'. Photographs by Stefan Moses with texts by Alexander Kluge. Wädenswil (Nimbus Verlag) 2014.

[16] Stefan Moses in discussion in Munich, 7th March 2017.

[17] Ibid.

[18] Wolfgang Ullrich, 'Denn Bedeutung schlummert überall' [Because meaning lies dormant everywhere], in: *Die ZEIT* No. 3/2013, 10th January 2013.

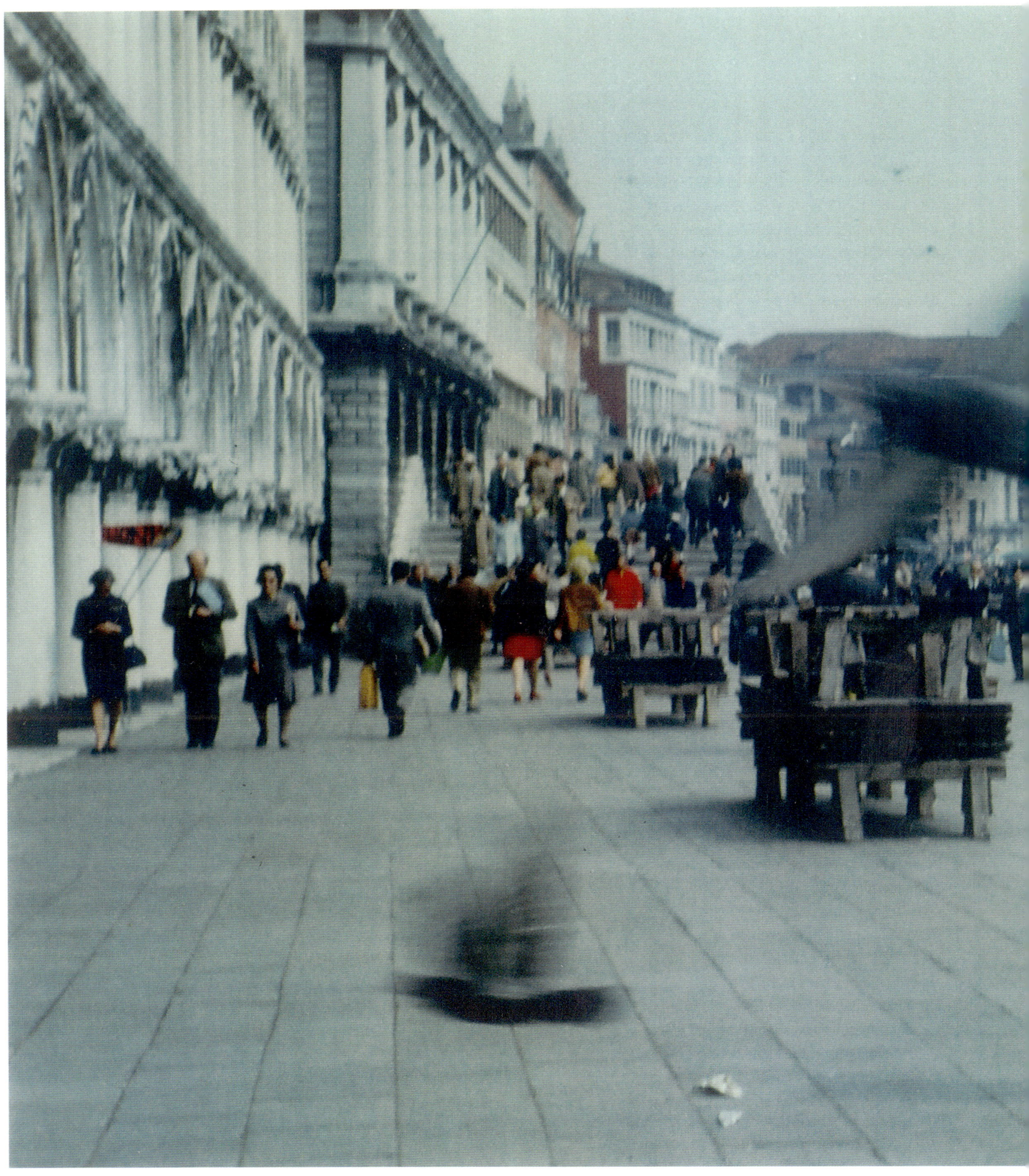

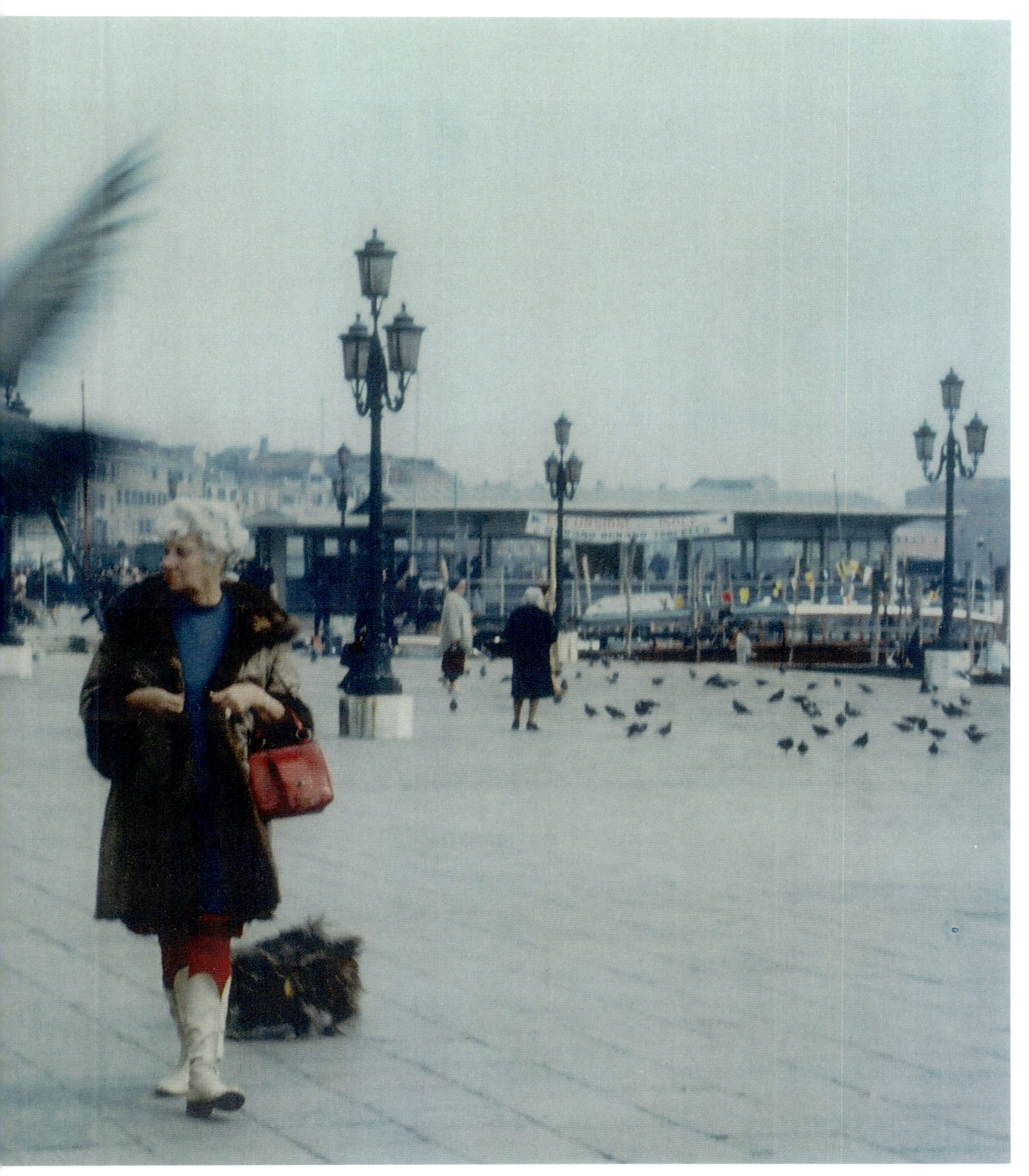

On the Riva degli Schiavoni.

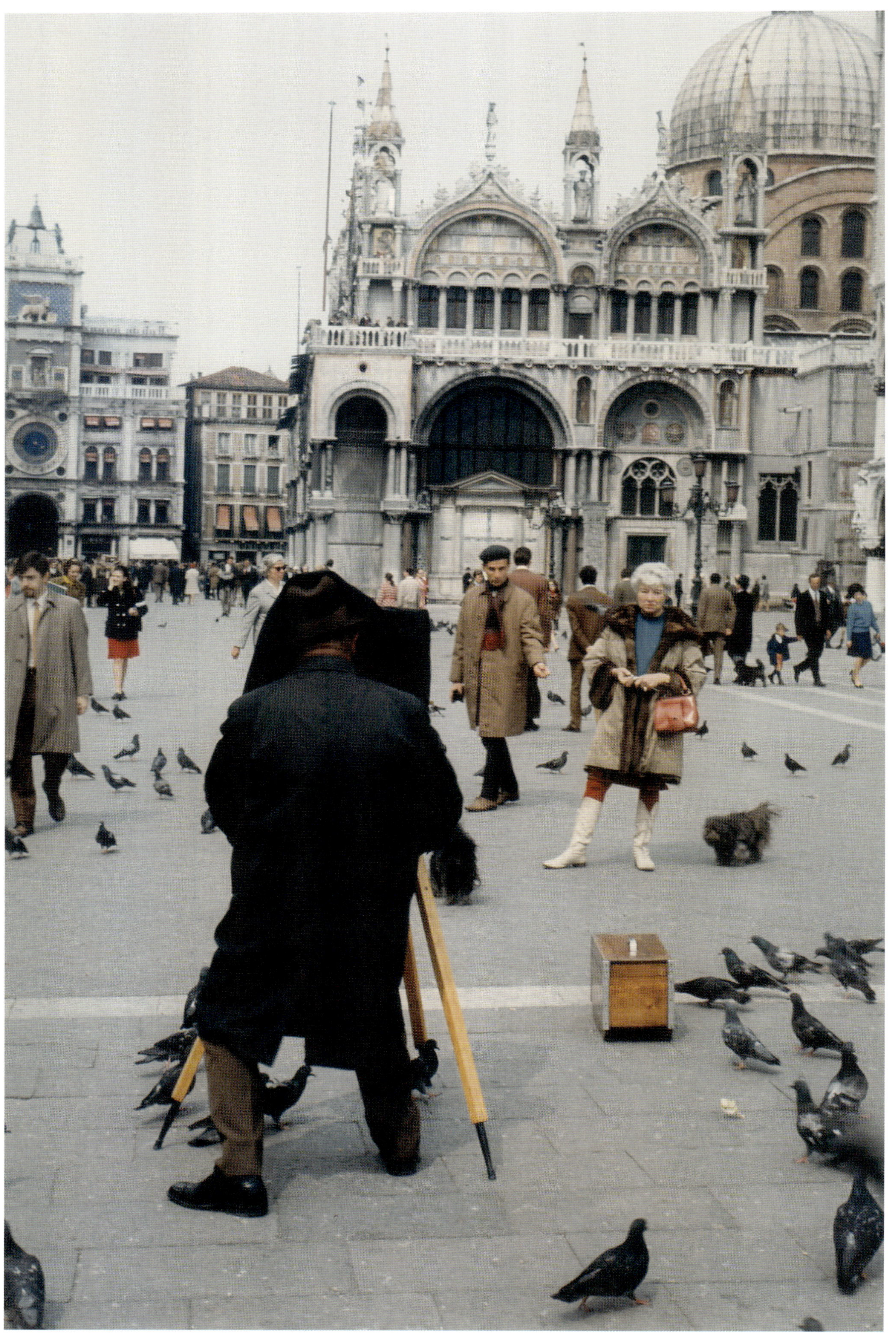

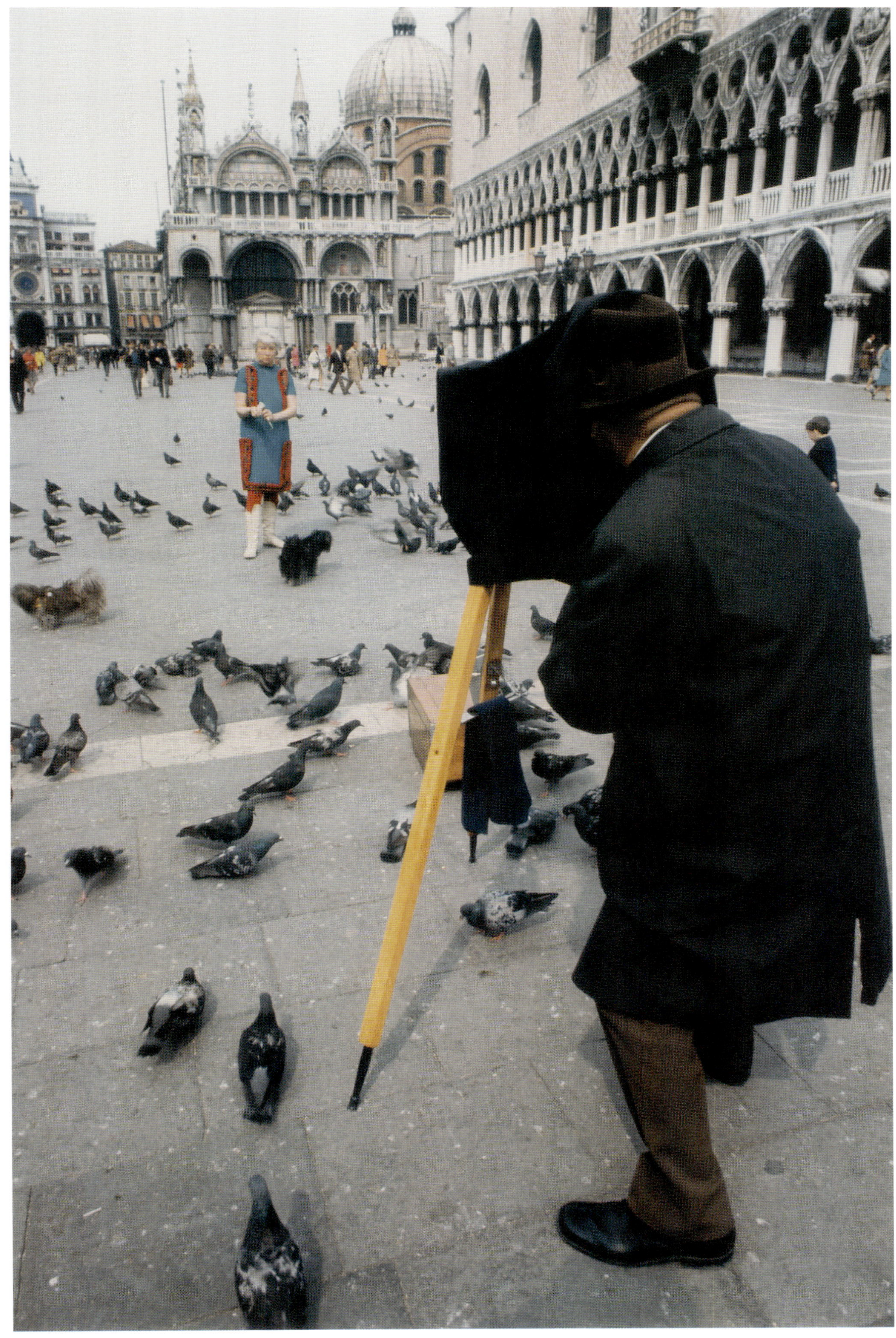

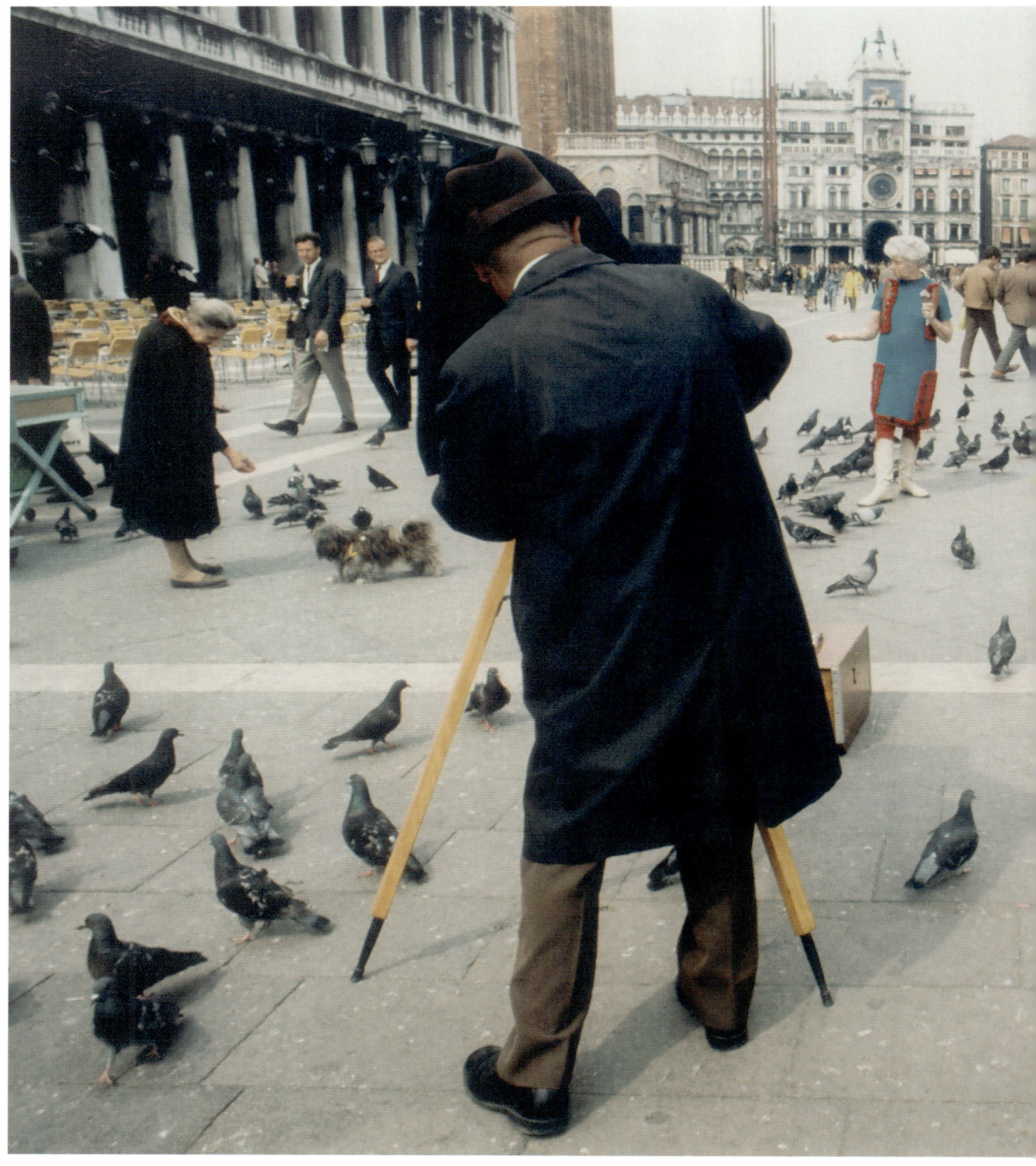

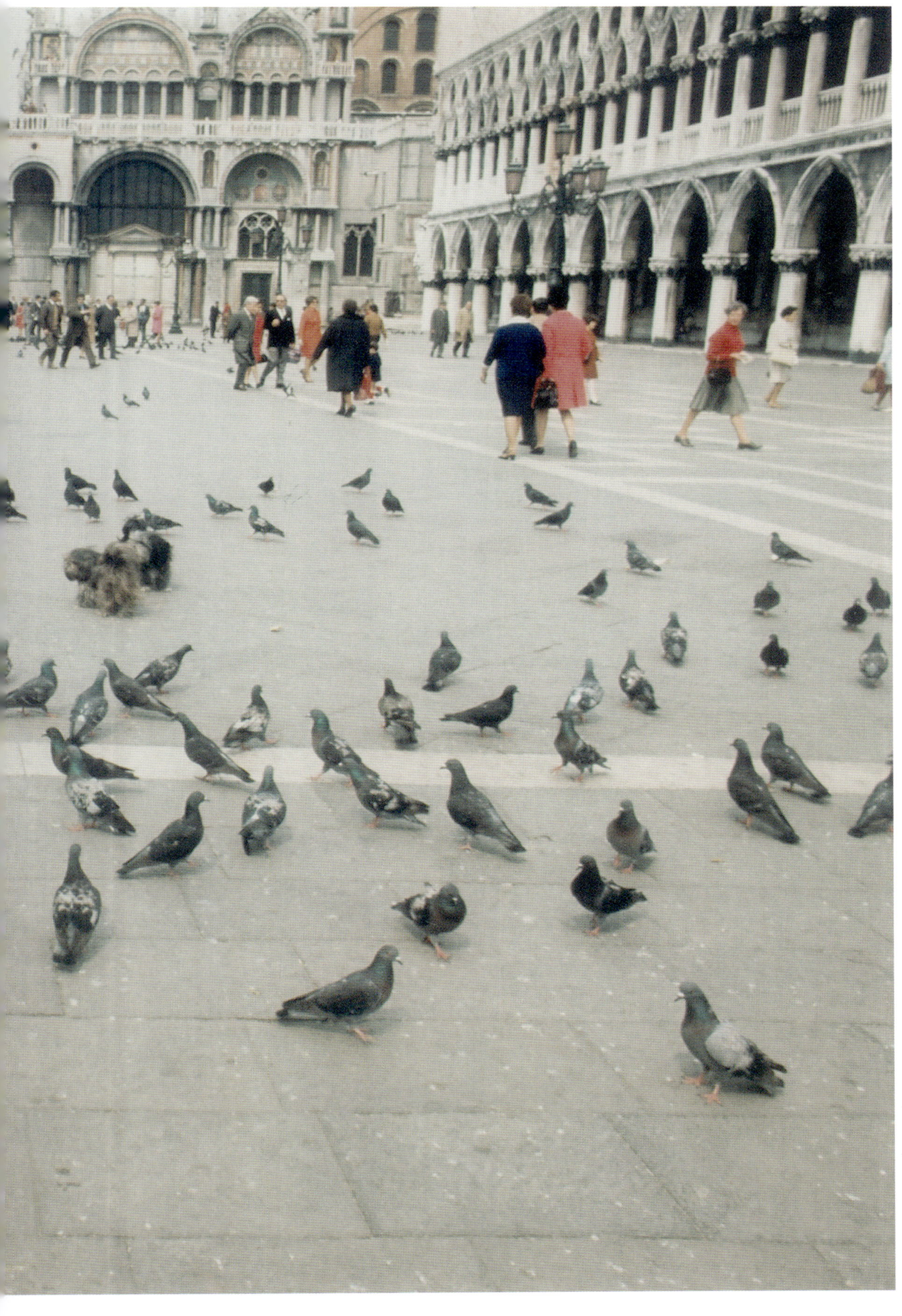

pp 24–27

On St Mark's Square

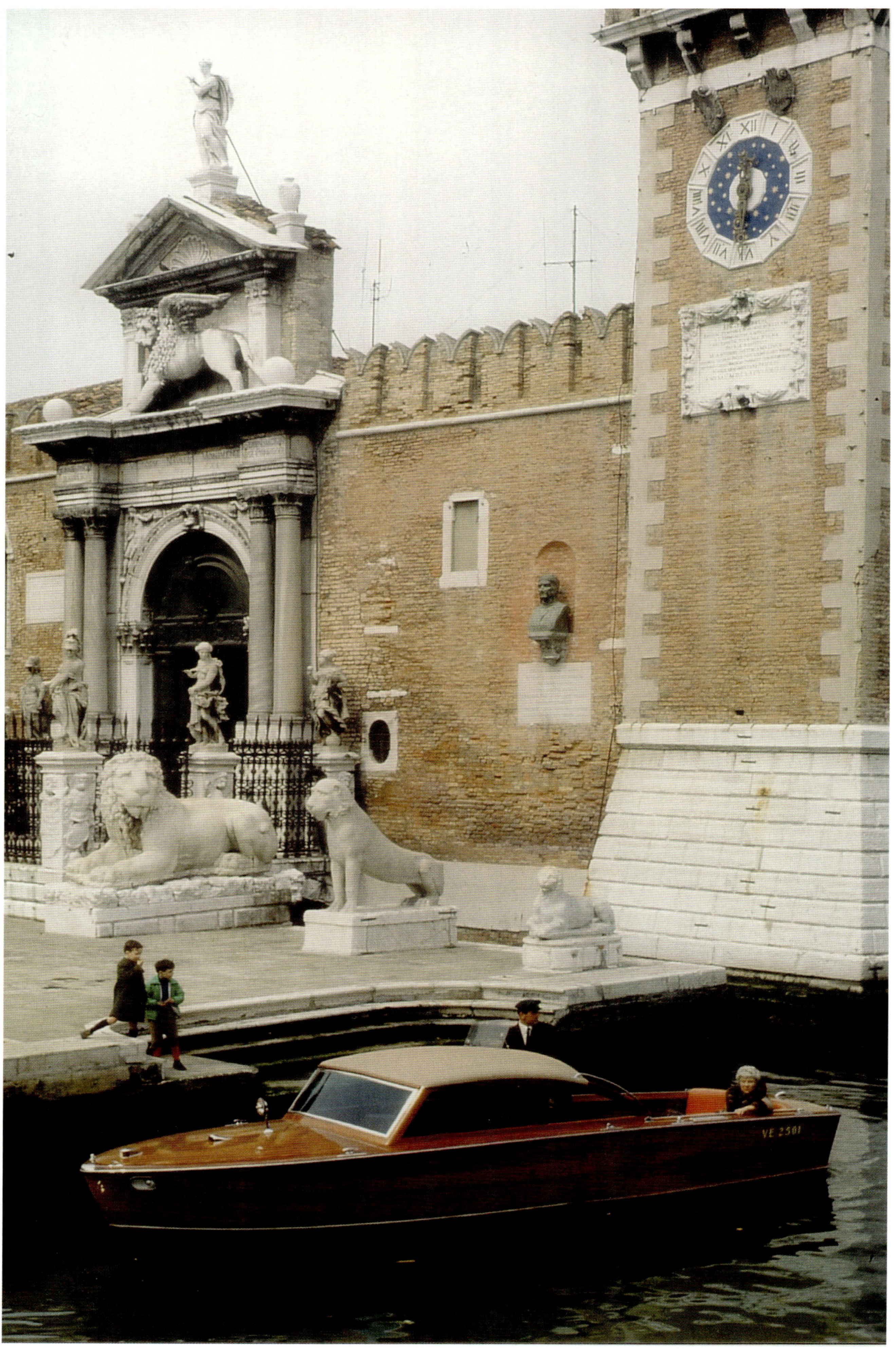

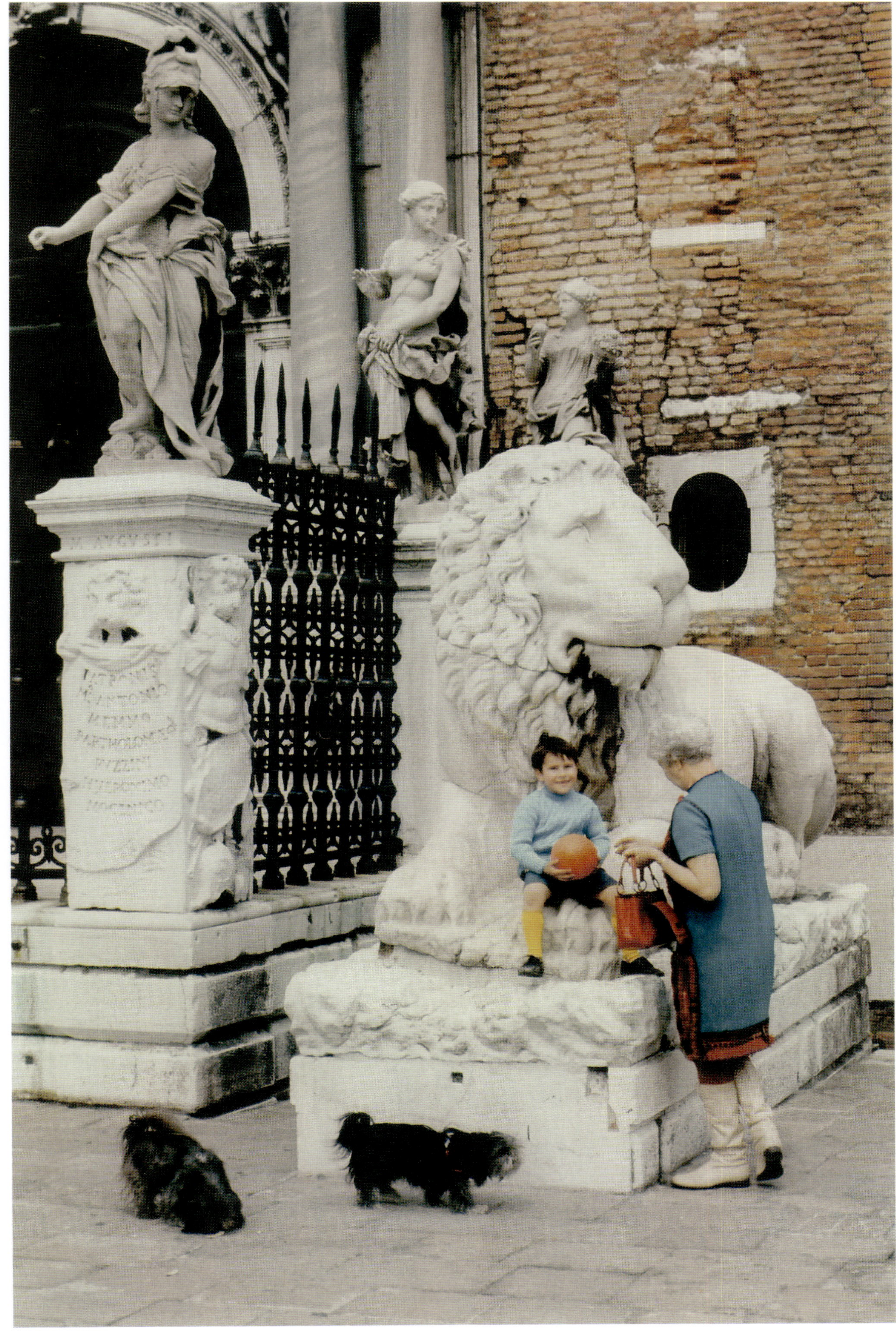

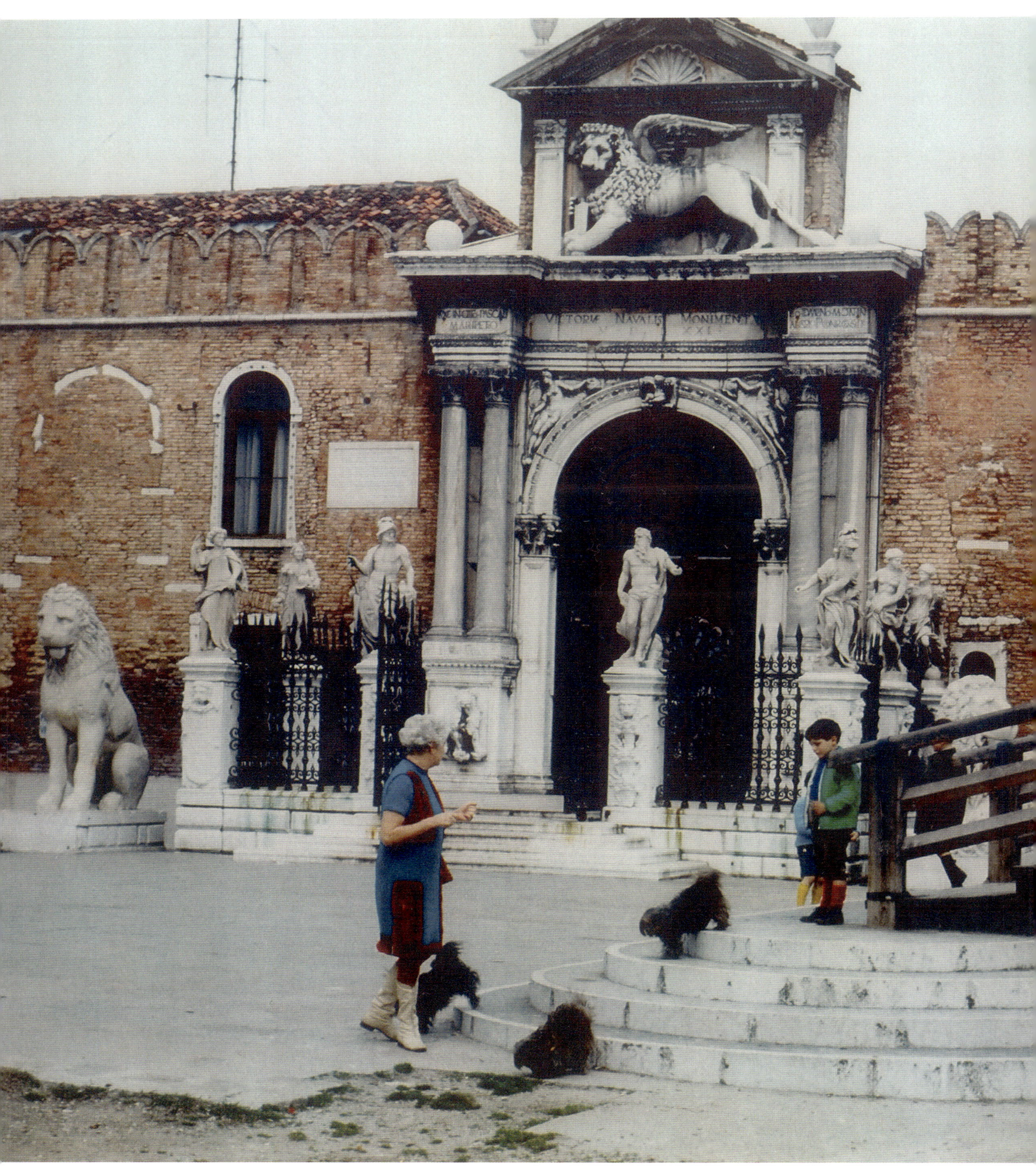

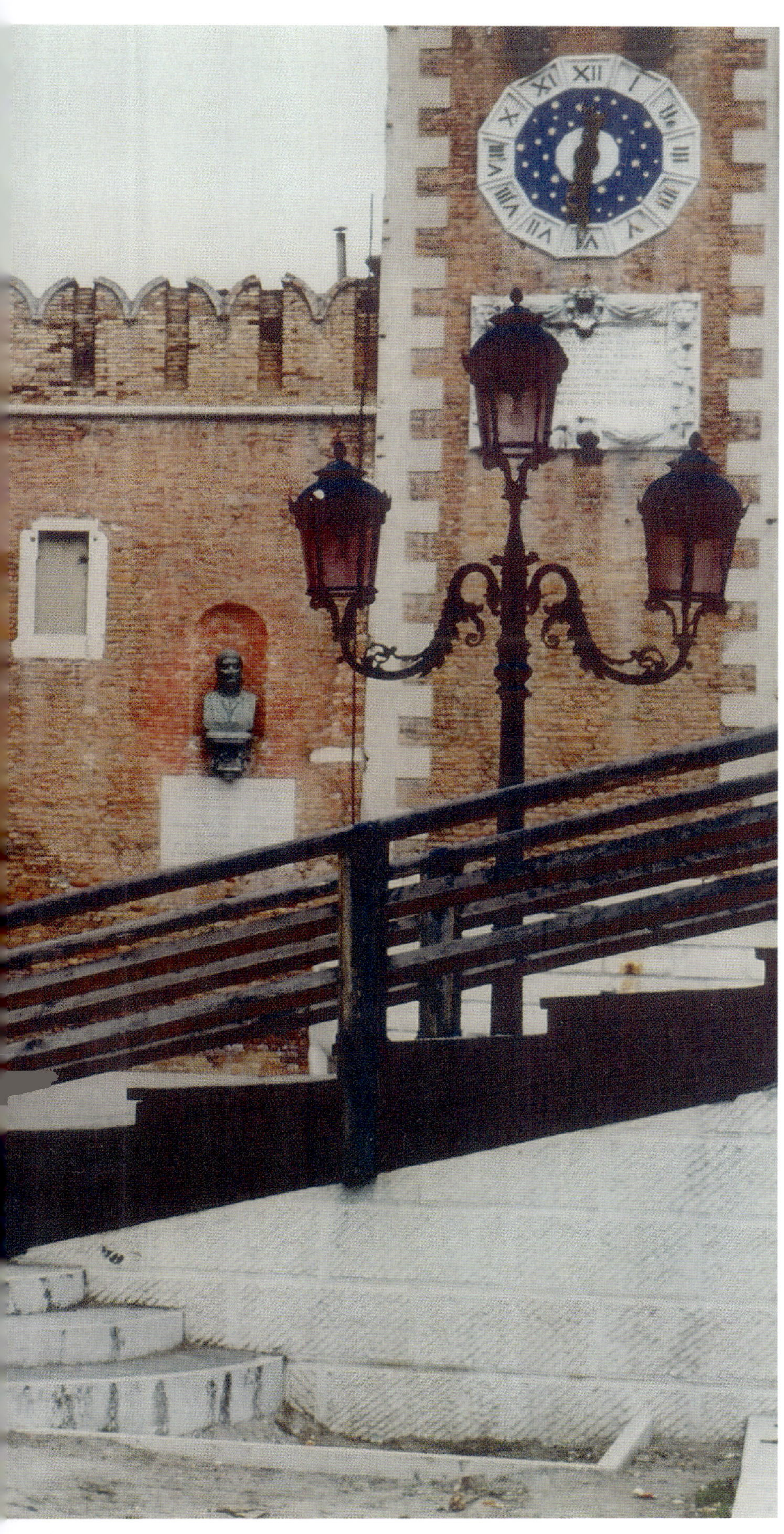

pp 28–33

Peggy visiting the monumental gate to the Arsenale di Venezia, one of the first buildings of the Renaissance.

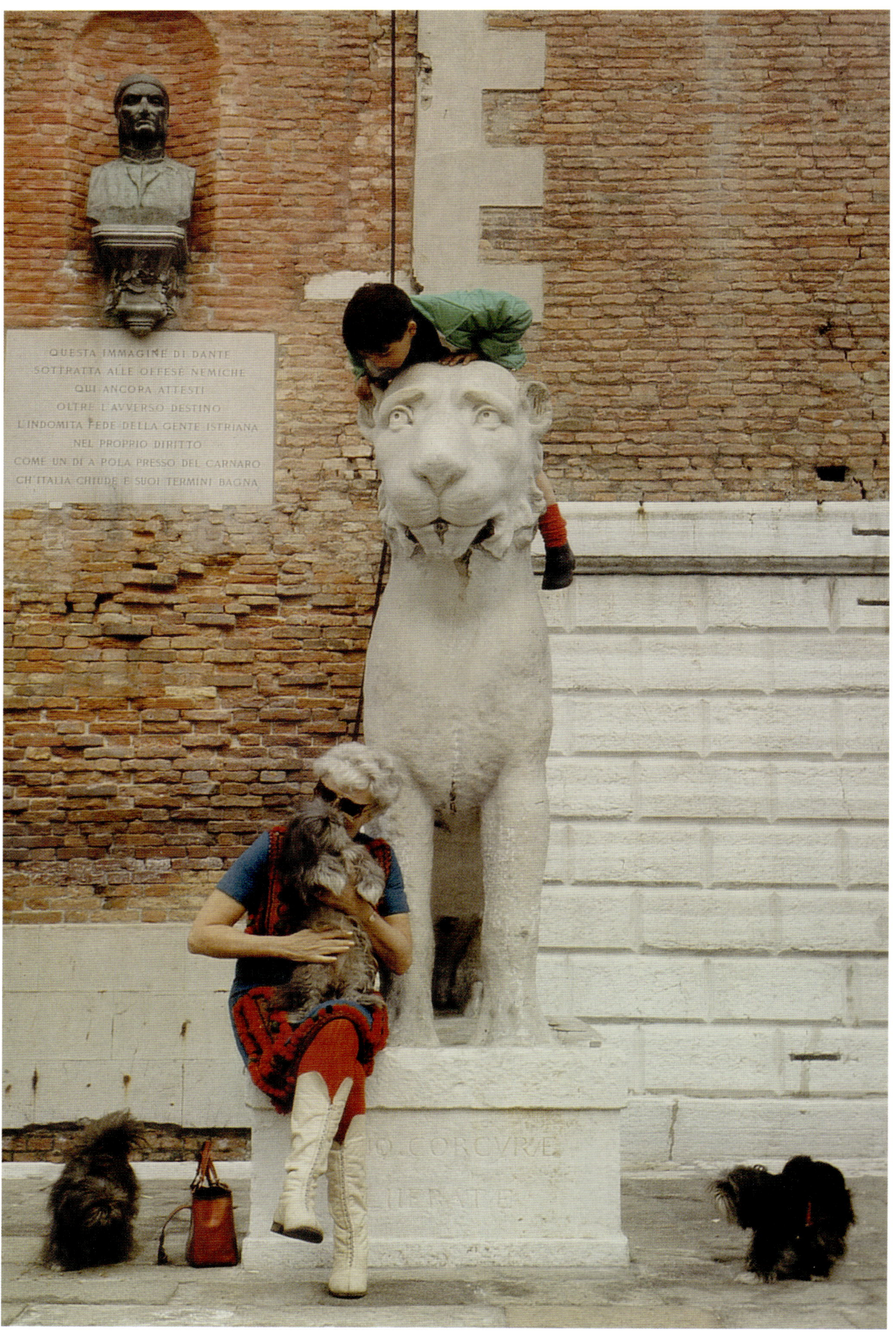
QUESTA IMMAGINE DI DANTE
SOTTRATTA ALLE OFFESE NEMICHE
QUI ANCORA ATTESTI
OLTRE L'AVVERSO DESTINO
L'INDOMITA FEDE DELLA GENTE ISTRIANA
NEL PROPRIO DIRITTO
COME UN DÌ A POLA PRESSO DEL CARNARO
CH'ITALIA CHIUDE E SUOI TERMINI BAGNA

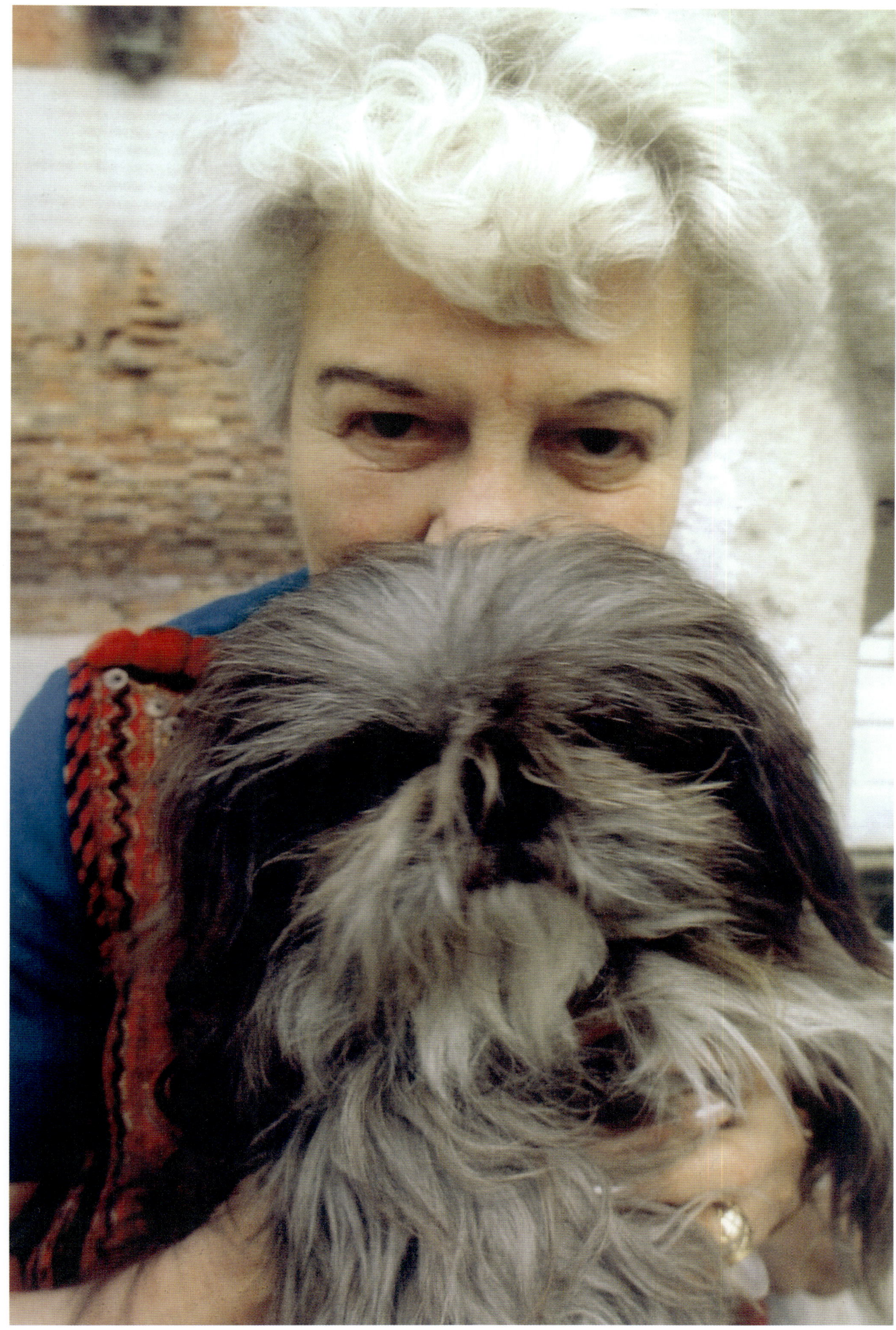

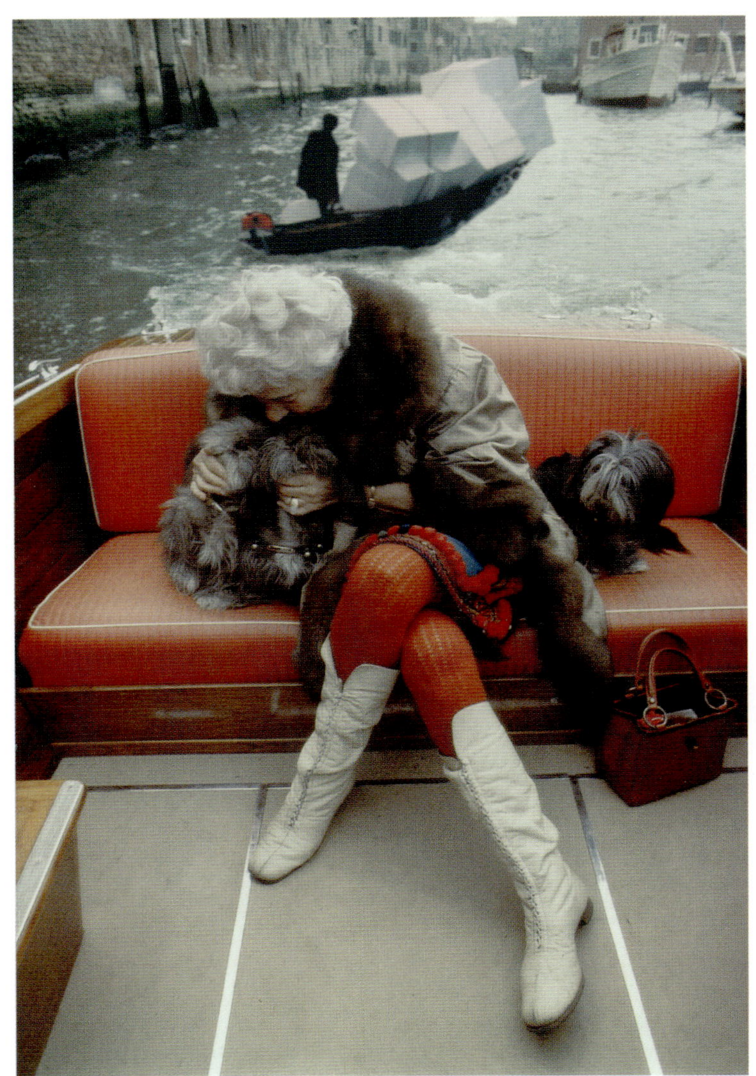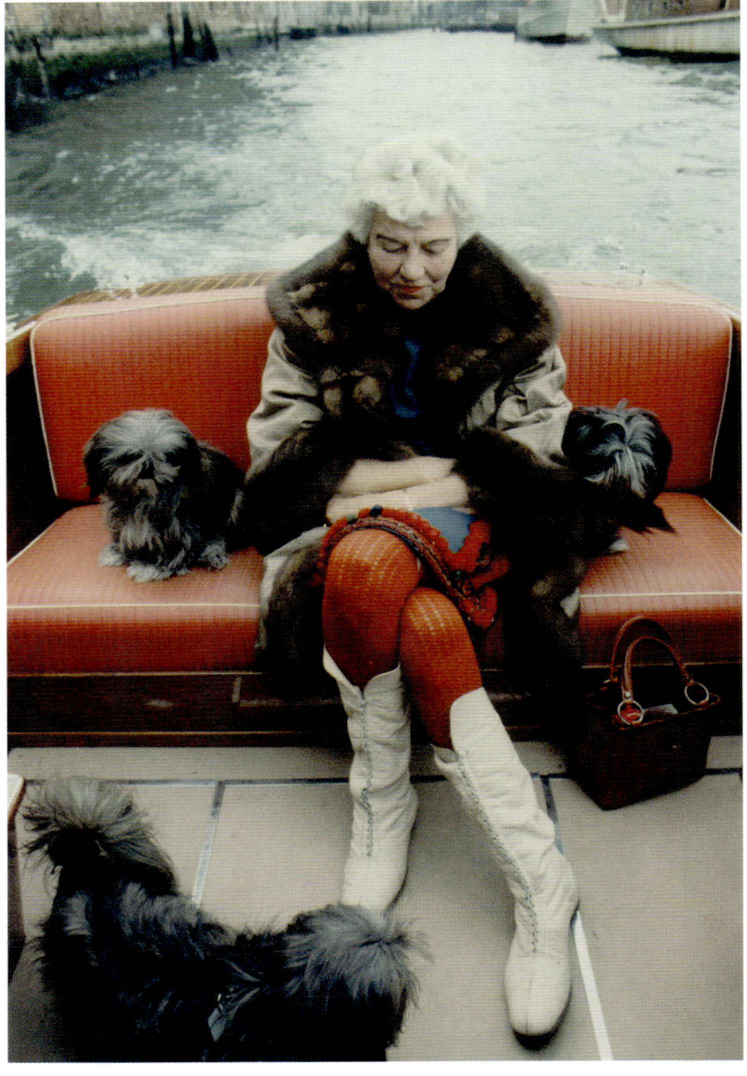

pp 34–43
In her motoscafo (water taxi).

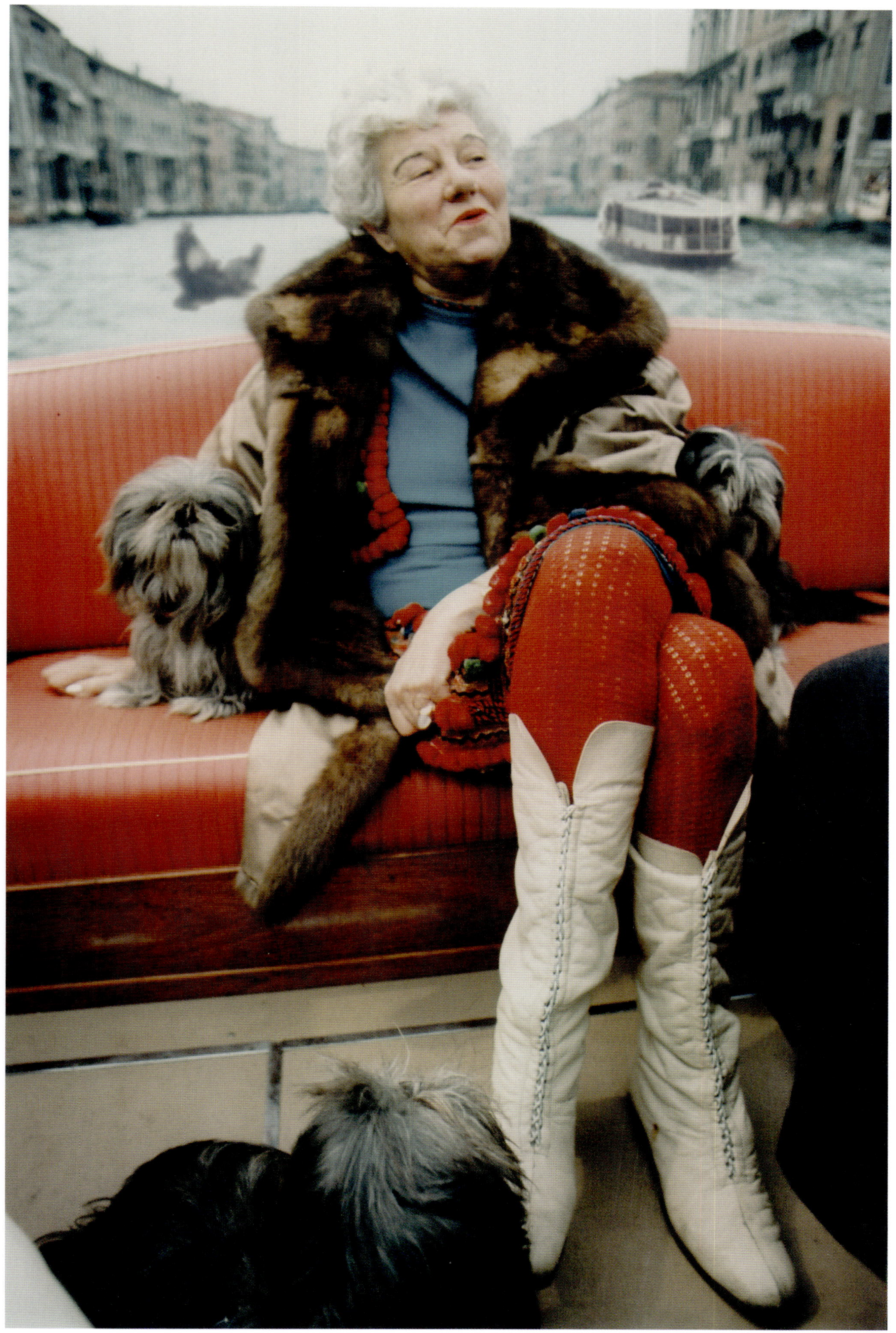

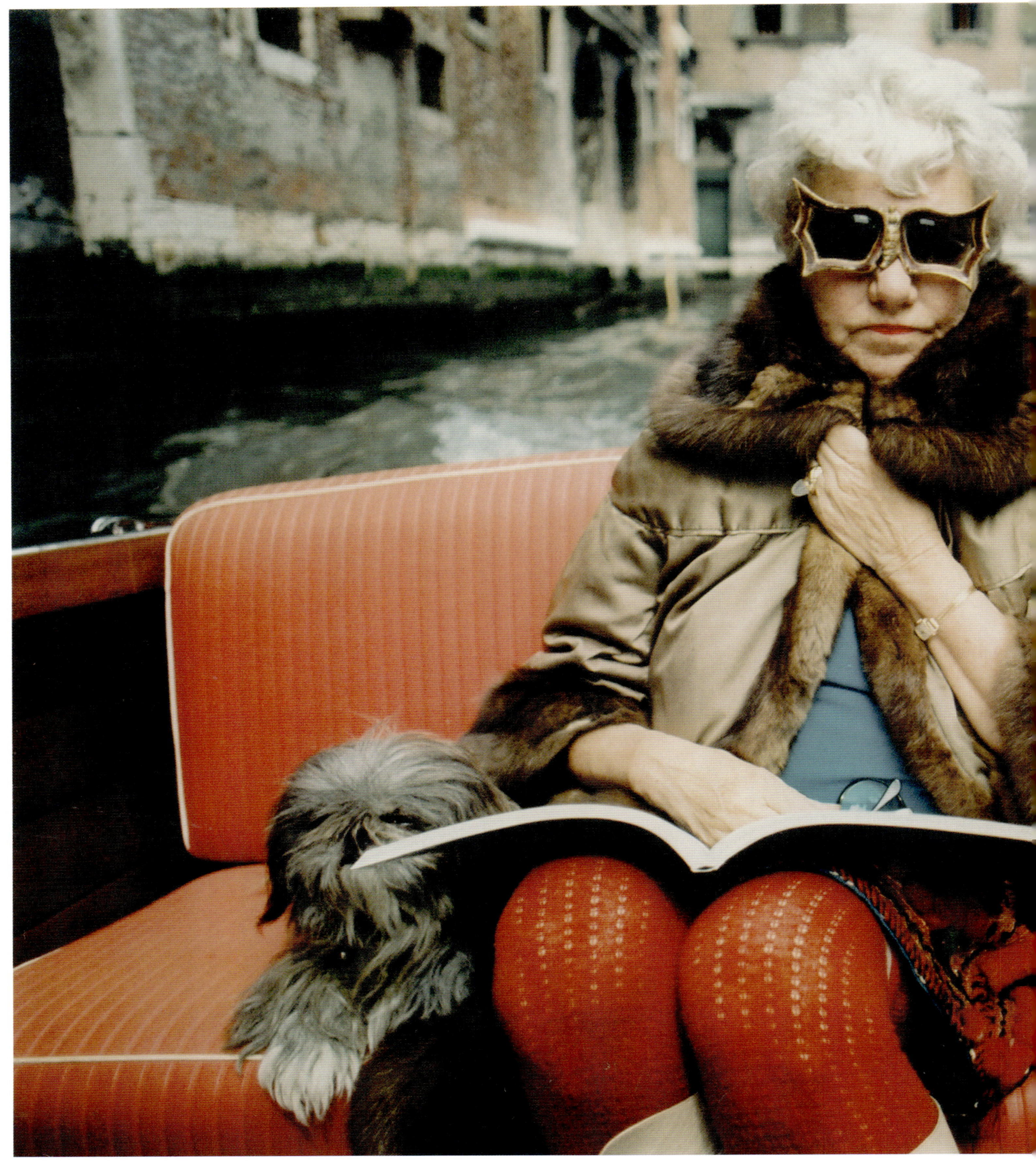

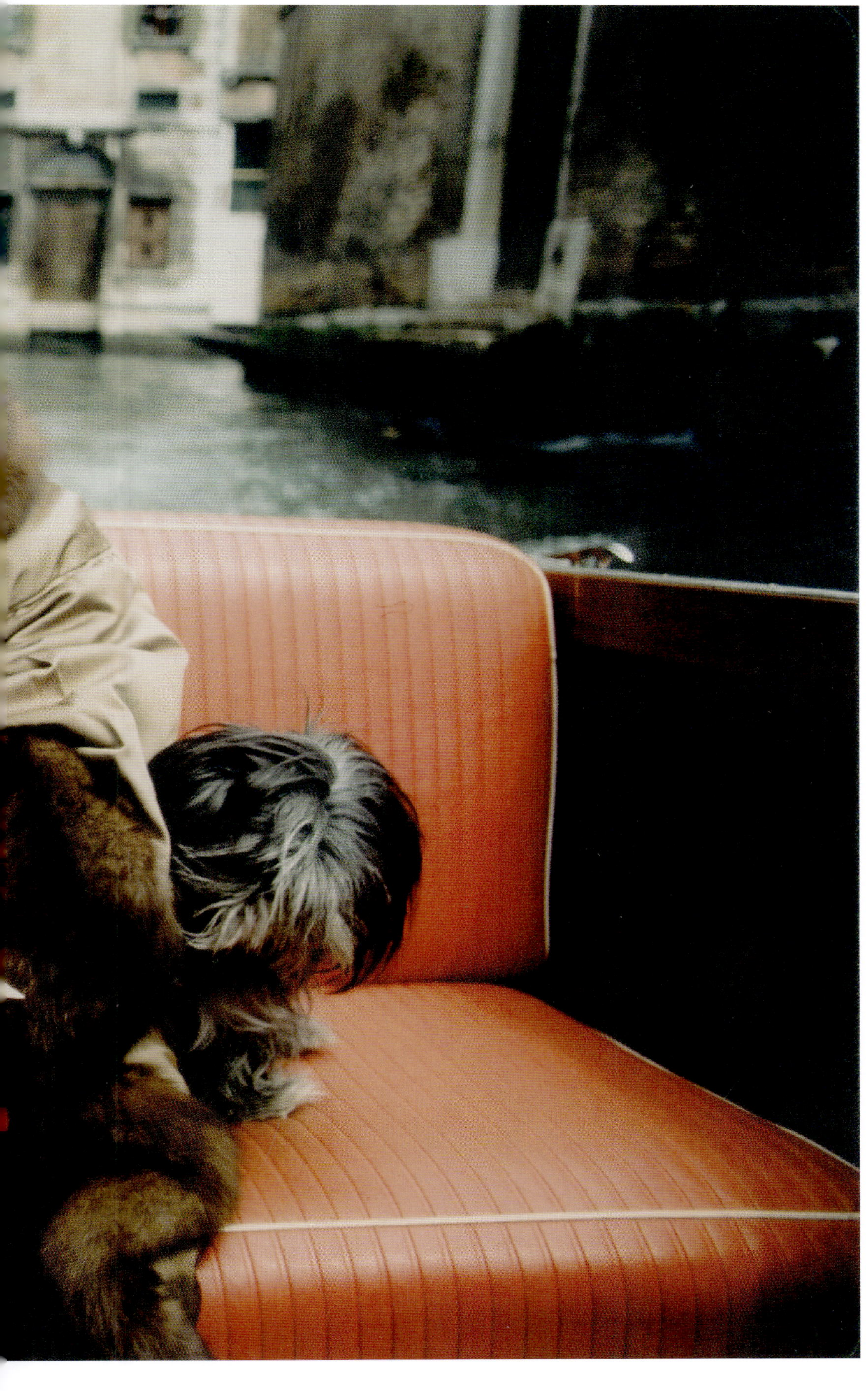

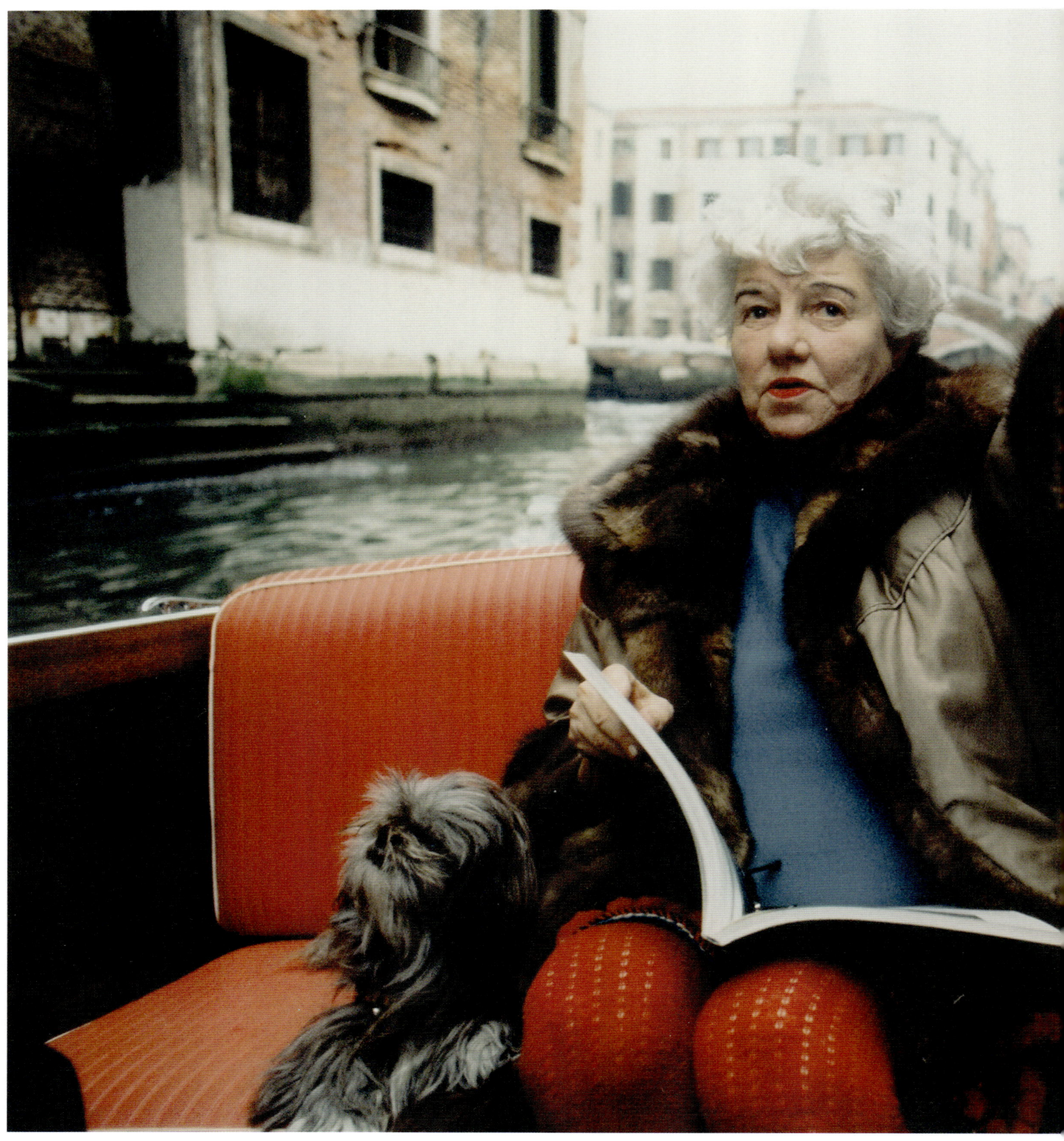

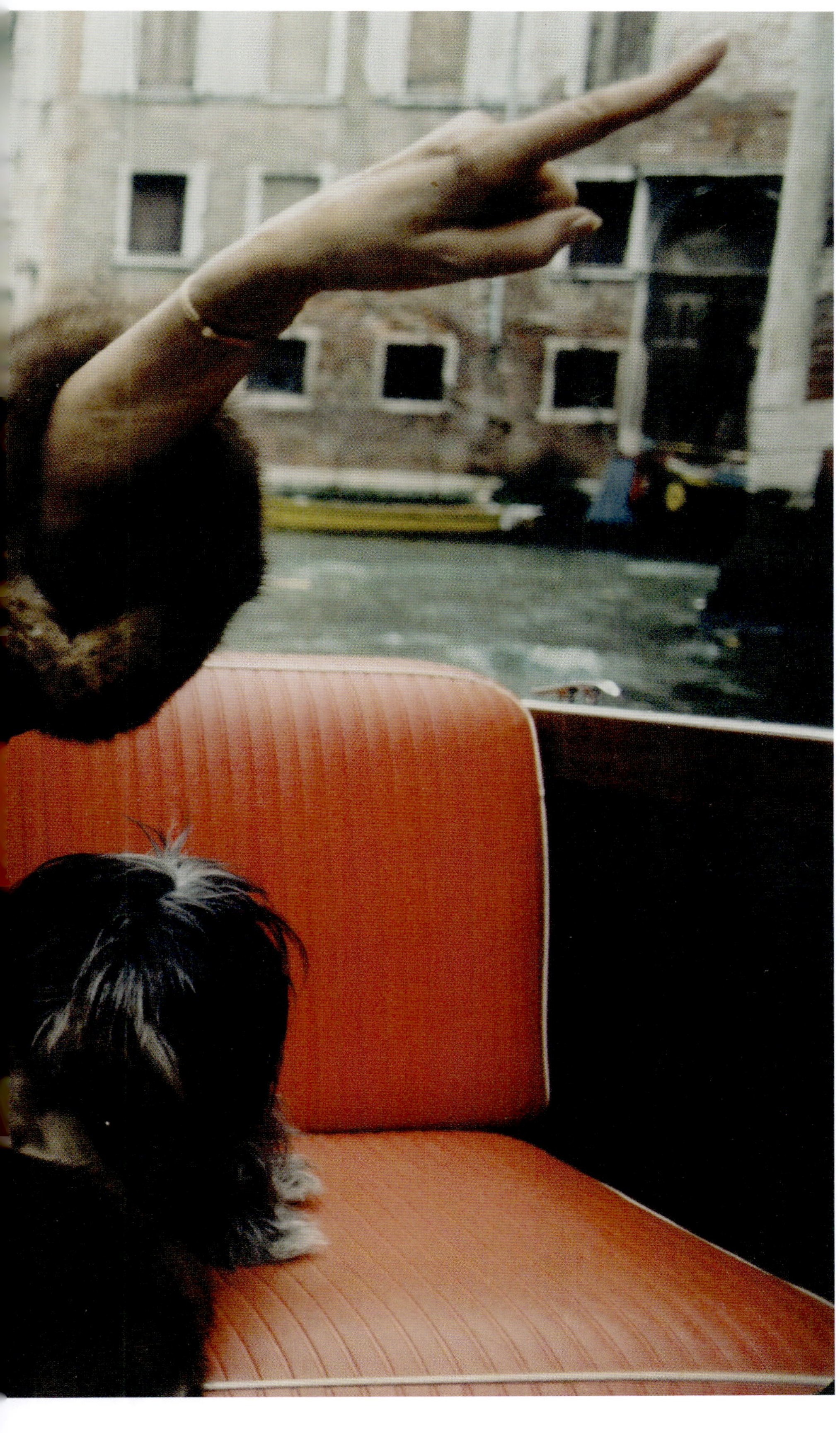

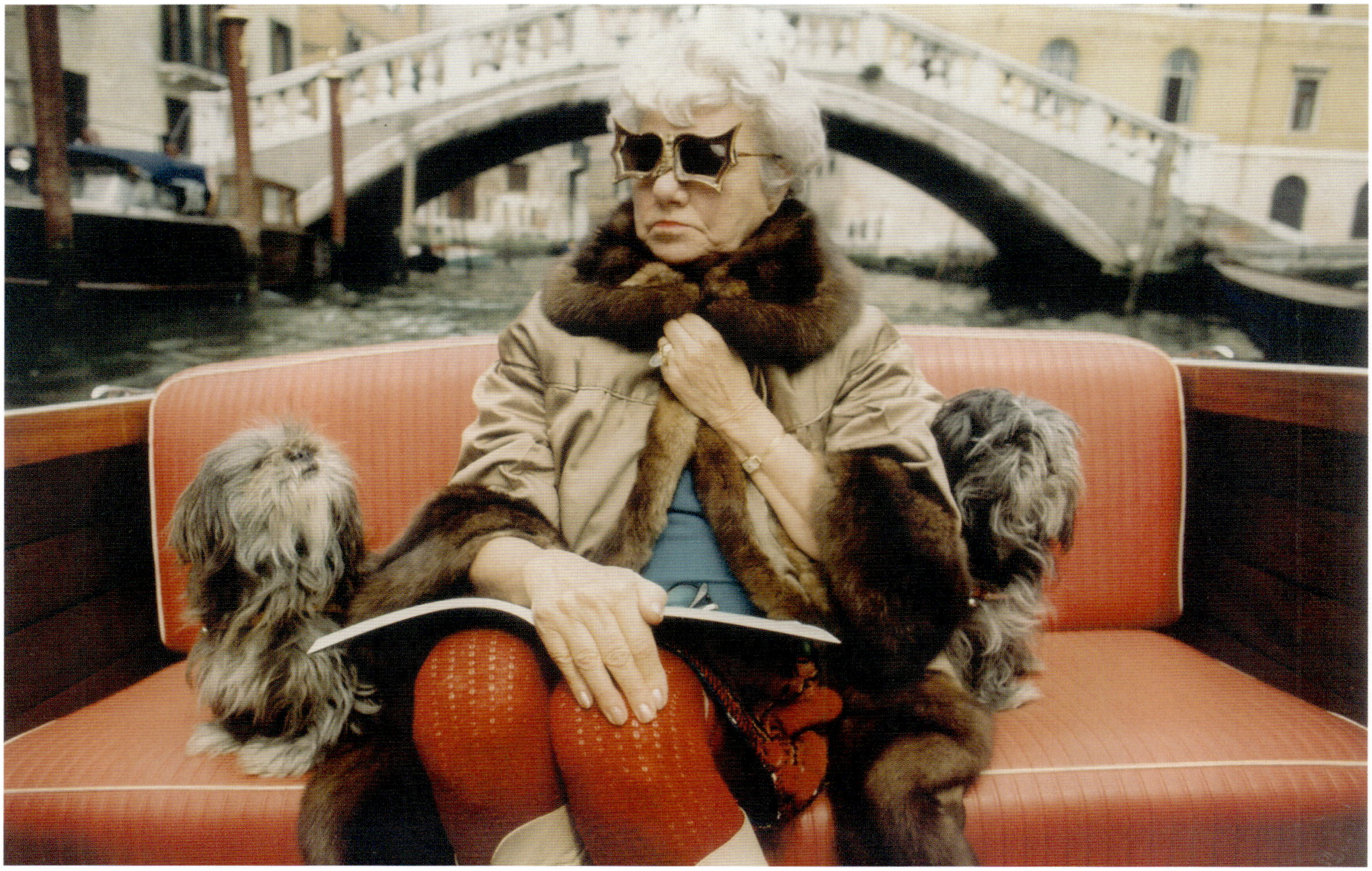

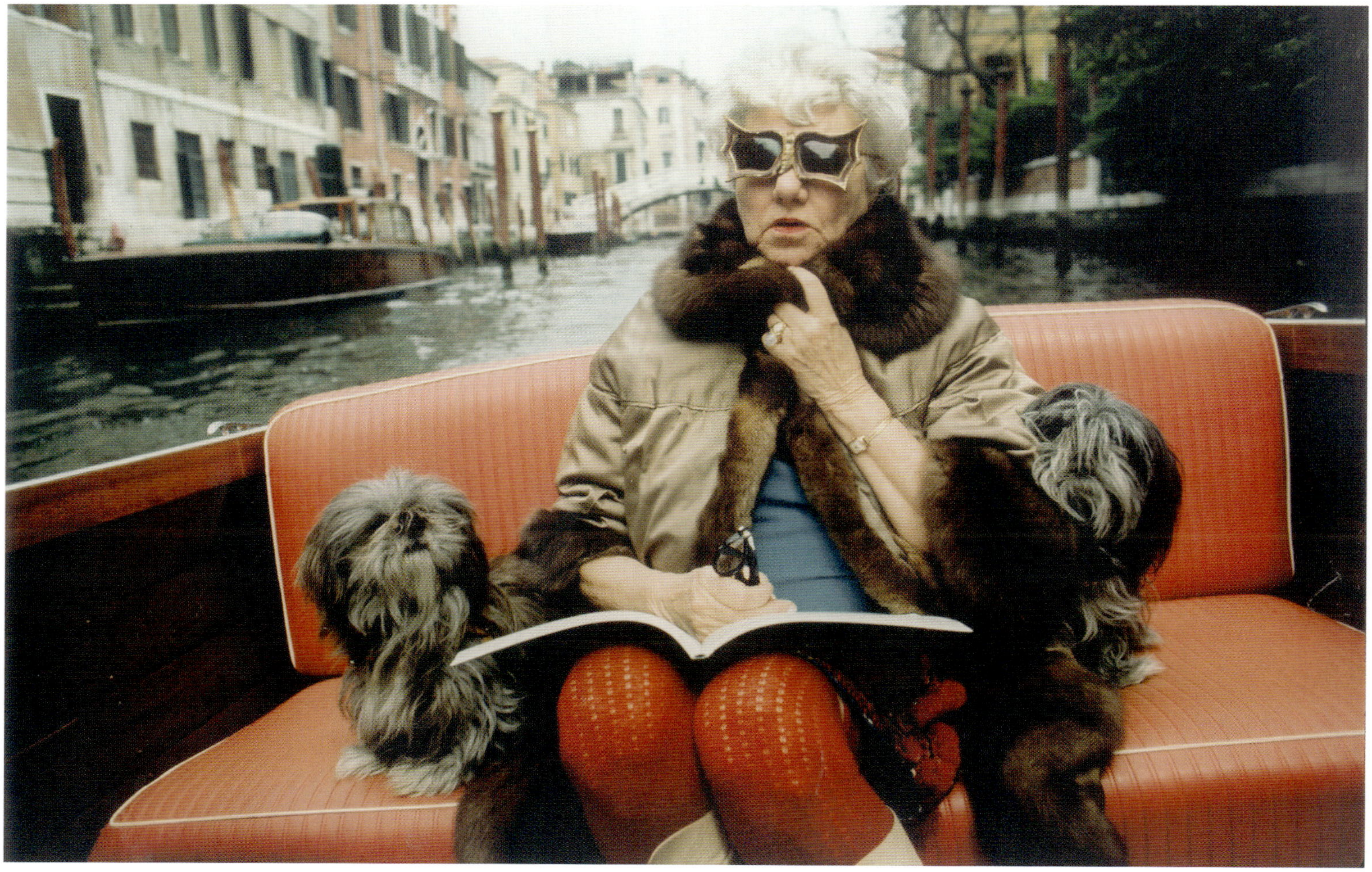

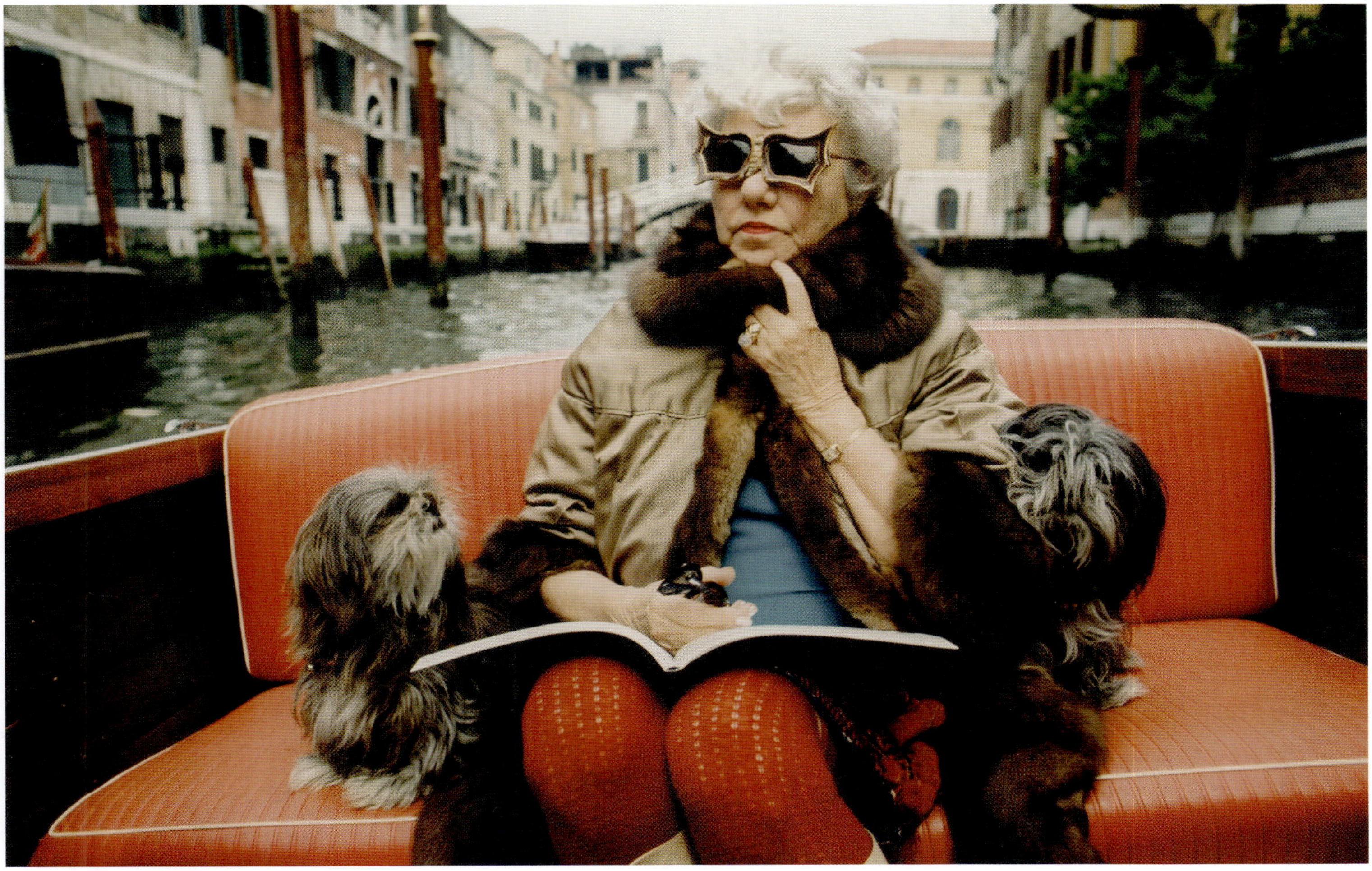

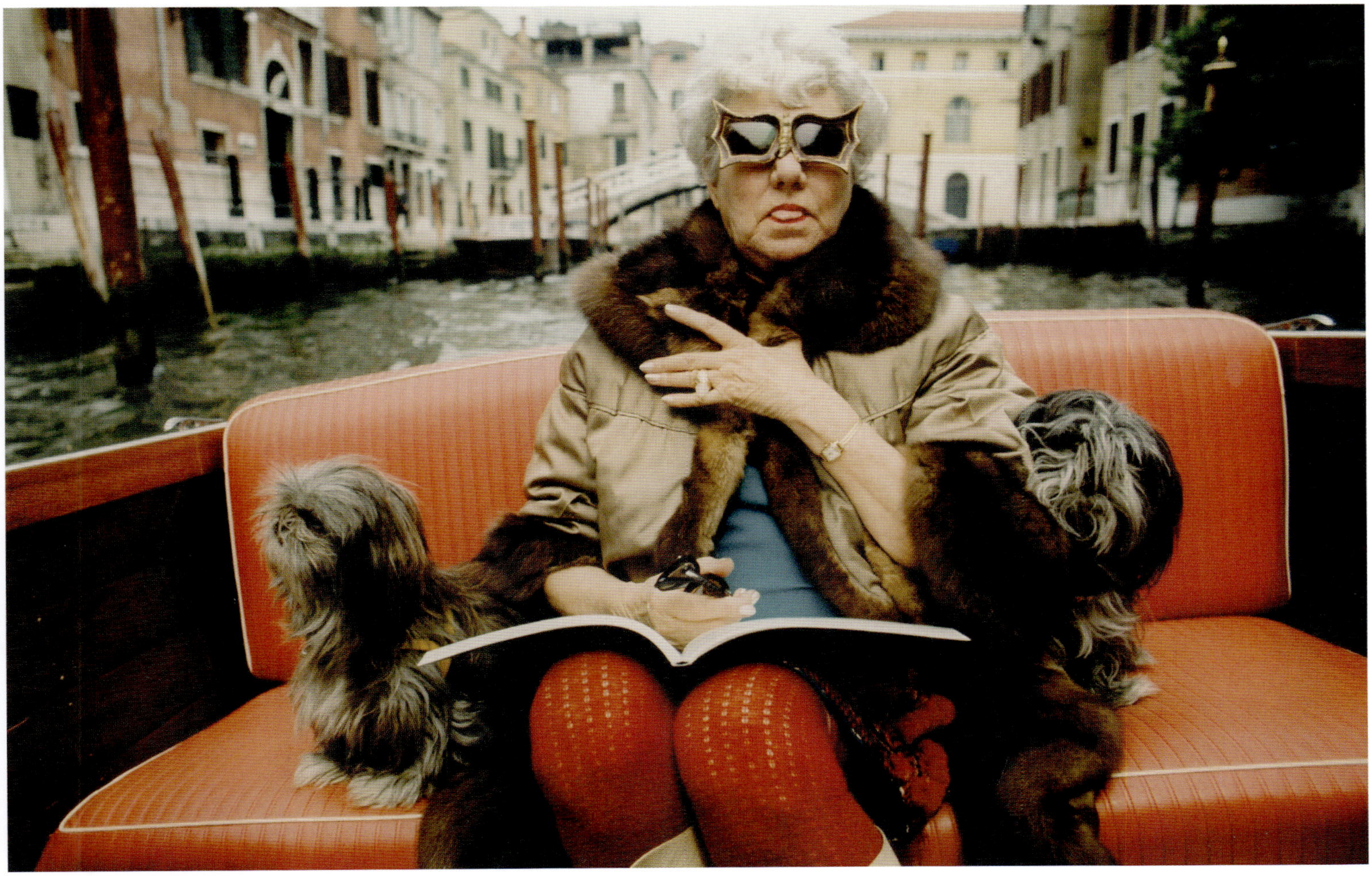

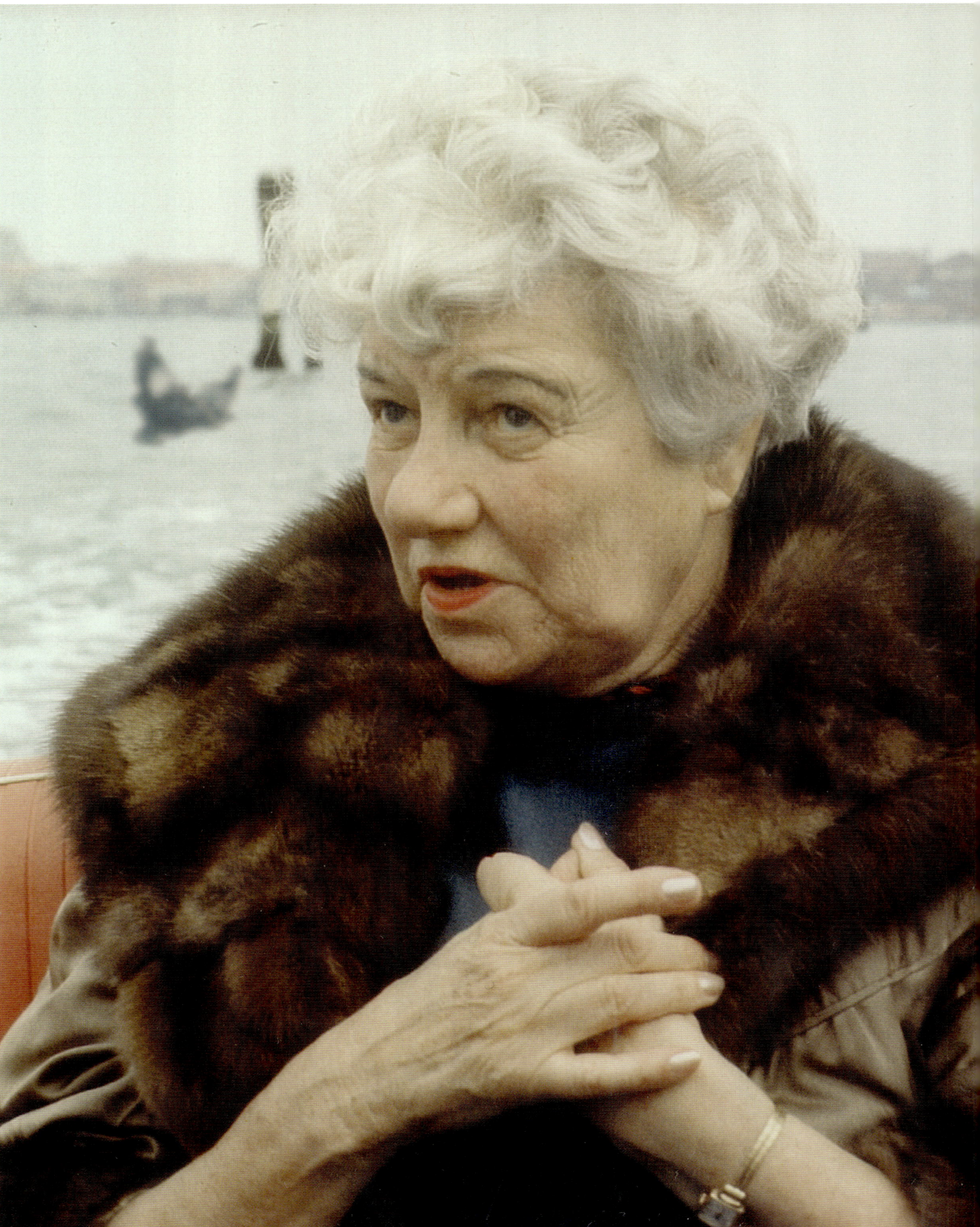

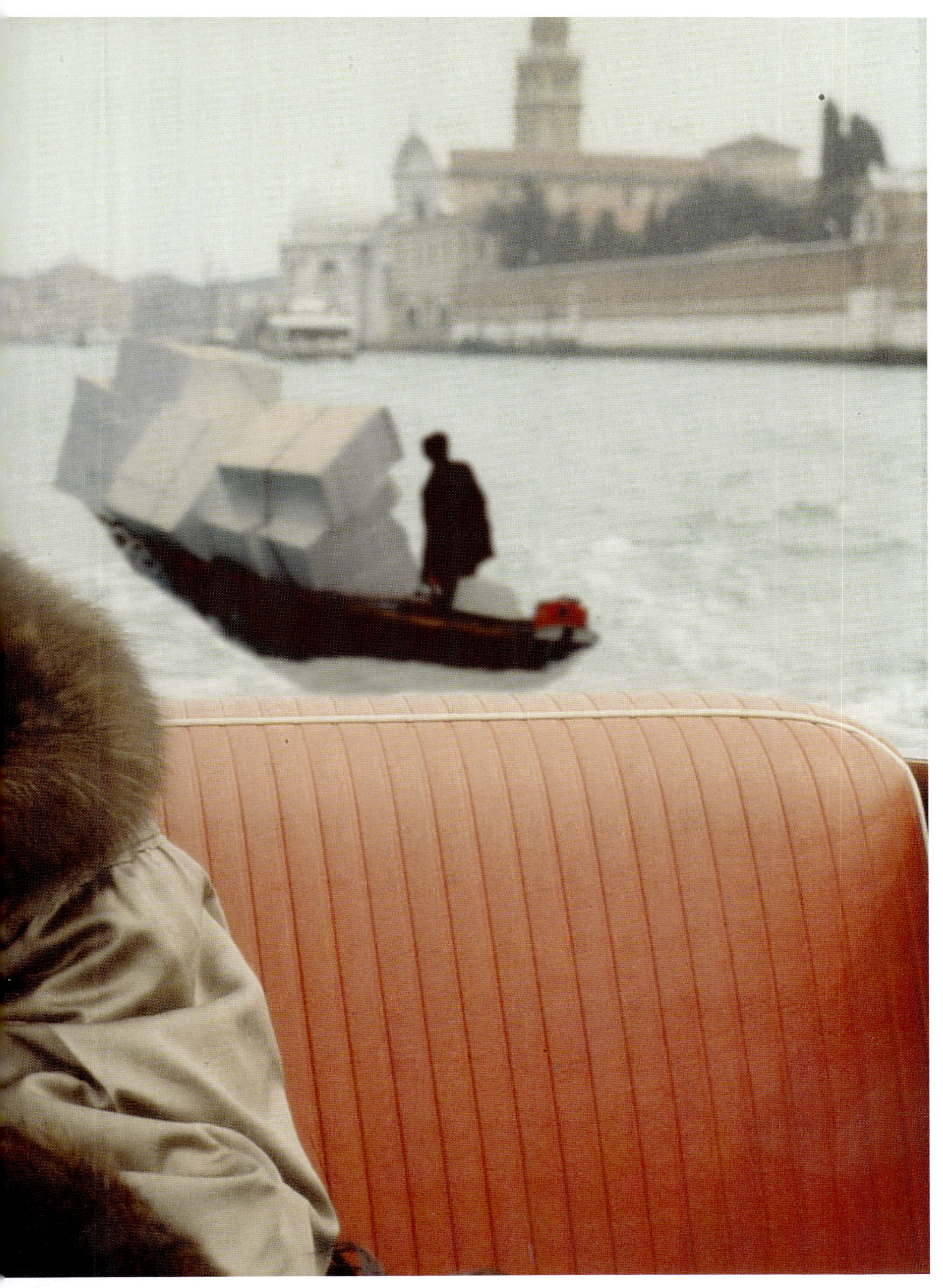

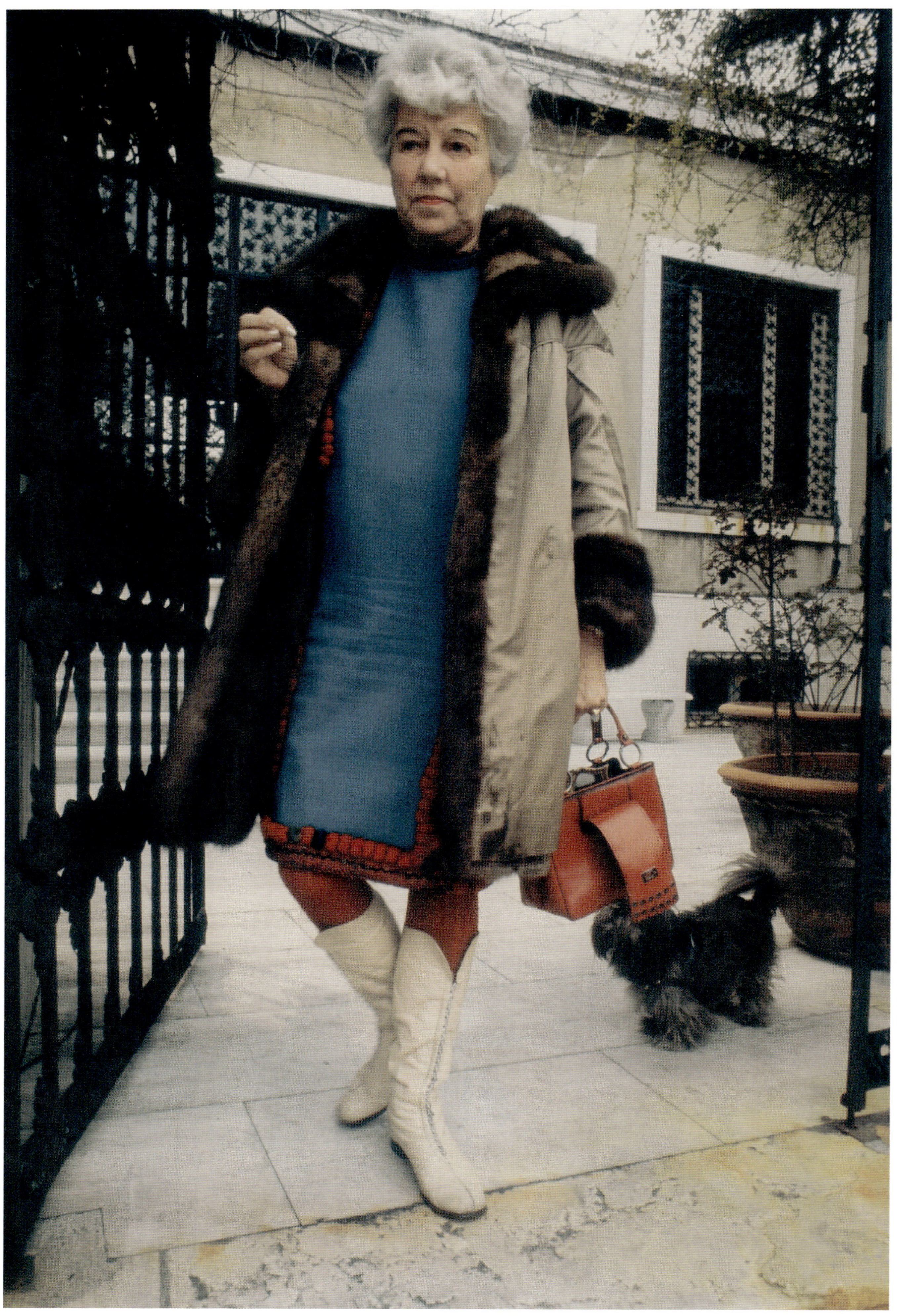

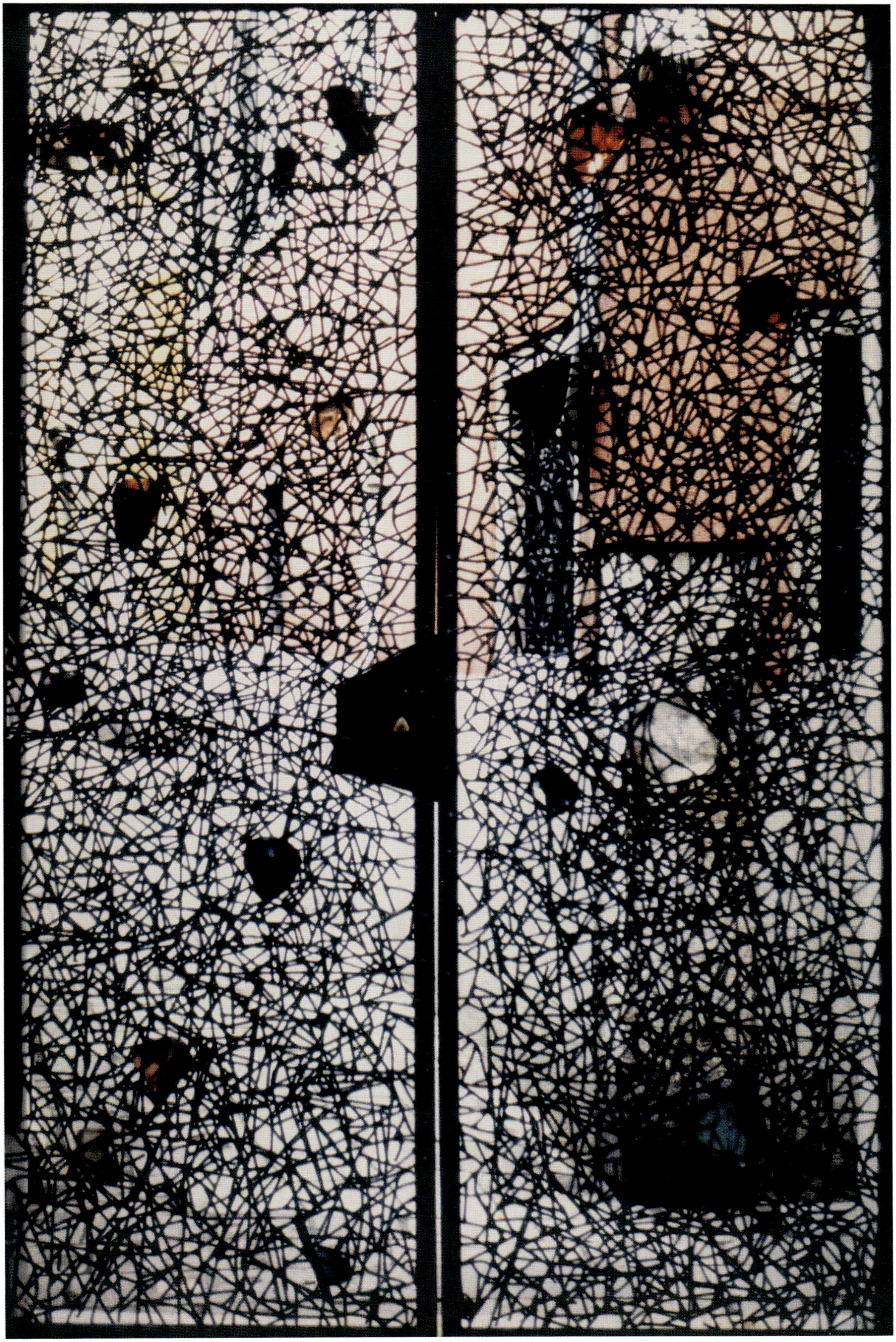

The gate onto Calle San Cristoforo by Claire Falkenstein (1961).
Peggy once called it the 'Gate to Paradise'.

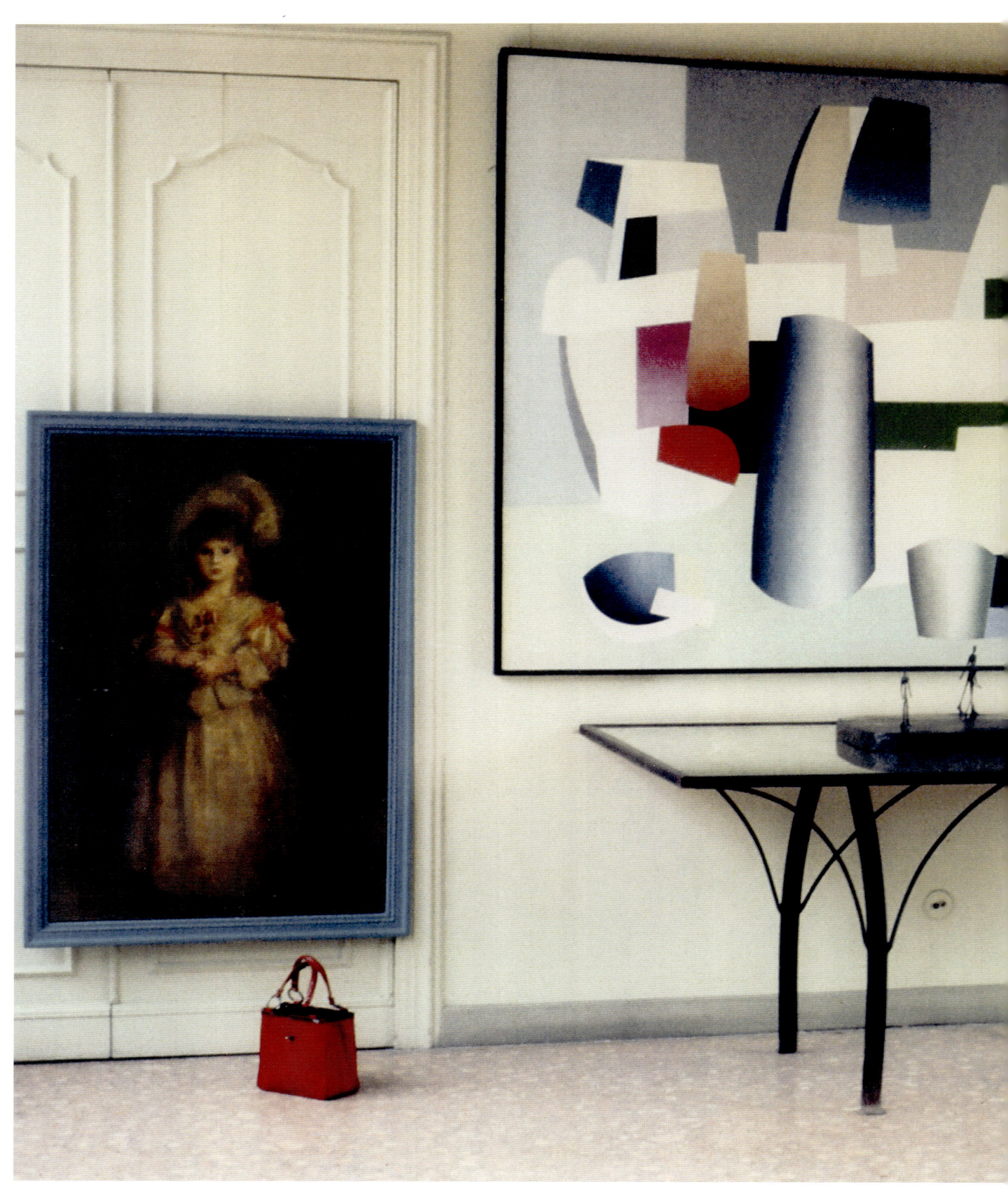

The palace entrance area. From left to right: Peggy Guggenheim in a 'Van Dyck' costume, portrait by Franz von Lenbach (c. 1903); Jean Hélion: *Composition* (1935); Alberto Giacometti's *Piazza* (1947–1948)

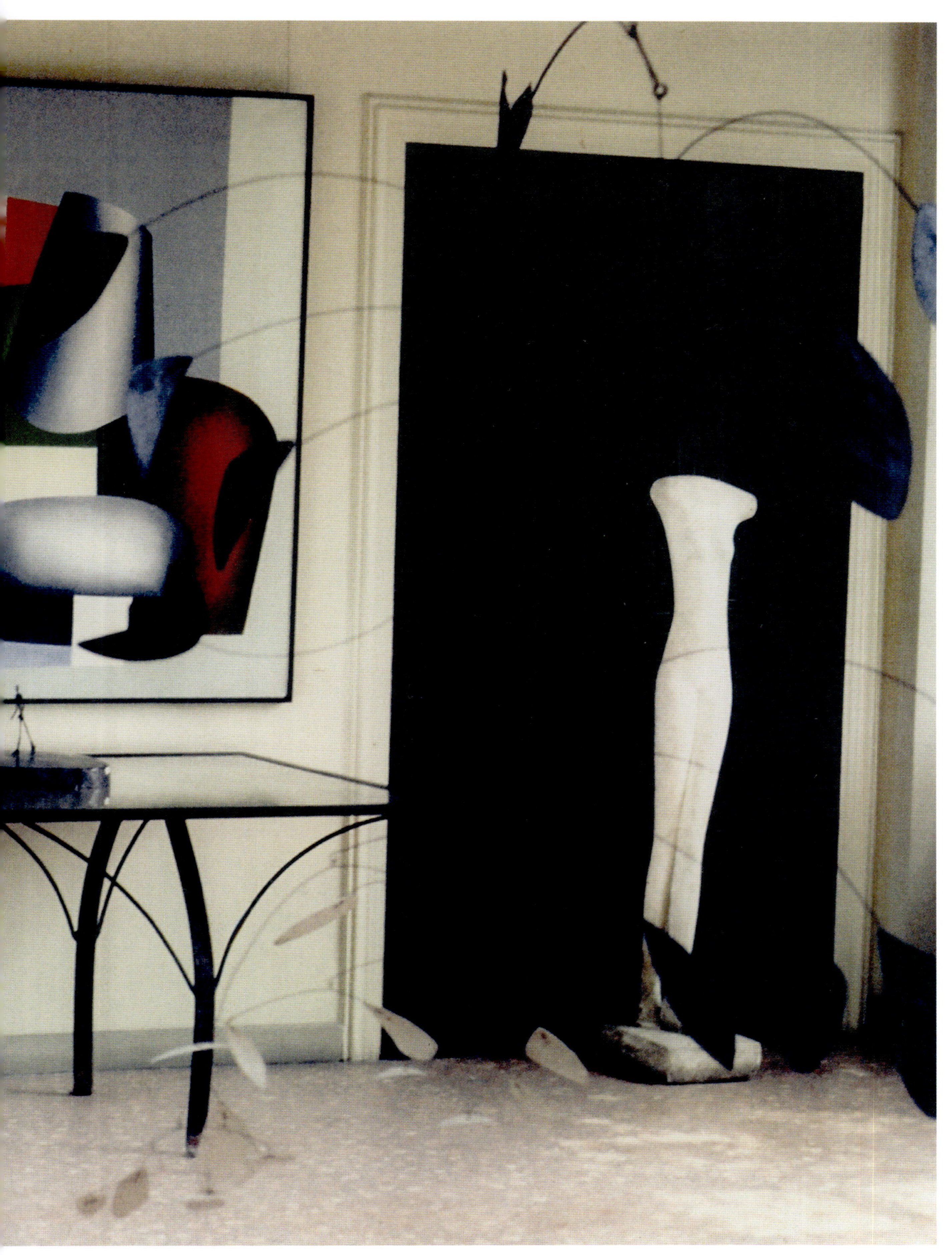

is to be seen on the Venetian glass table, and on the right is his *Gehende Frau* [Walking Woman] (1936). Alexander Calder's *Mobile Arc of Petals* (1941) is hanging in the foreground.

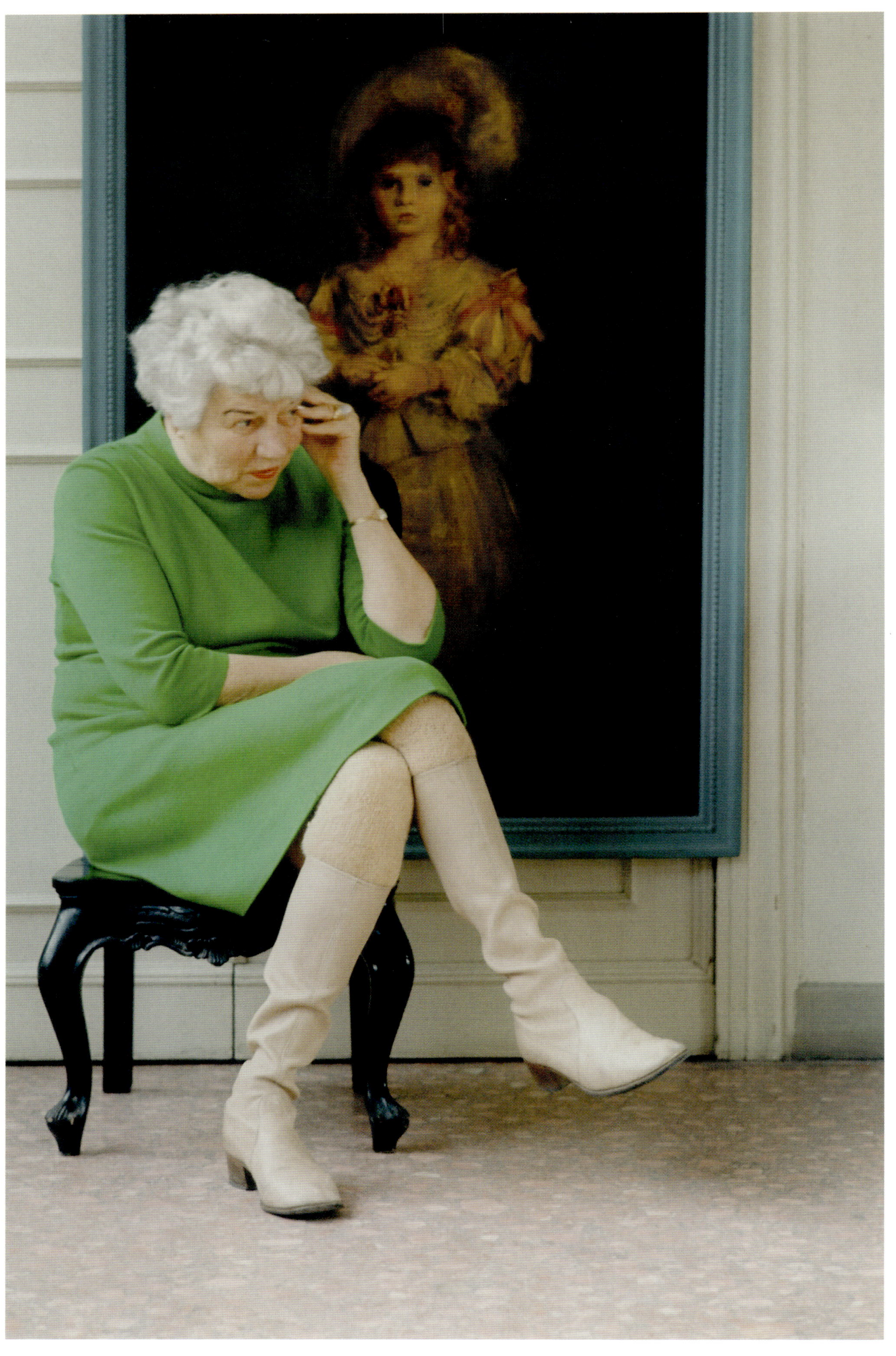

  In front of the portrait of her as a child (Franz von Lenbach, c. 1903).

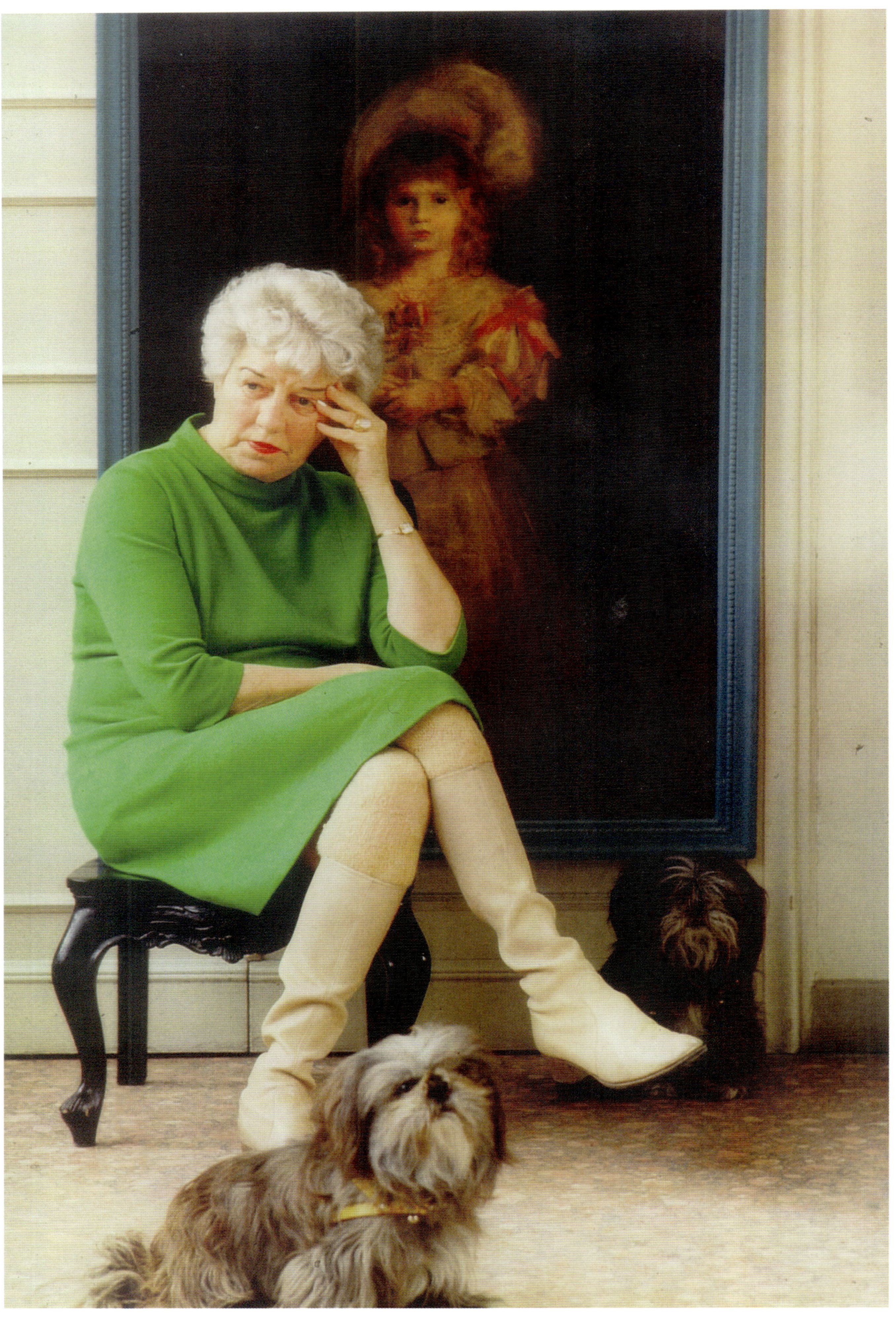

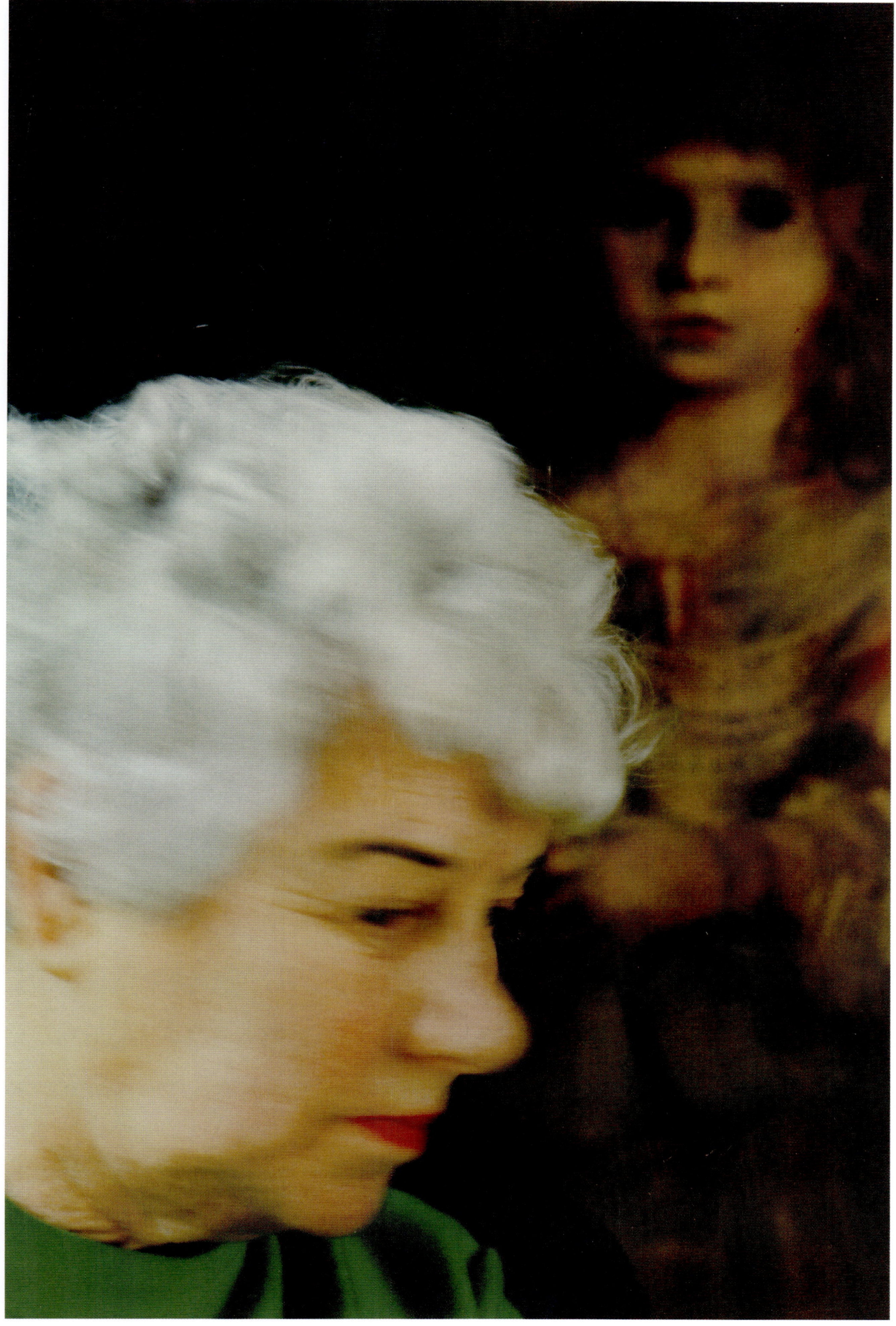

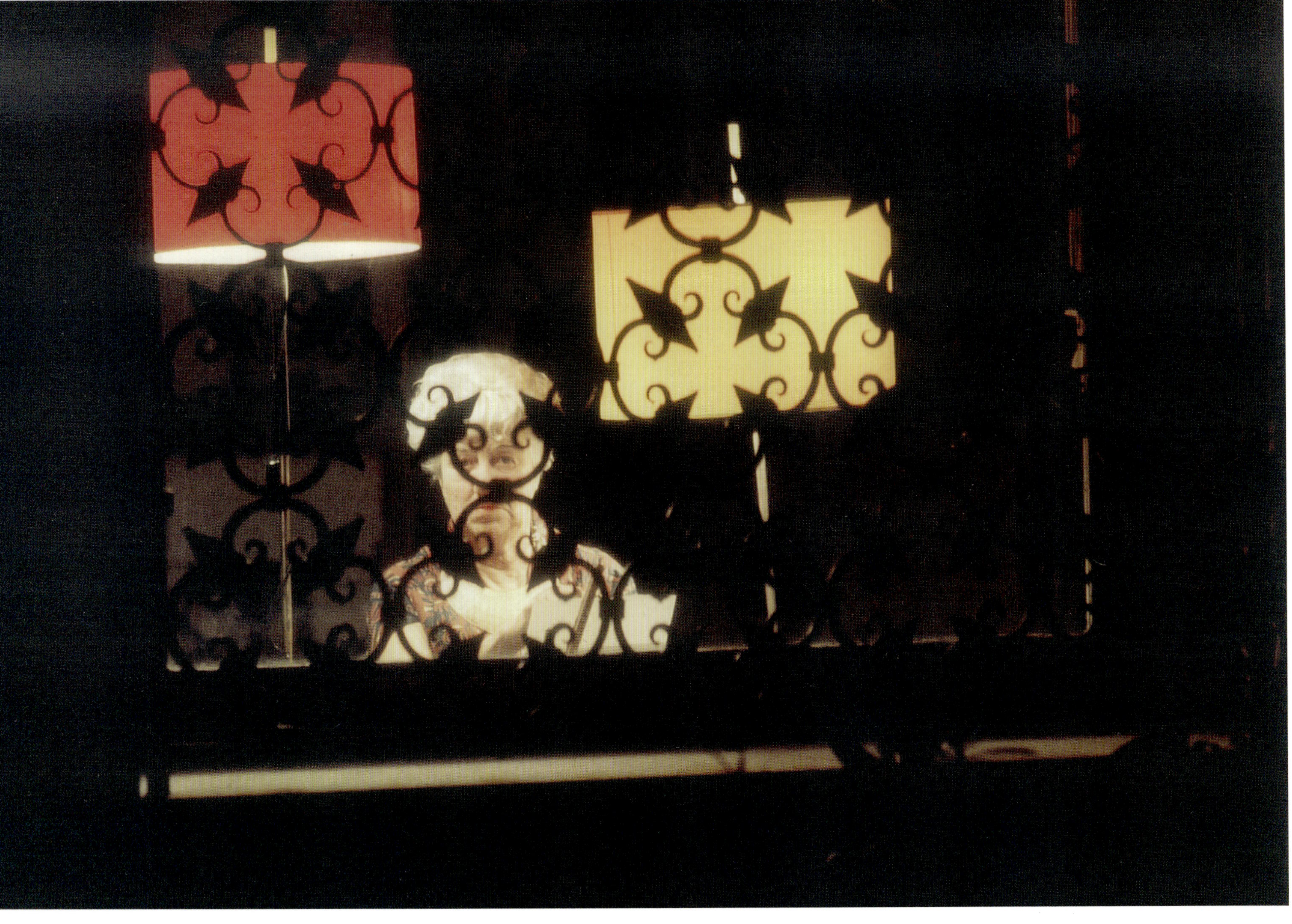

Late evening, at her desk in the library.

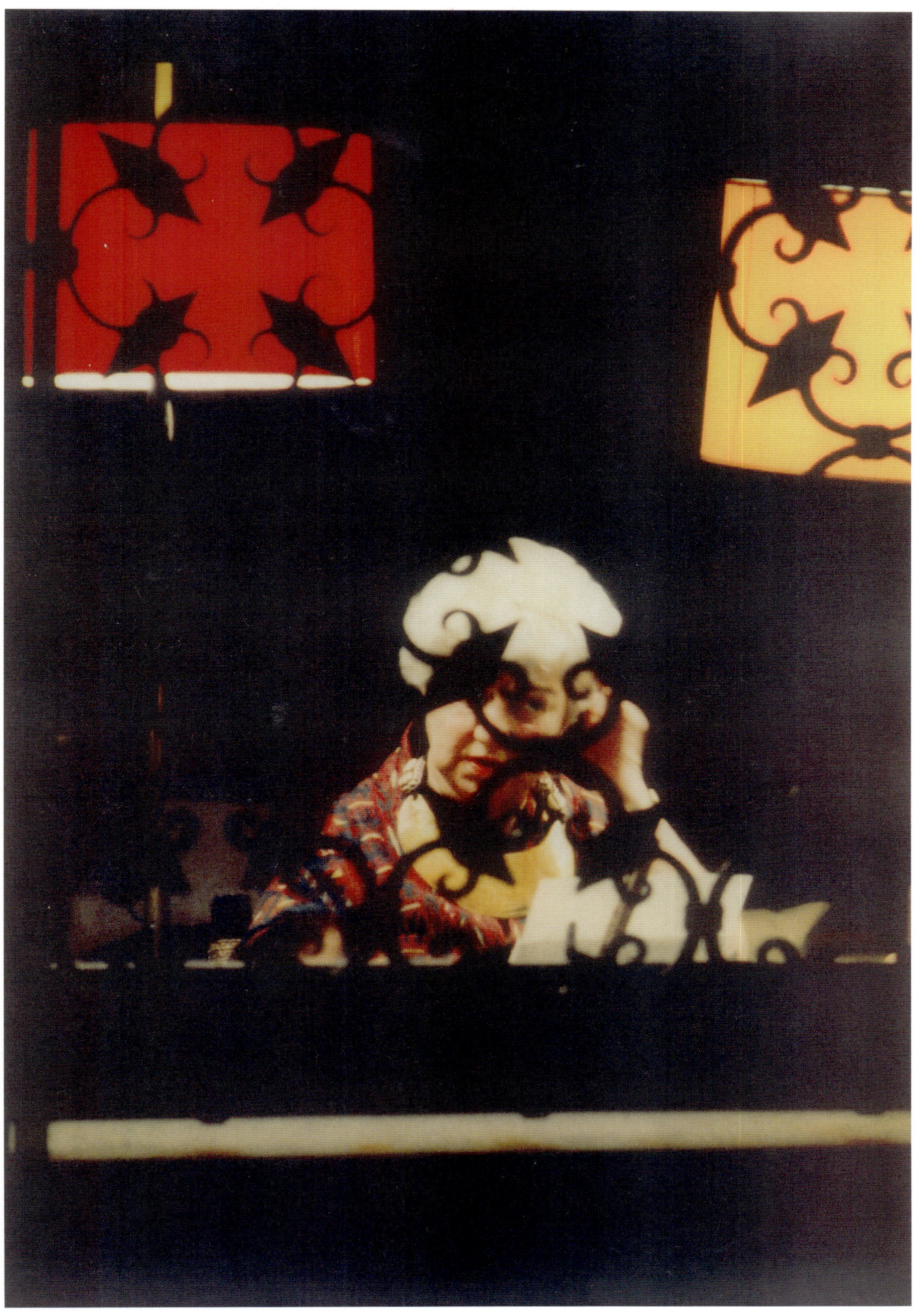

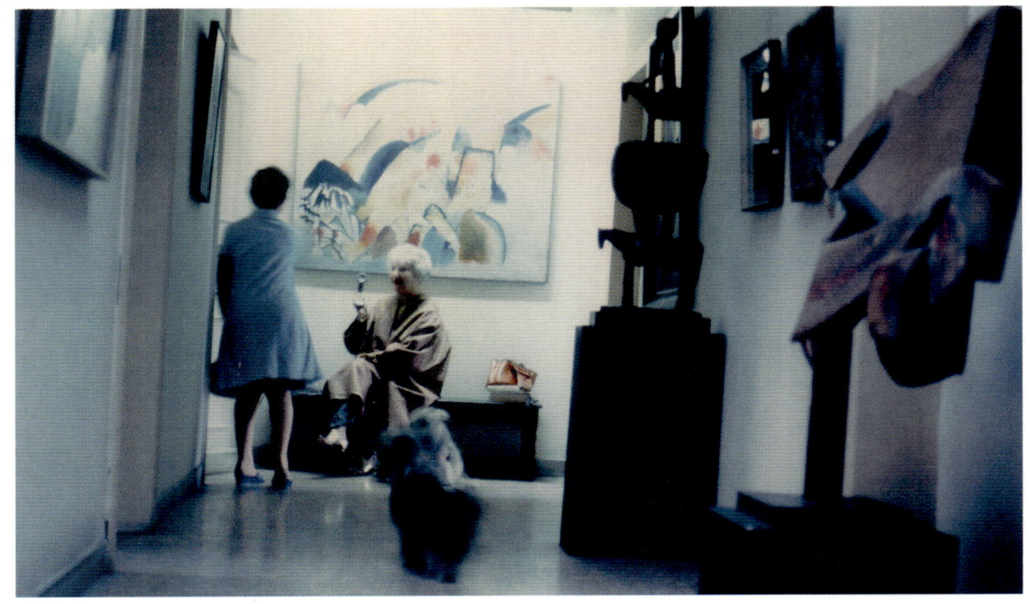

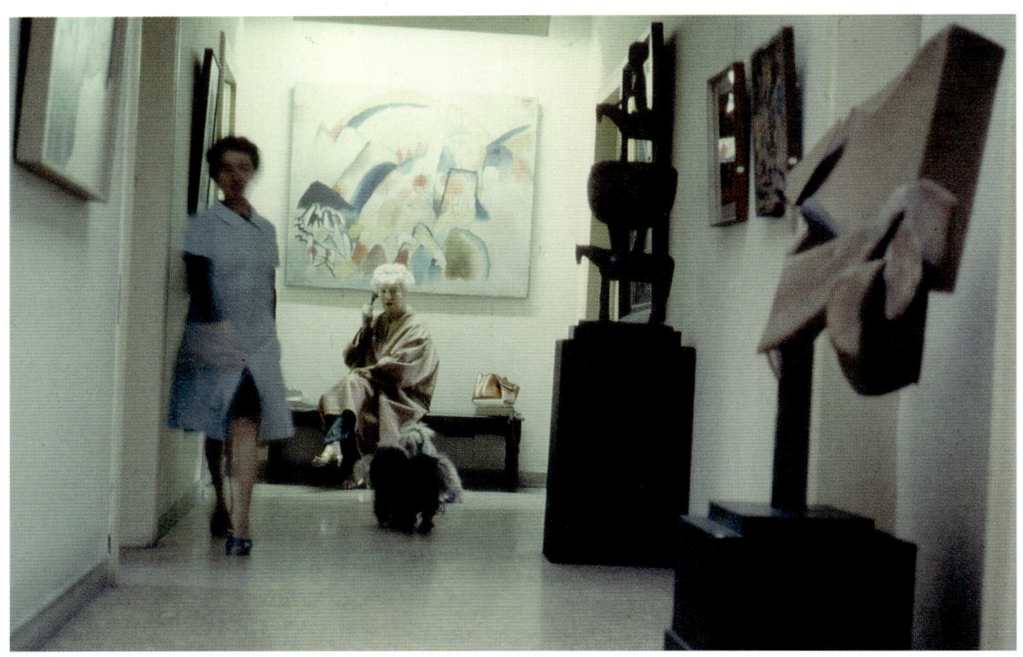

Peggy on the phone. Behind her is Wassily Kandinsky's *Landschaft mit Roten Flecken II* [Landscape with Red Spots II] (1913), and on the right in the foreground is Umberto Boccioni's *Dinamismo di un Cavallo in Corsa + Case* [Dynamism of a Speeding Horse + Houses] (1915).


Peggy still on the phone. In the foreground you can see a carved wooden bowl with lid. It comes from the Dogon people of Mali, Africa.

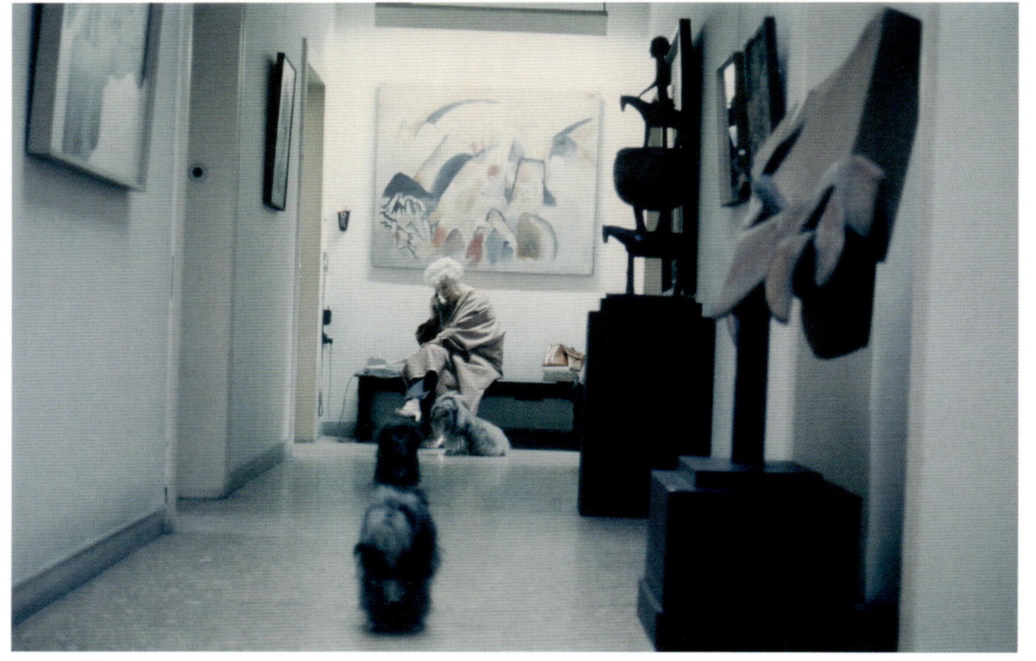

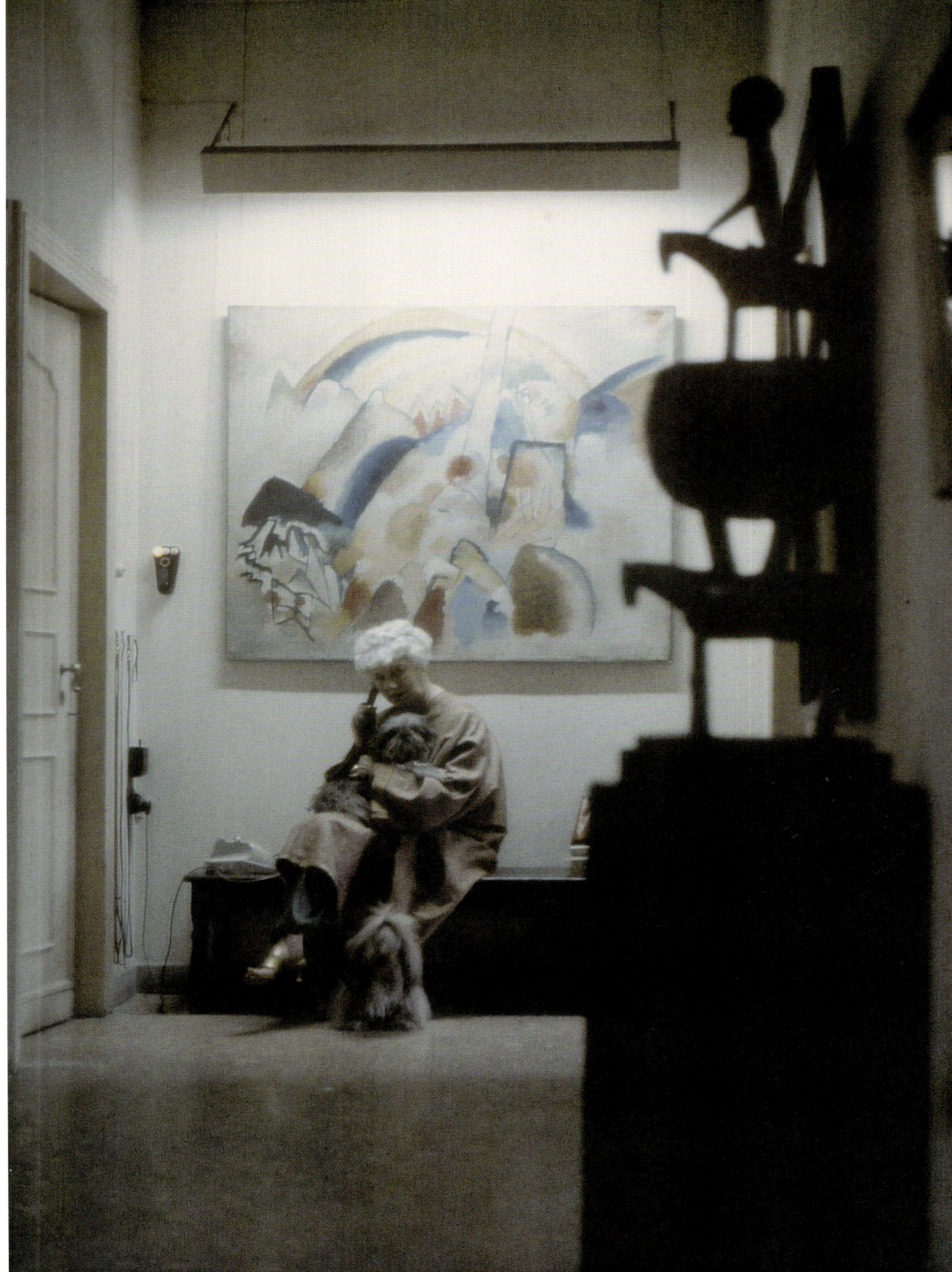

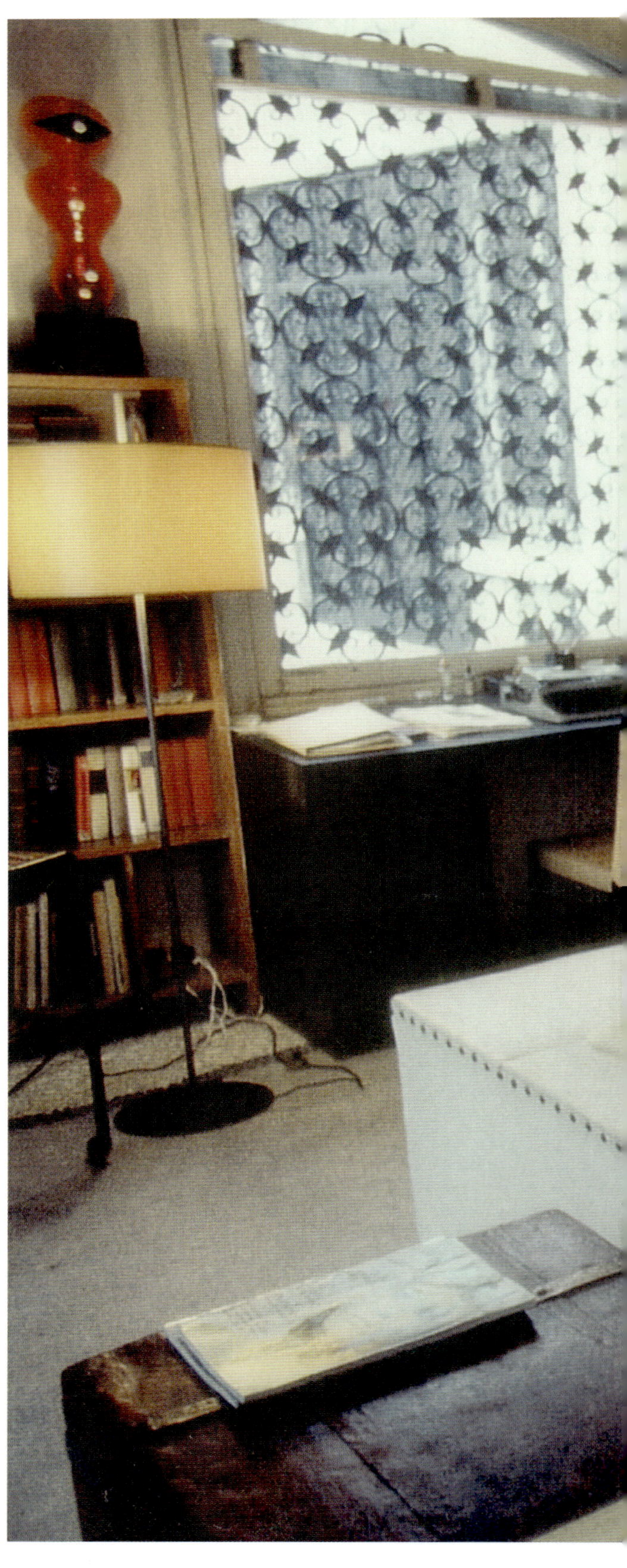

pp 56–59

Giuseppe Santomaso shows Peggy his painting *Vita Segreta* [Secret Life] (1958) in the library. The picture now belongs to the Peggy Guggenheim Collection.

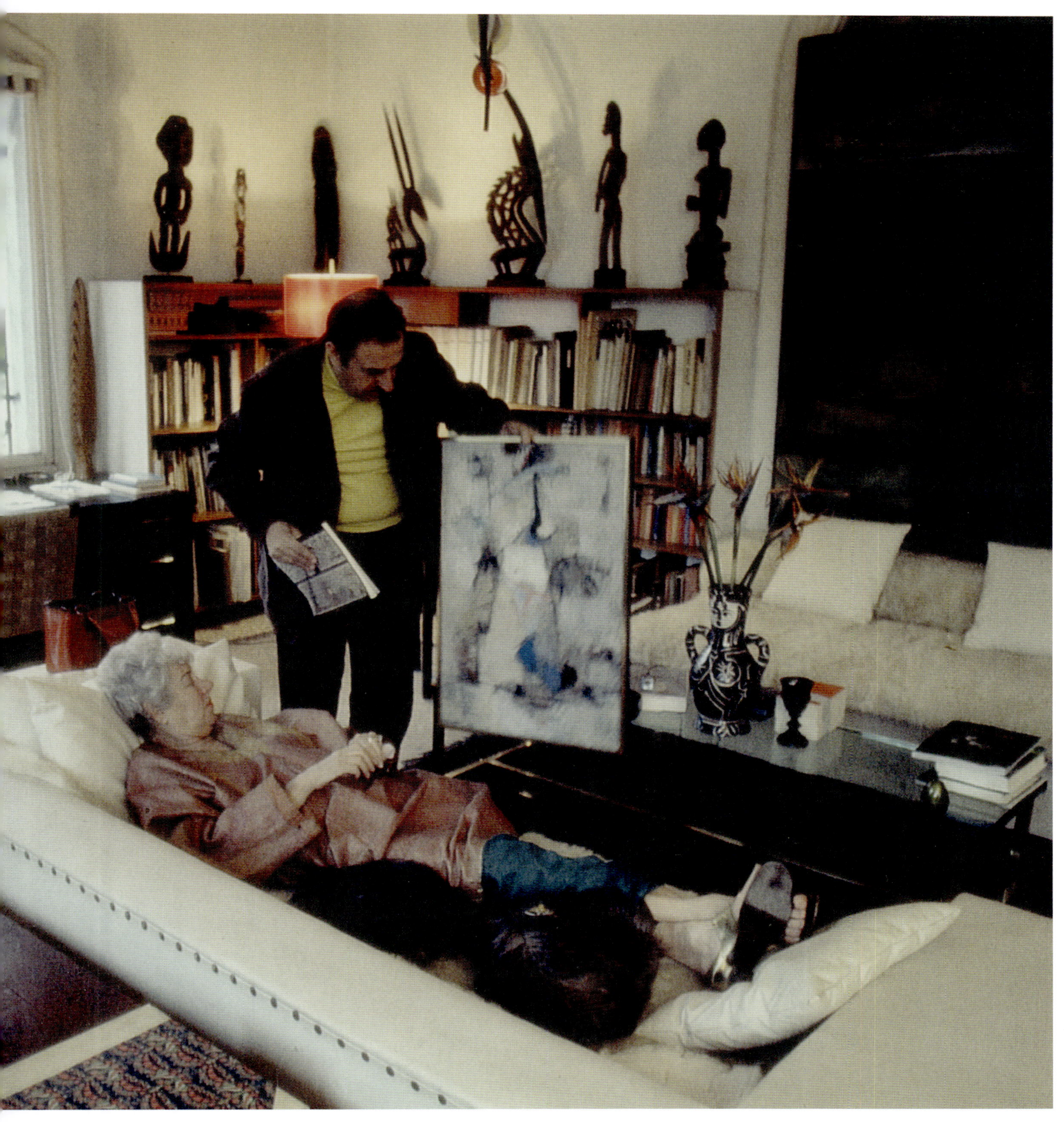

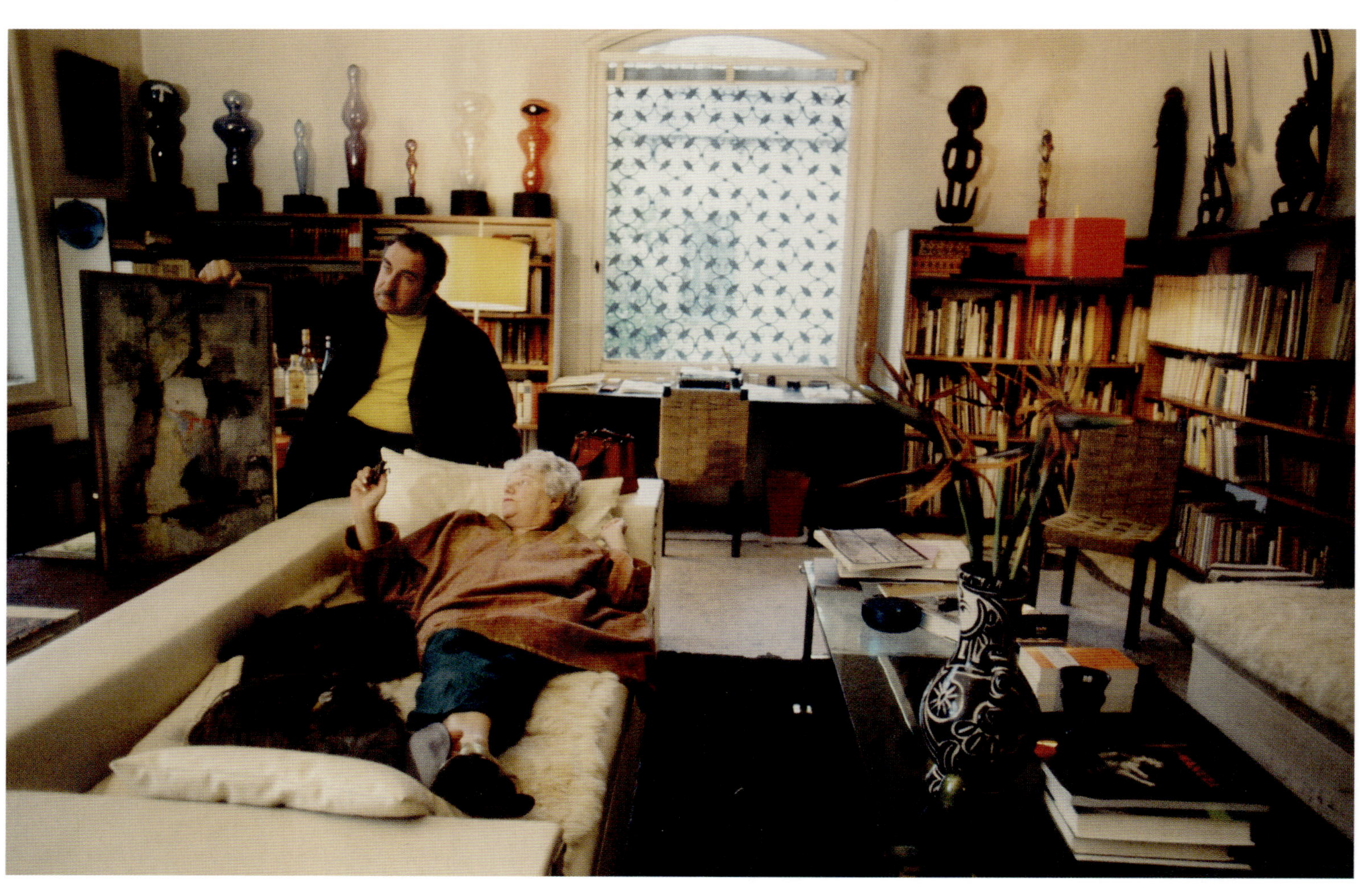

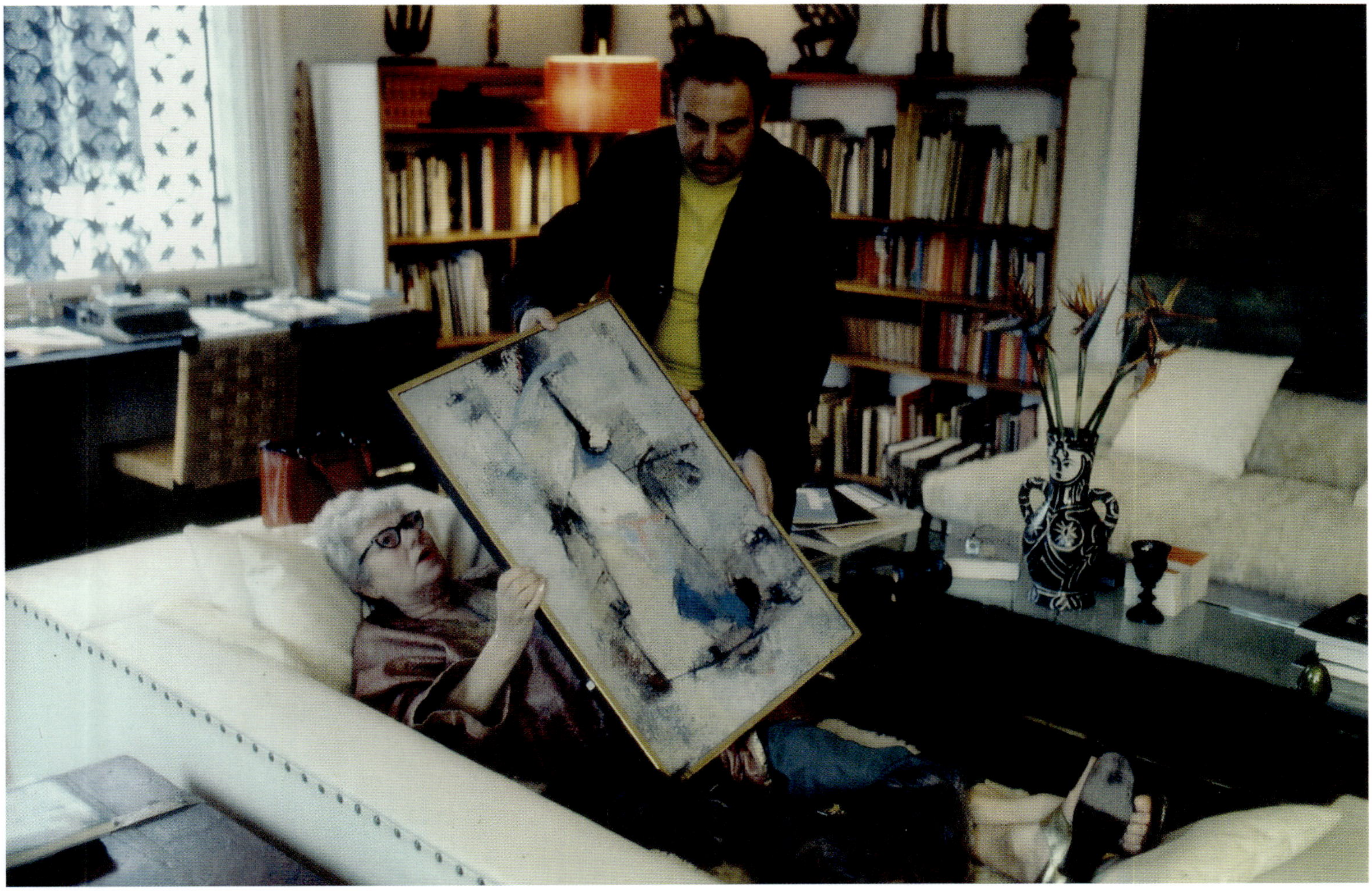

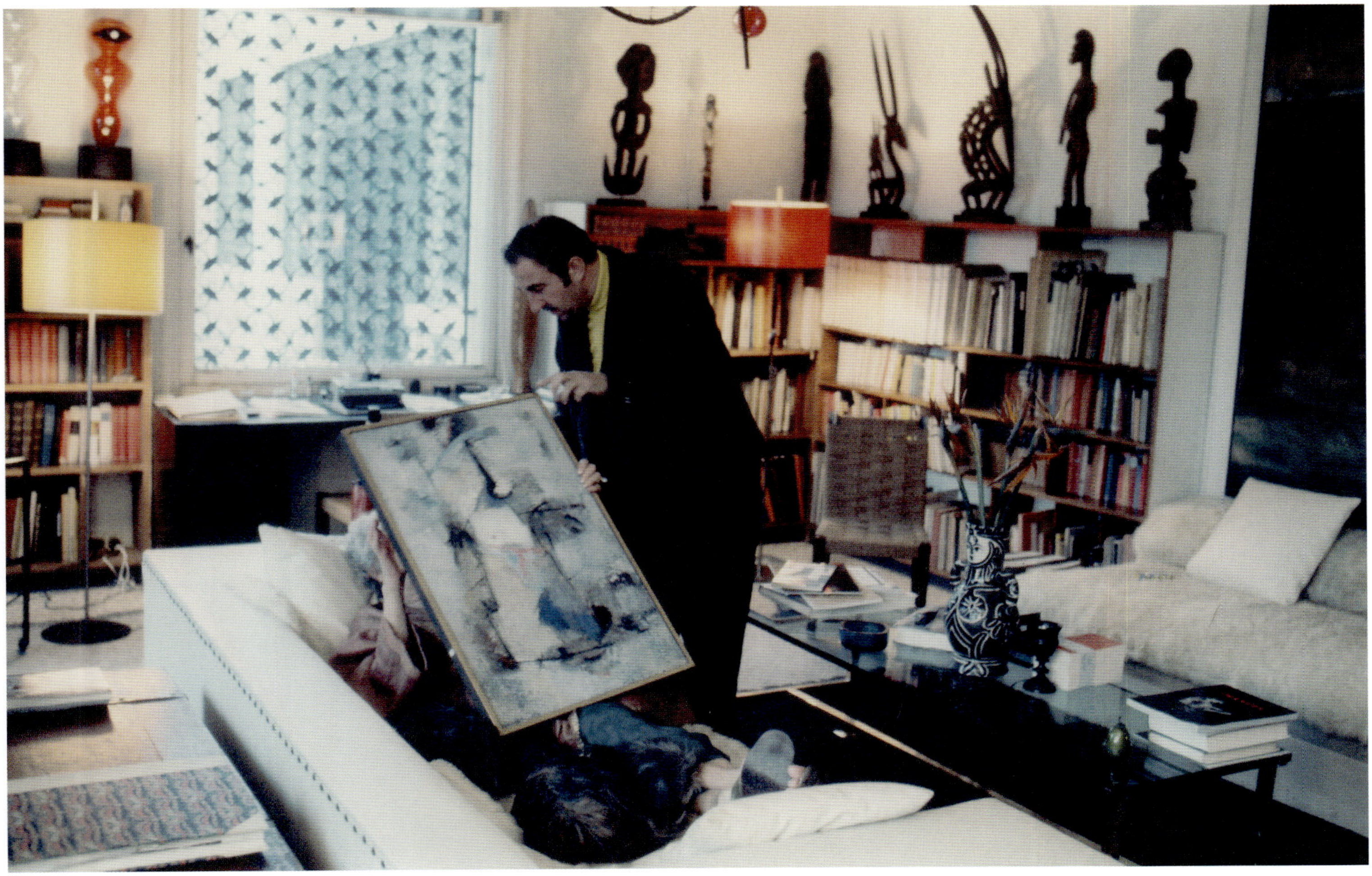

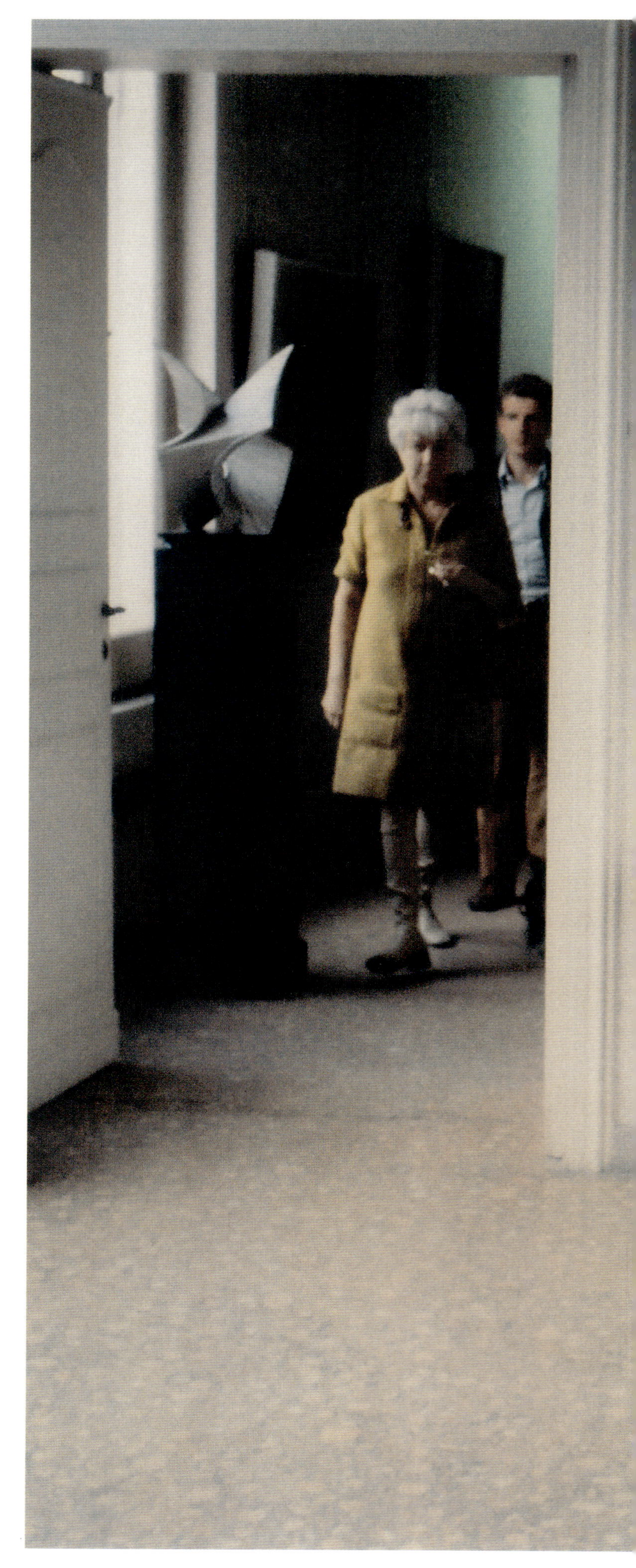

Peggy and the author Pierre Hoffmann
in the hall on the east side of the
Palazzo Venier dei Leoni.

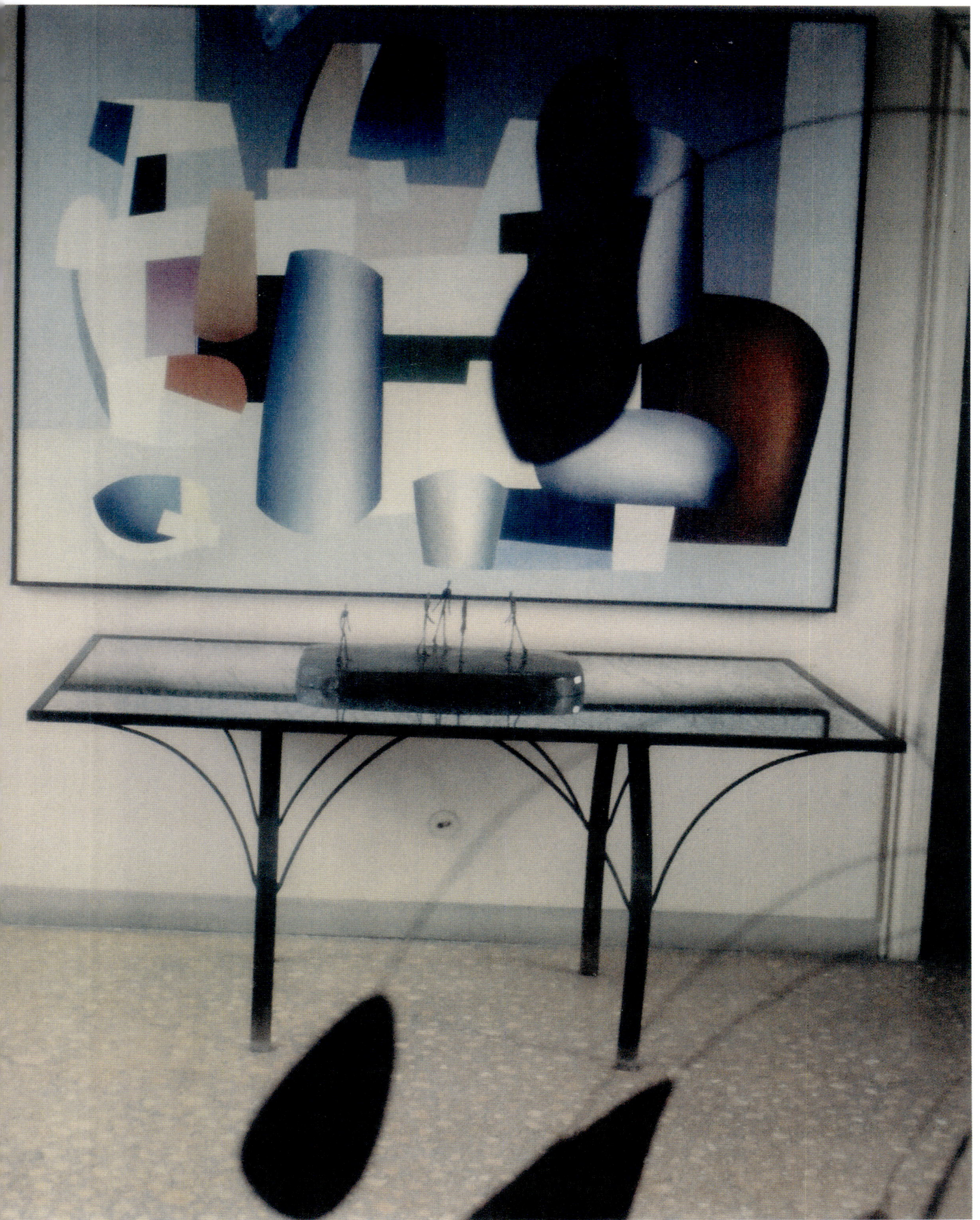

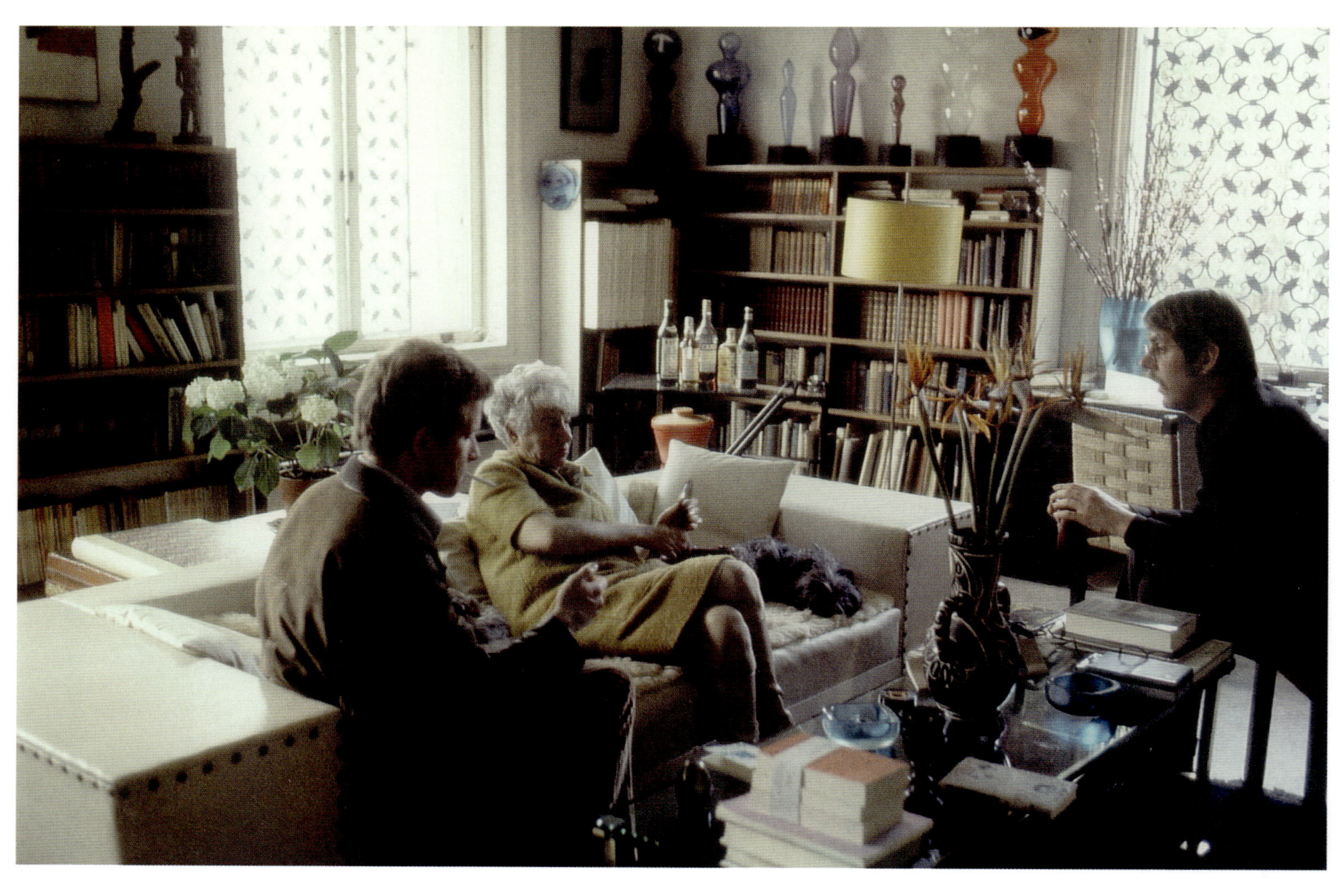

In her library, talking to the authors
Uli Weyland and Pierre Hoffmann.

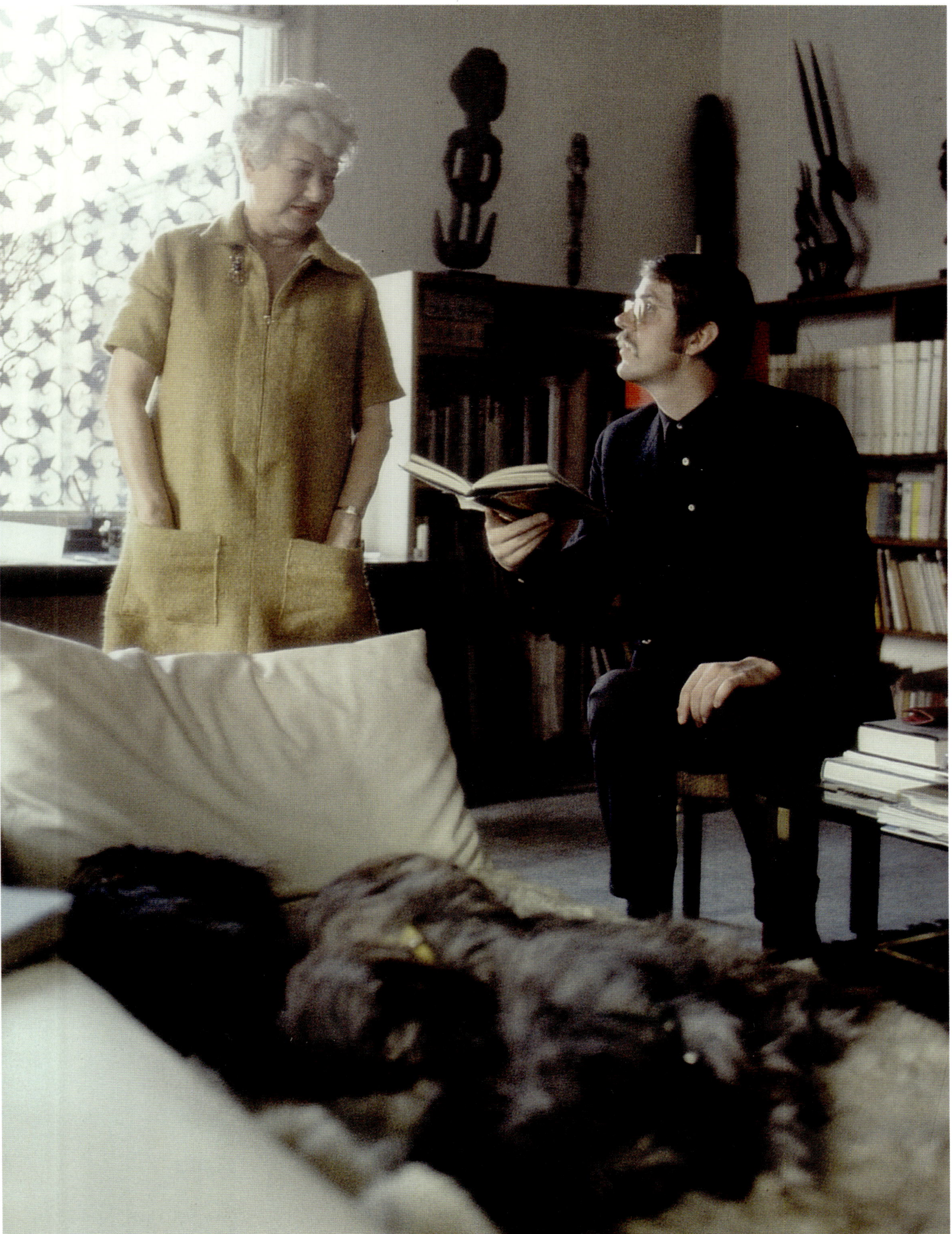

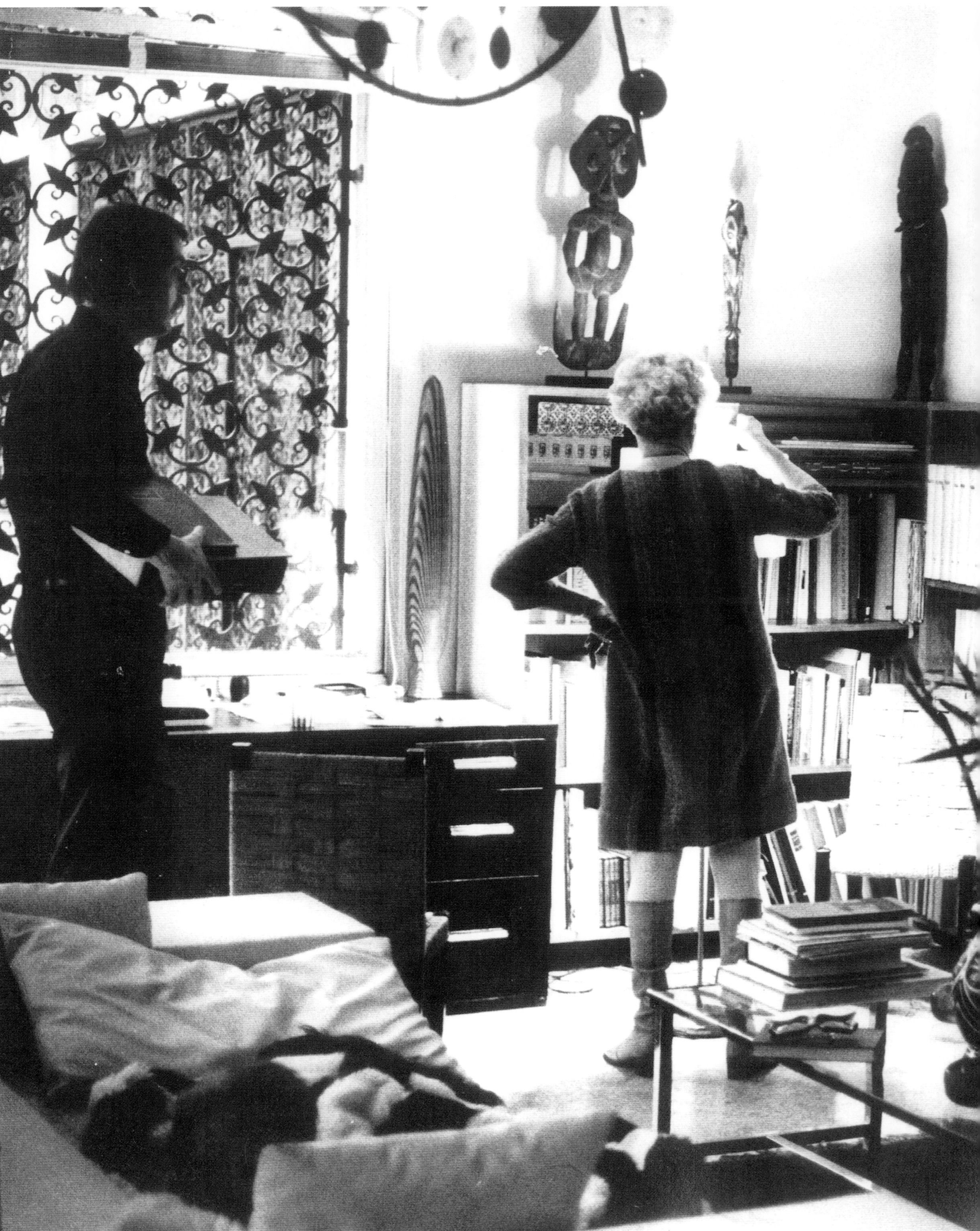

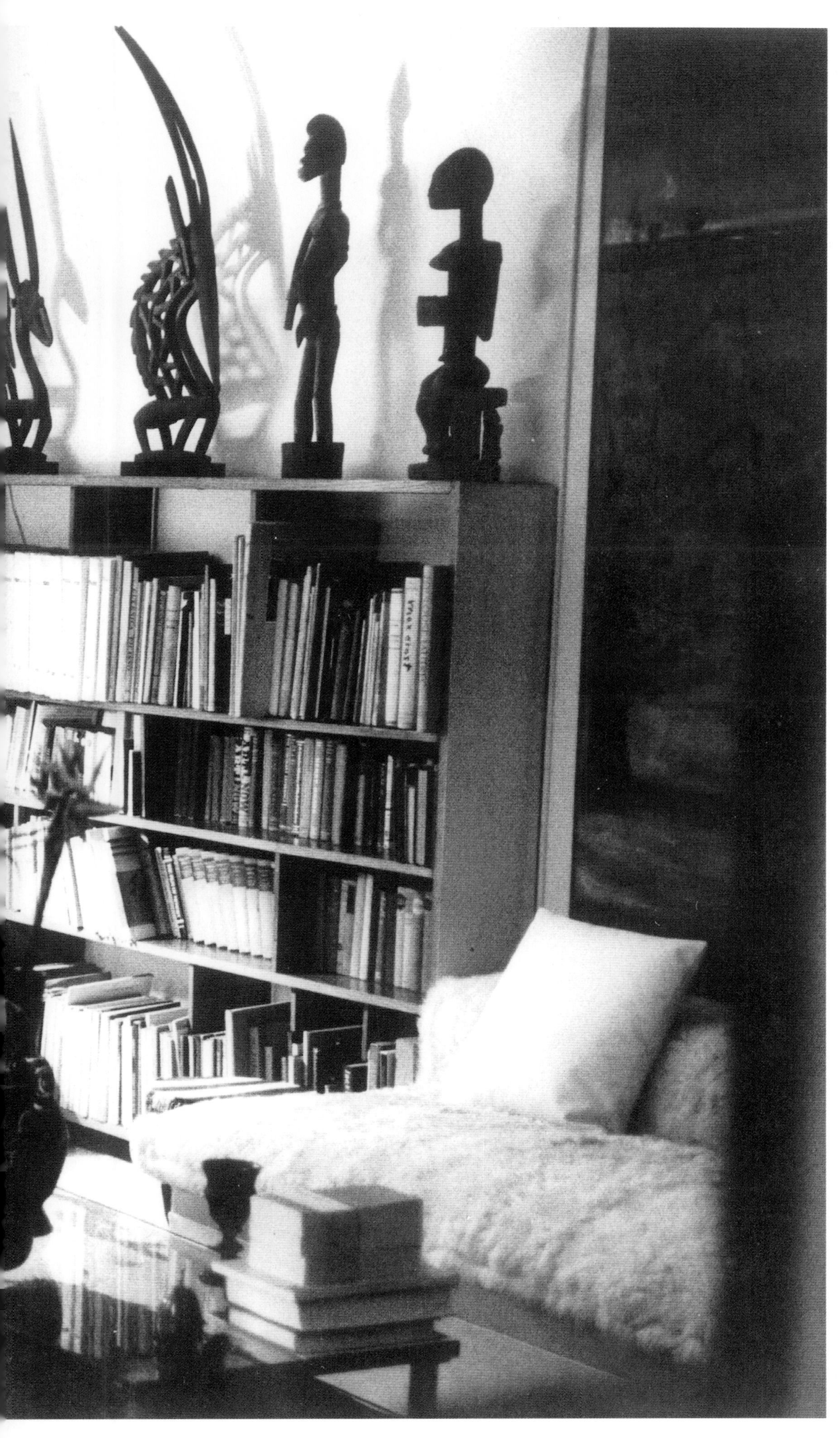

pp 64–67
In the library.

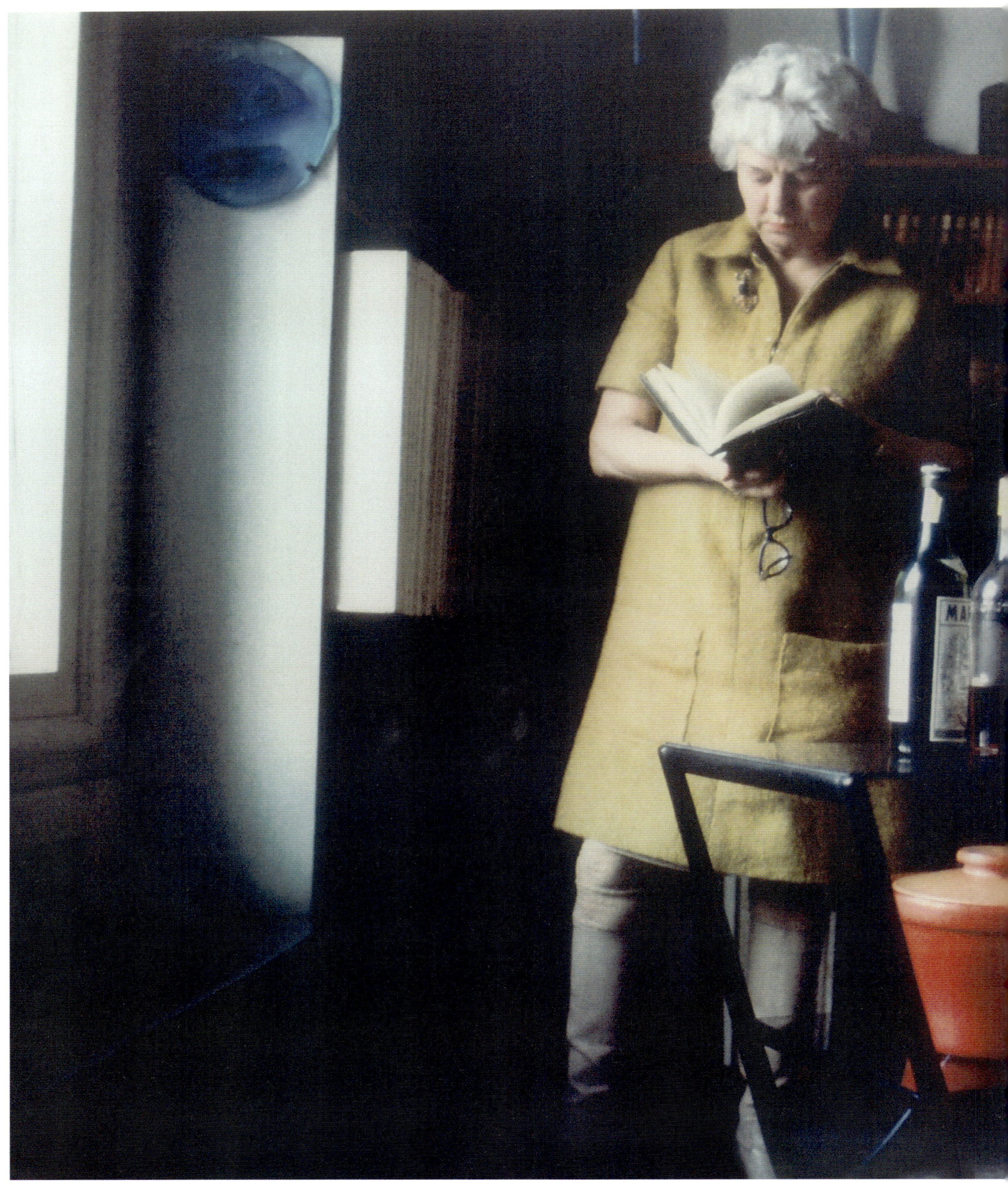

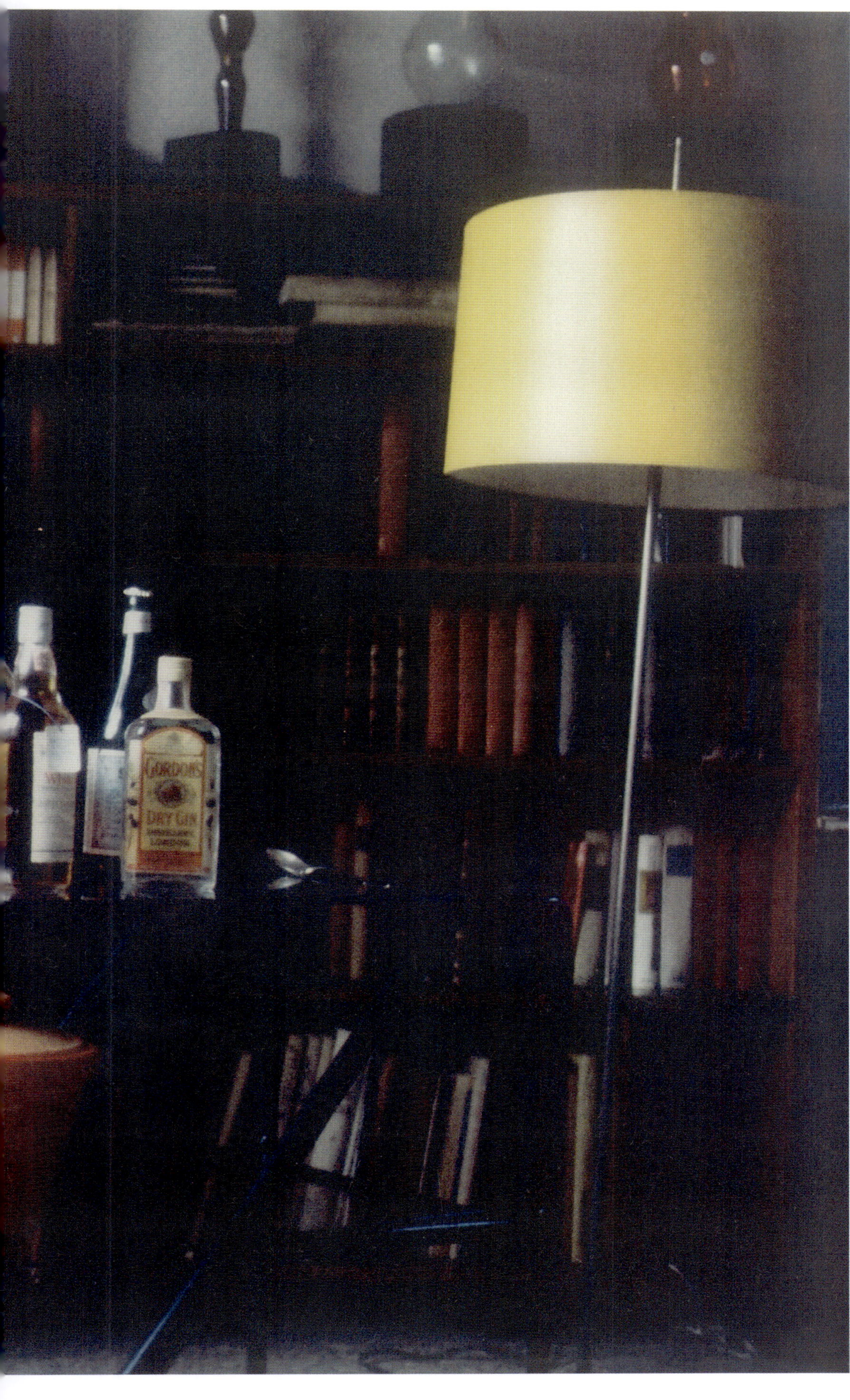

House cat Max meets *Taktile Struktur Rotierend*
[Tactile Rotating Structure] (1961) by Günther Uecker.

Right, and following pages
House cat Max with Henry Moore's *Three Standing Figures*.

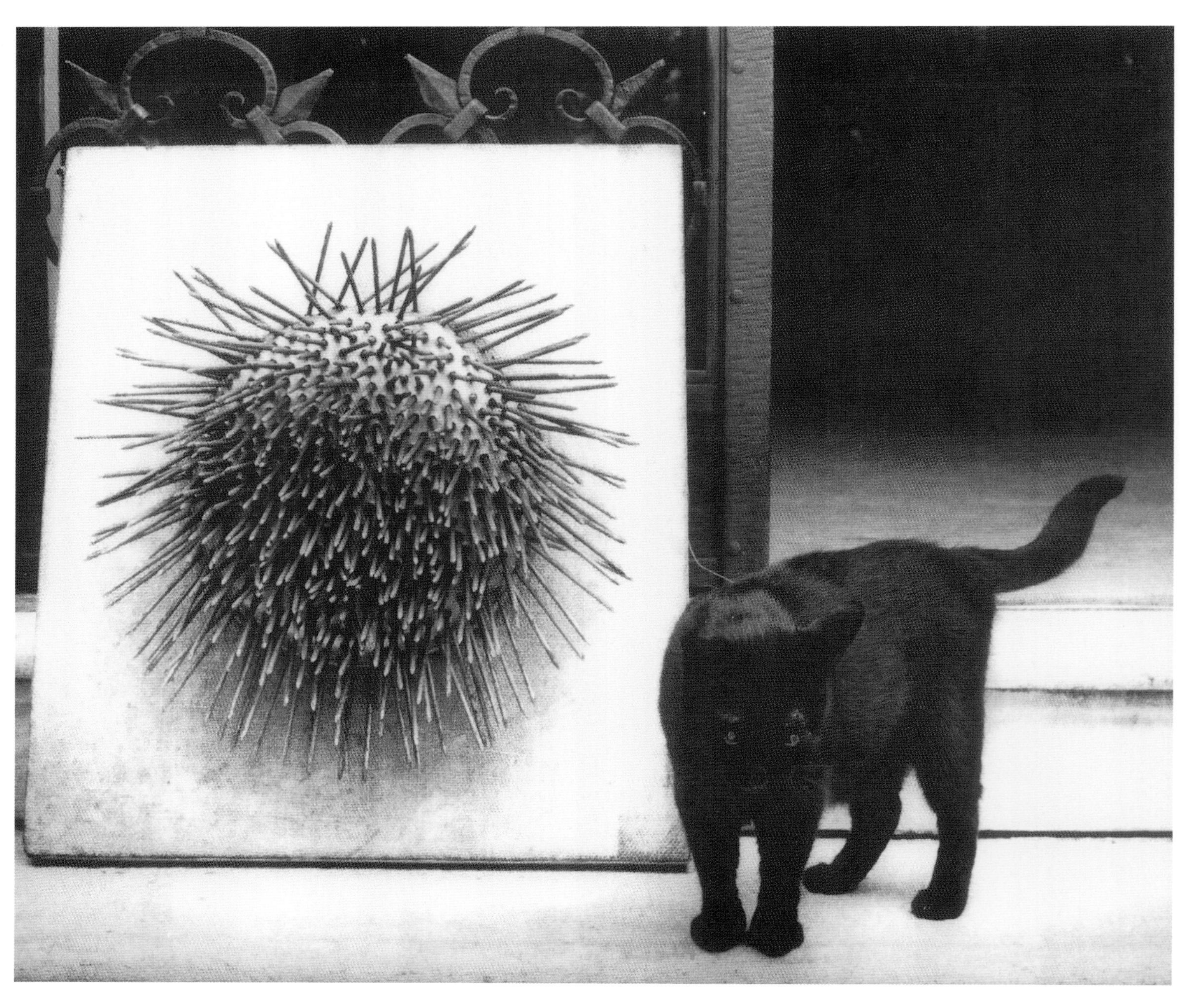

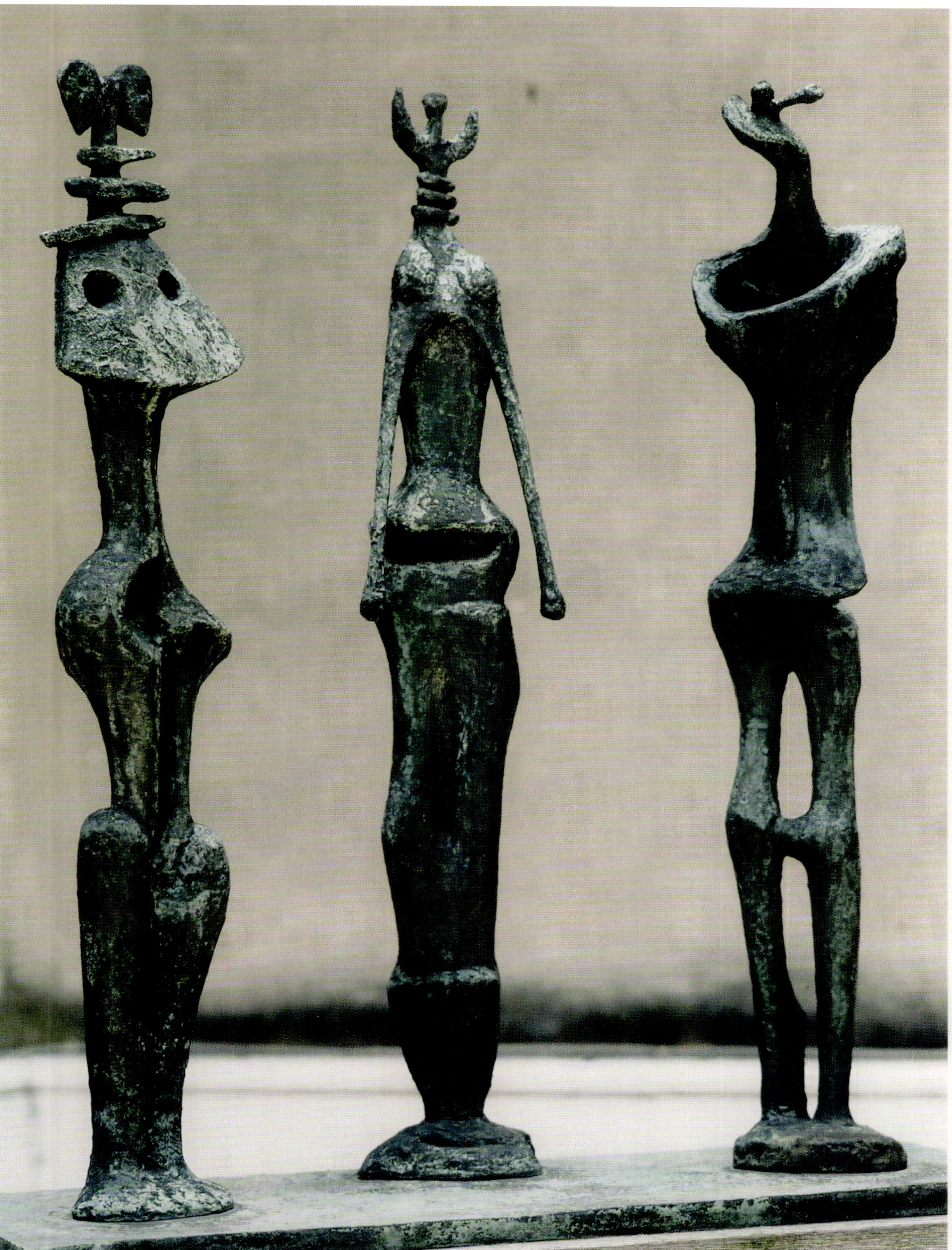

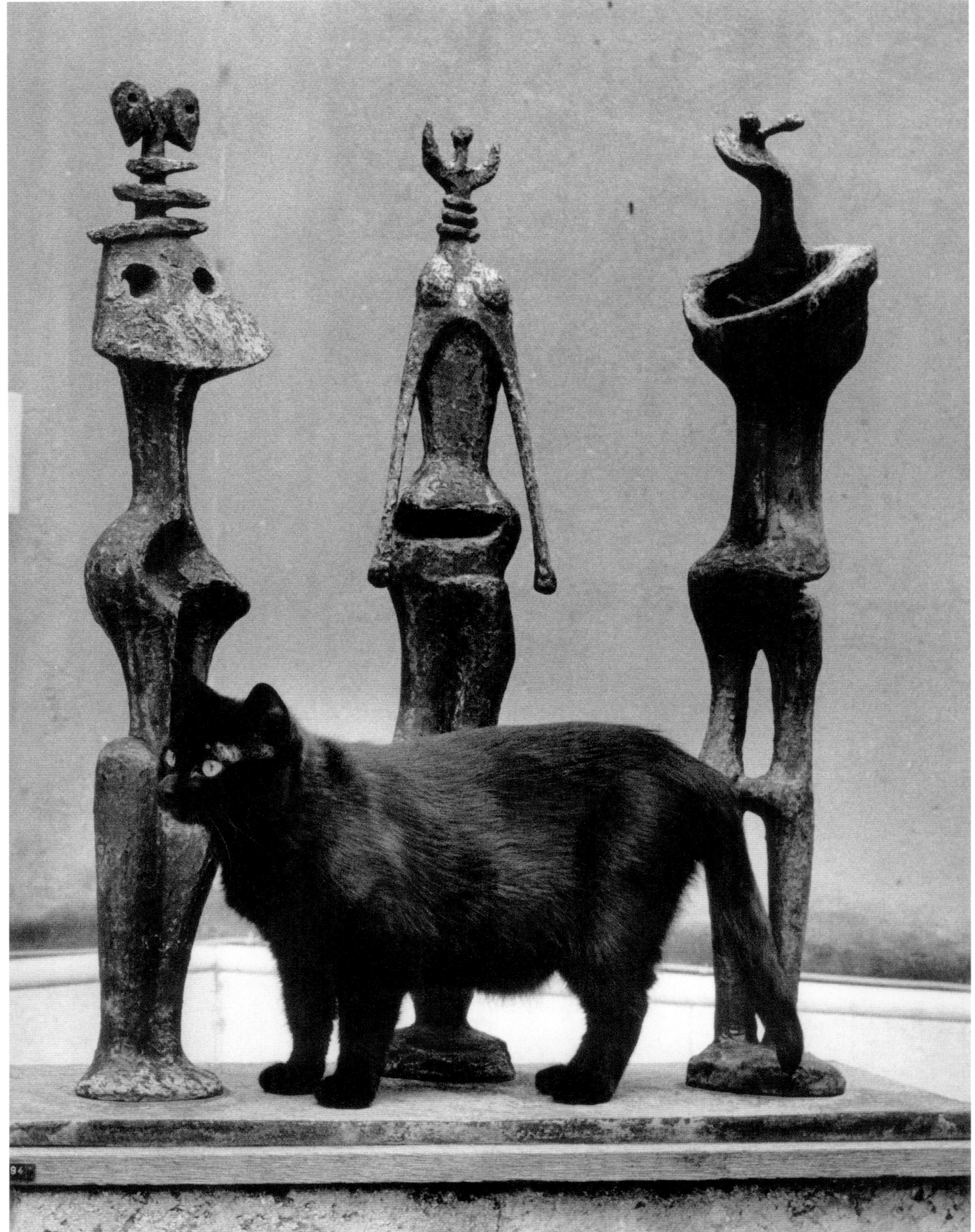

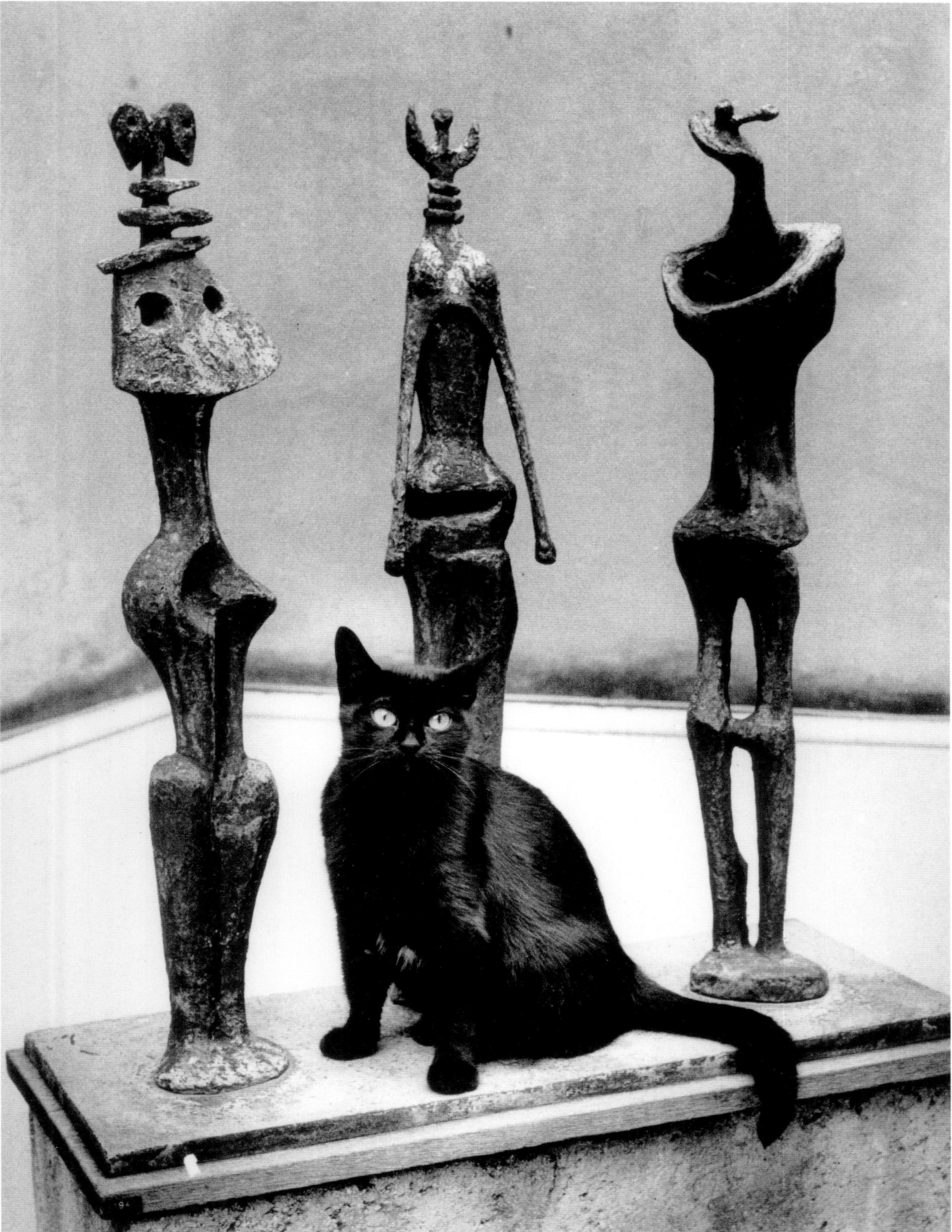

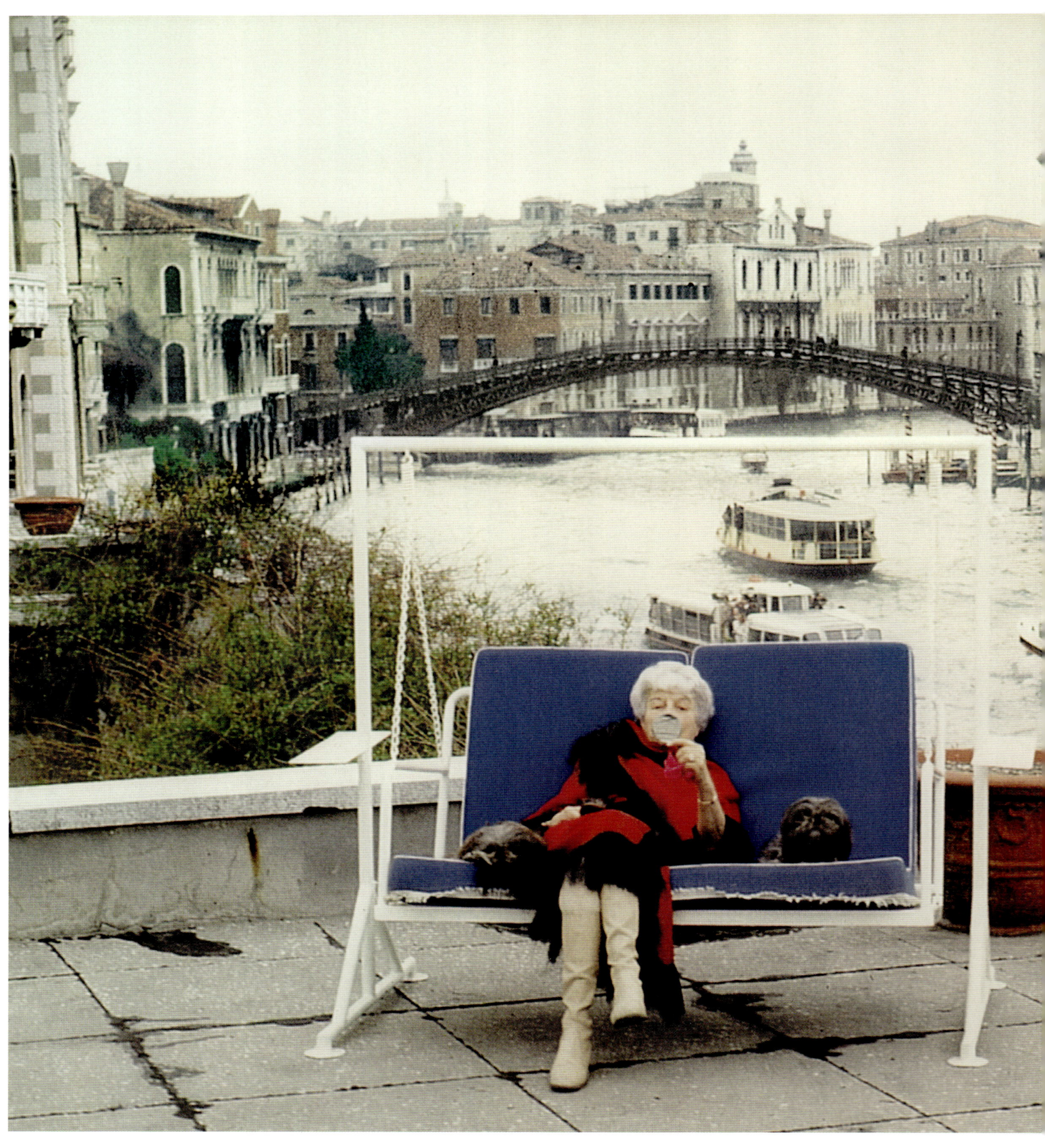

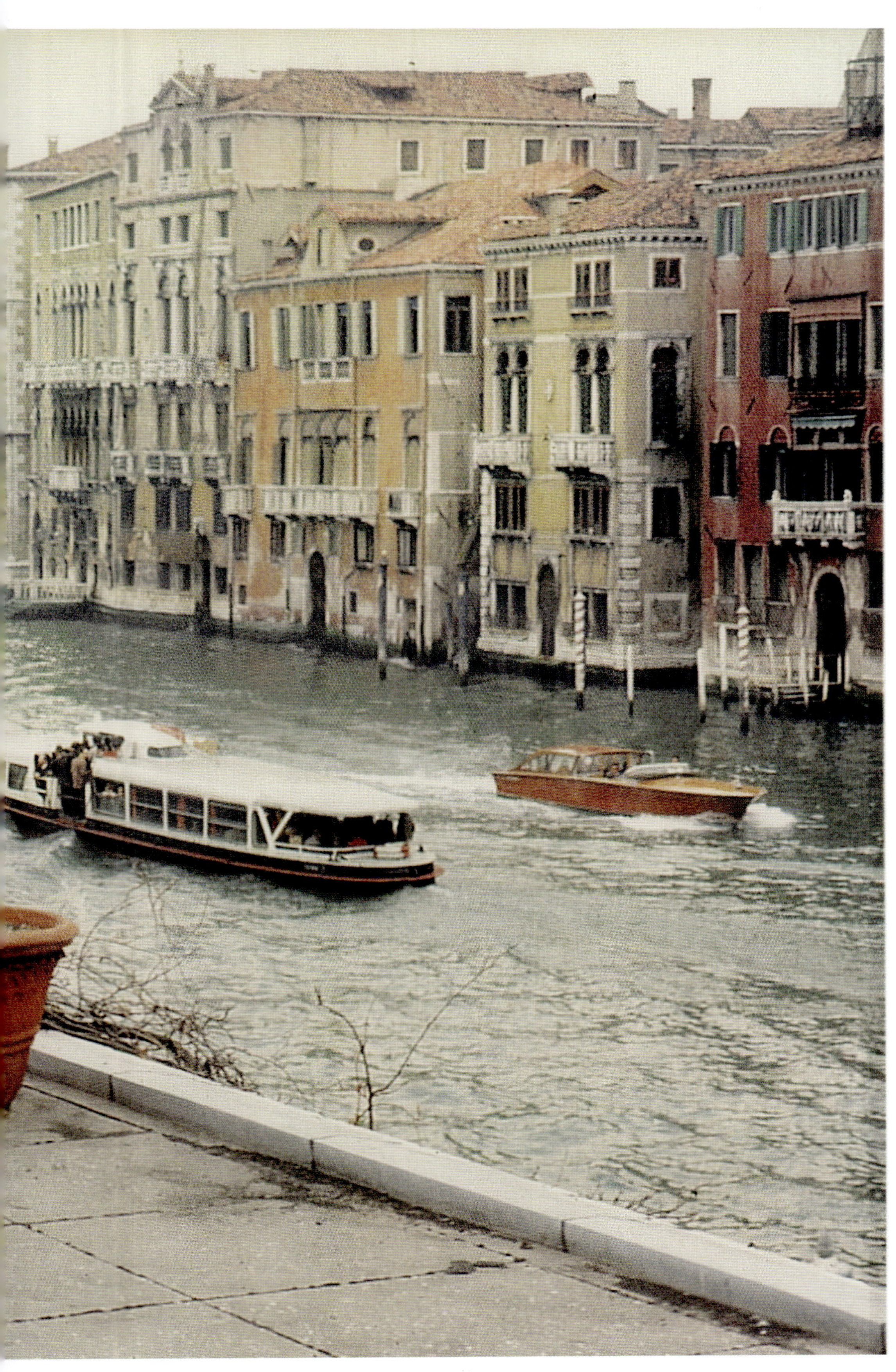

pp 72–75
Peggy in the Hollywood
swing seat on her
roof terrace.
The Ponte dell'Accademia
can be seen in the
background.

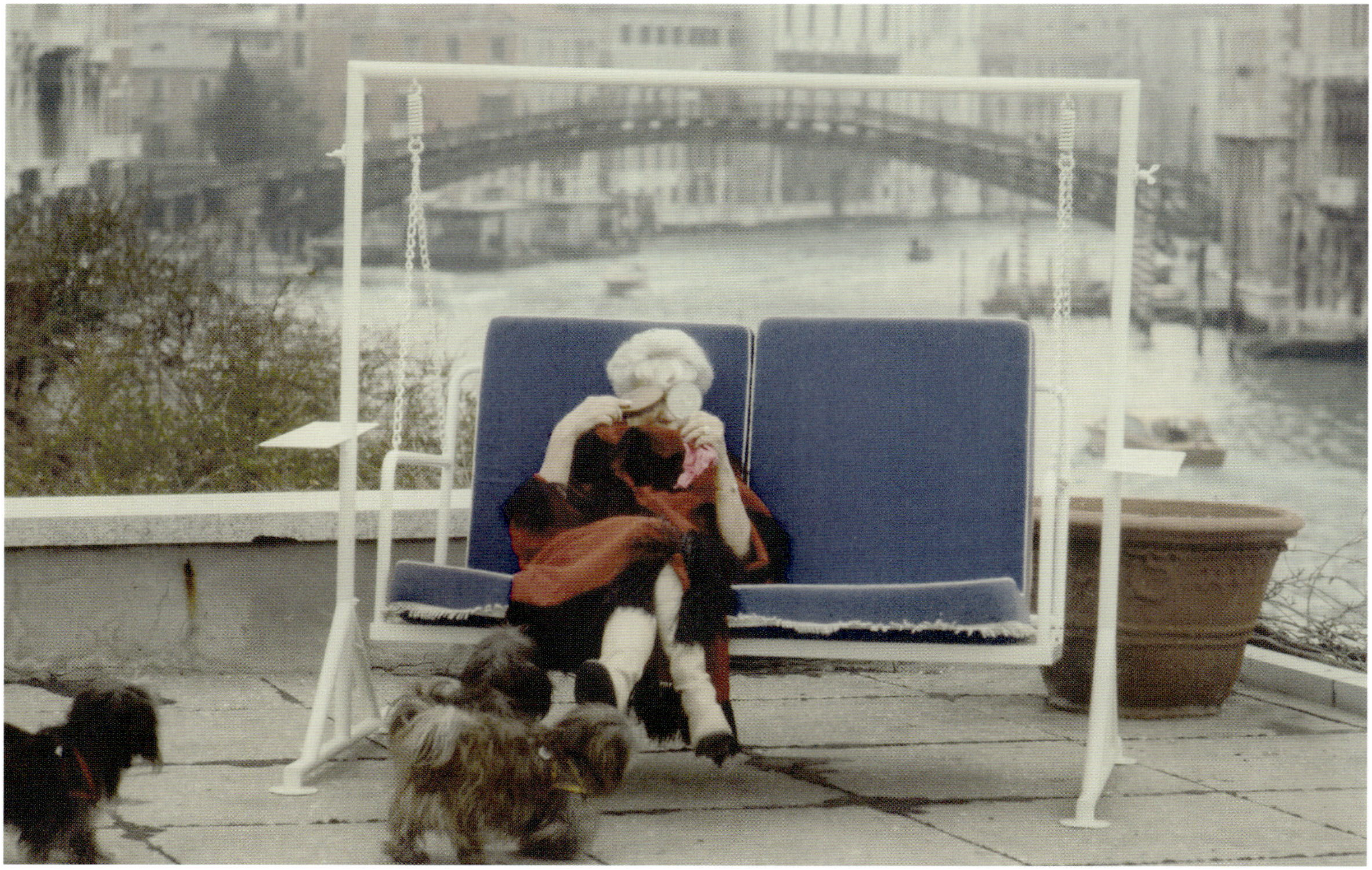

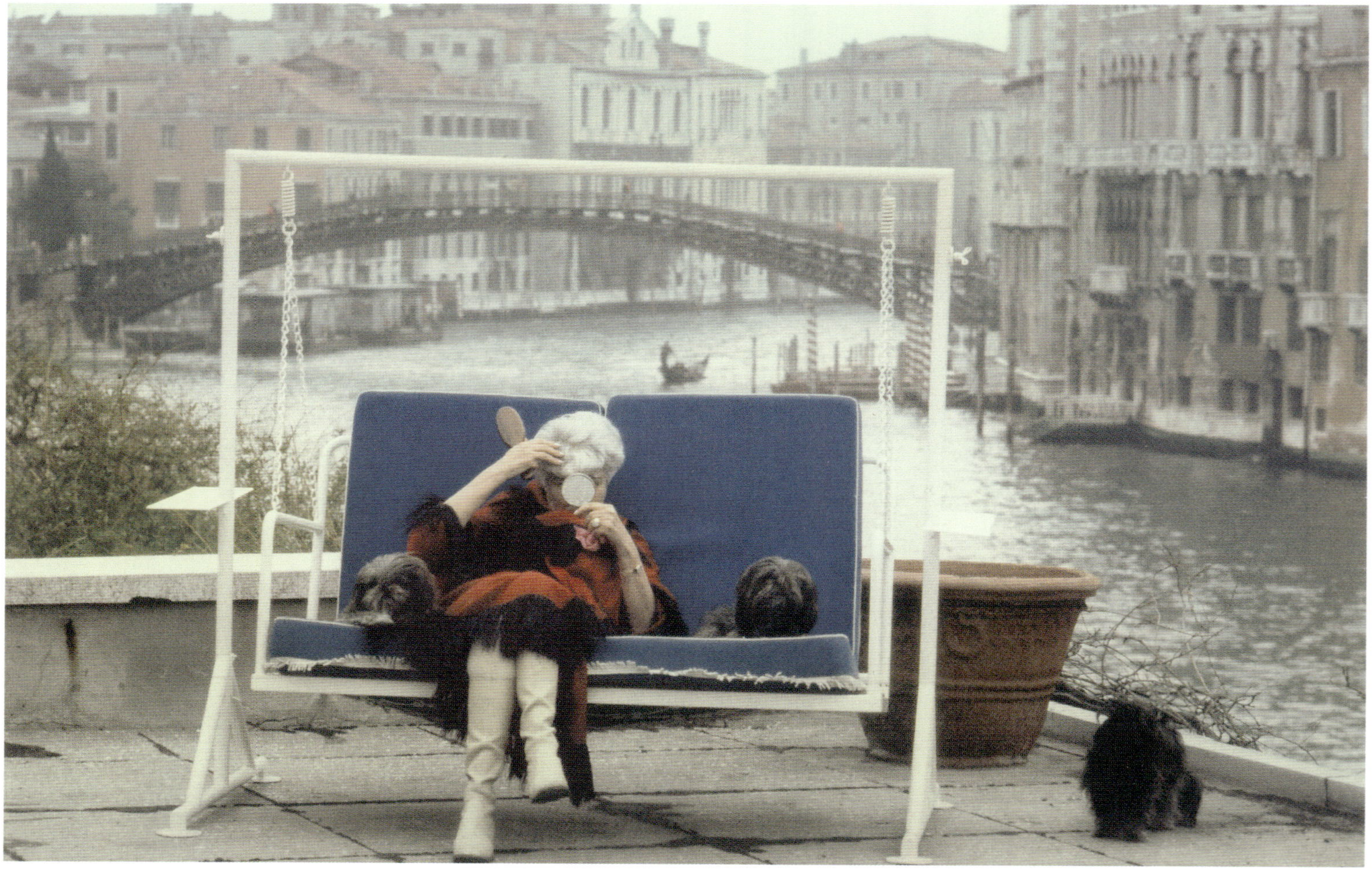

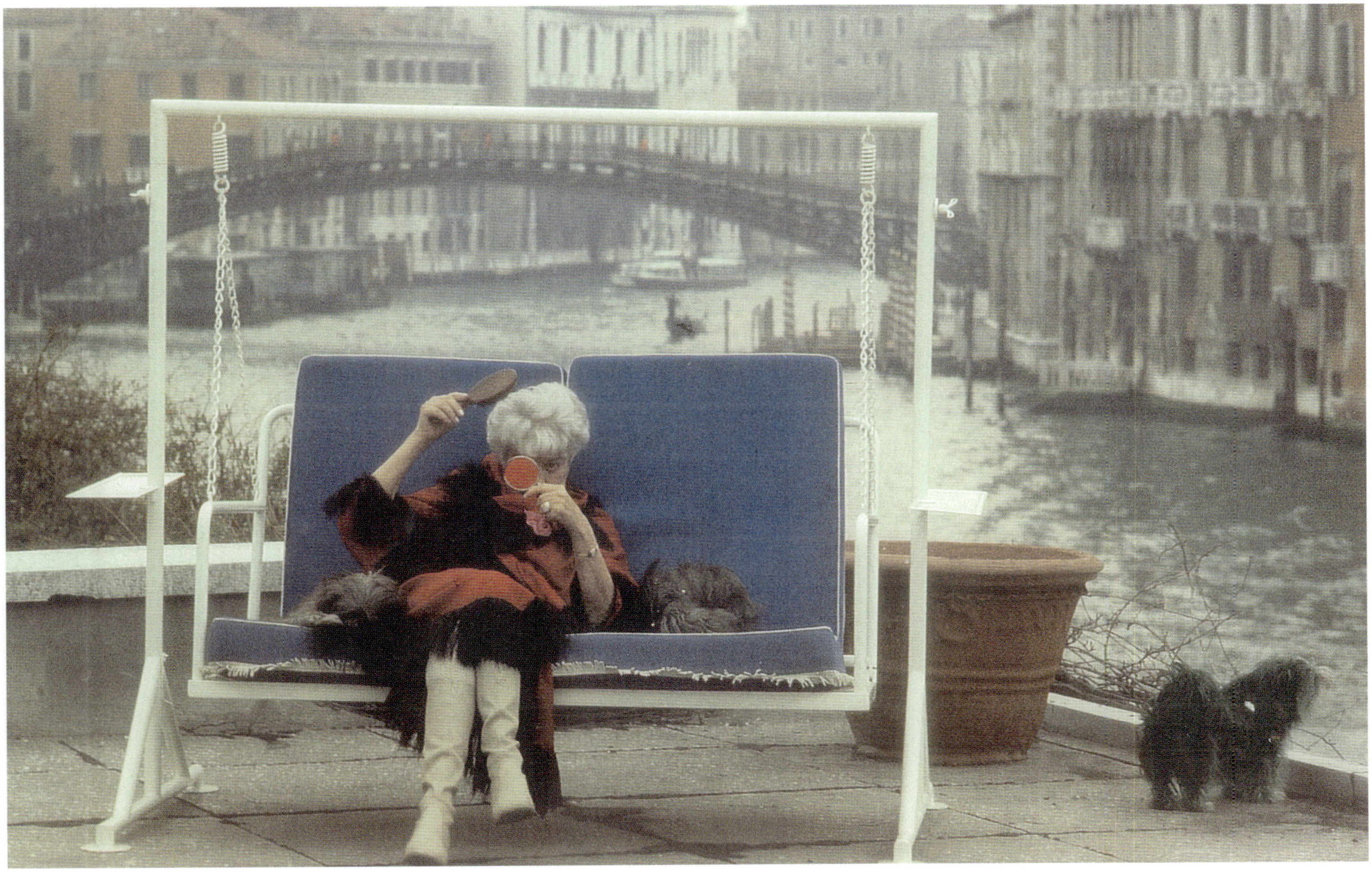

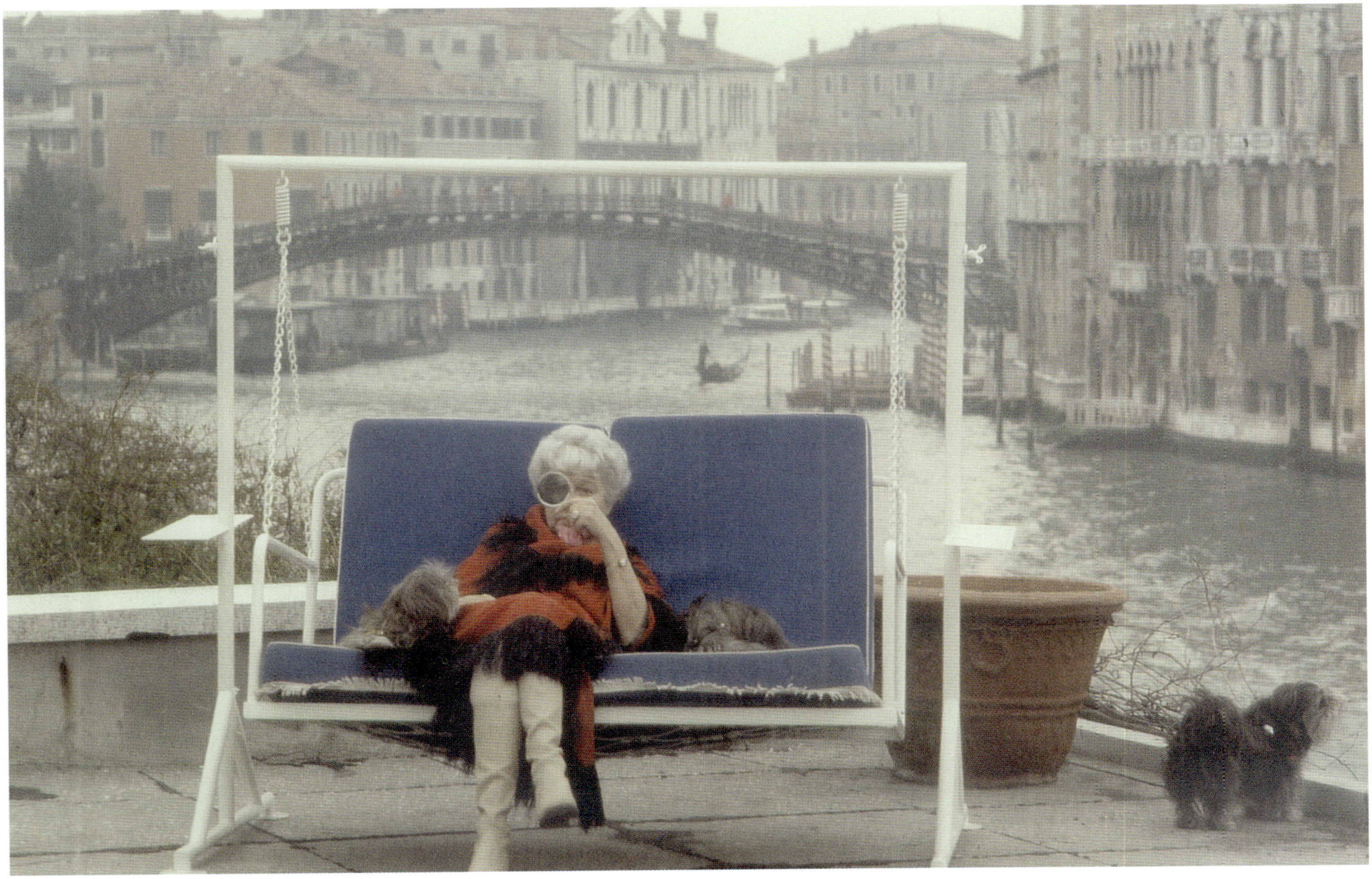

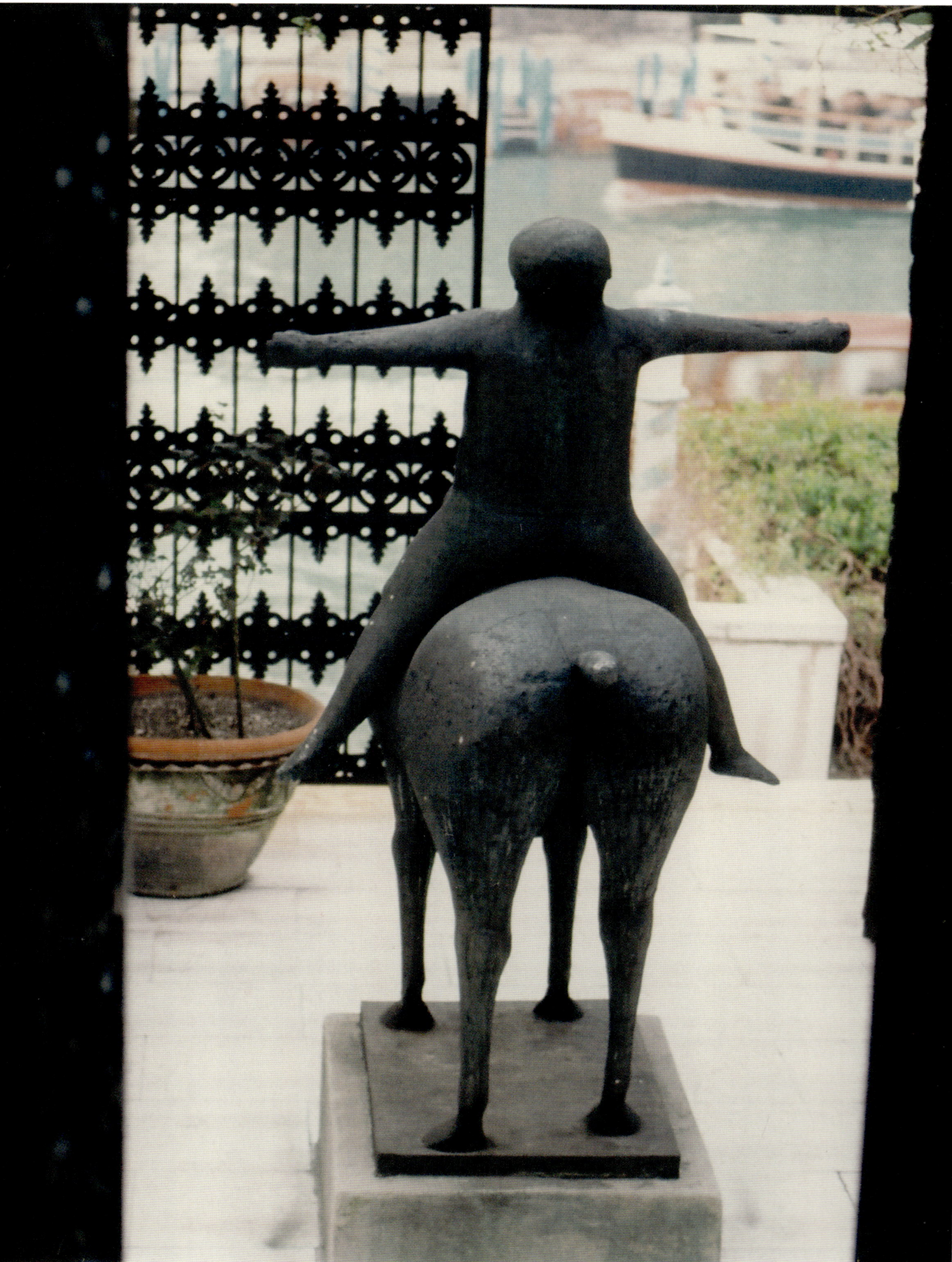

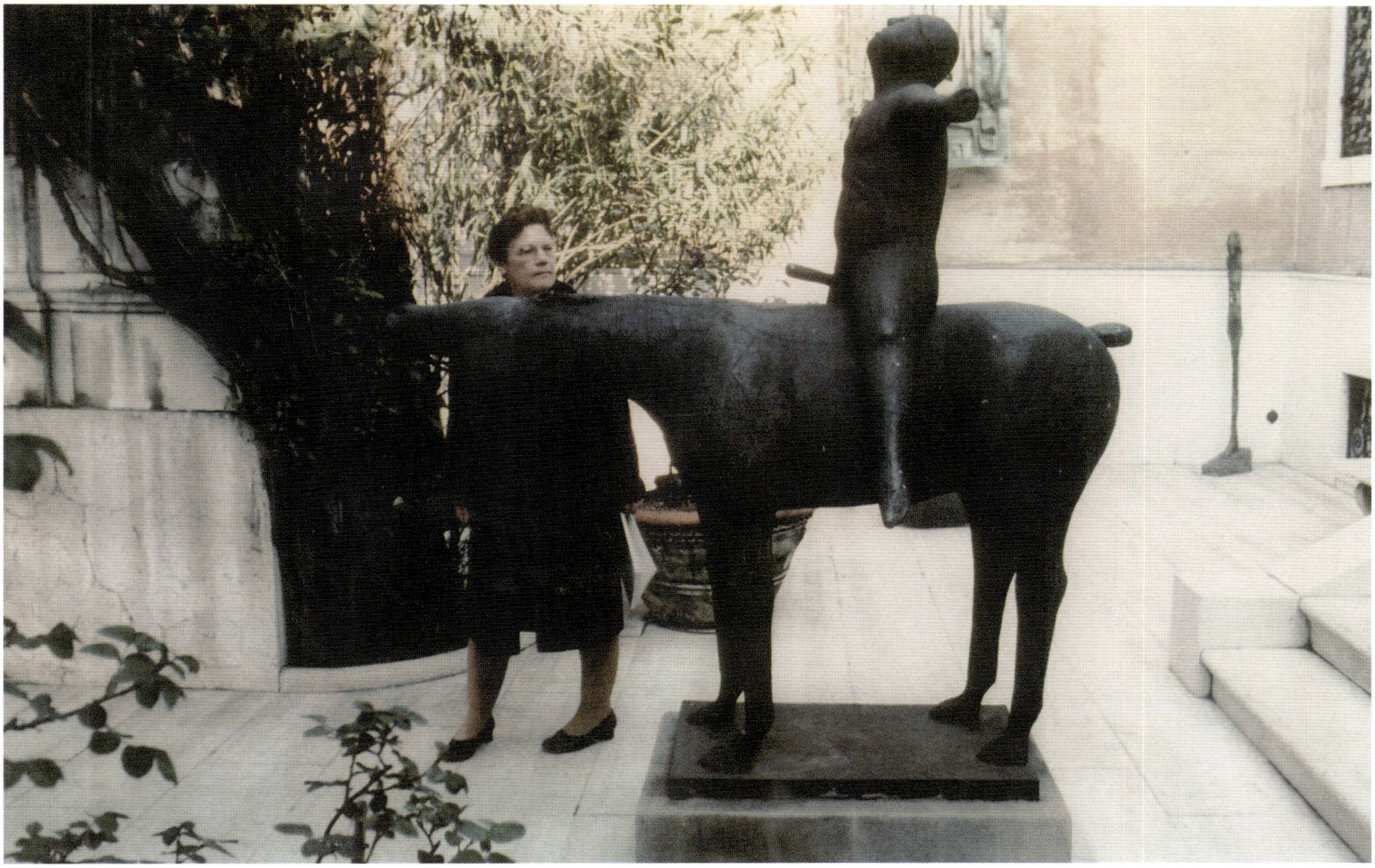

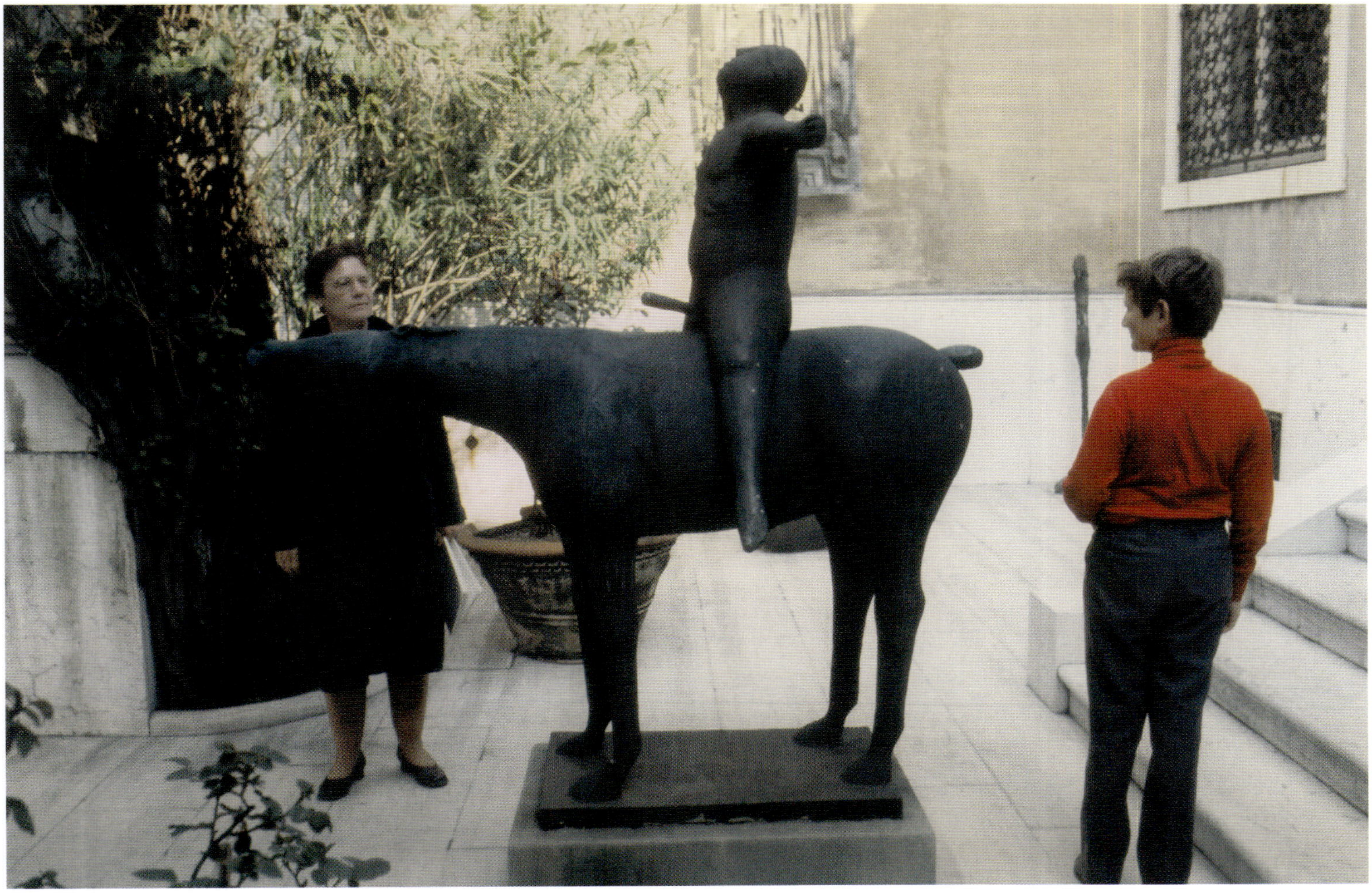

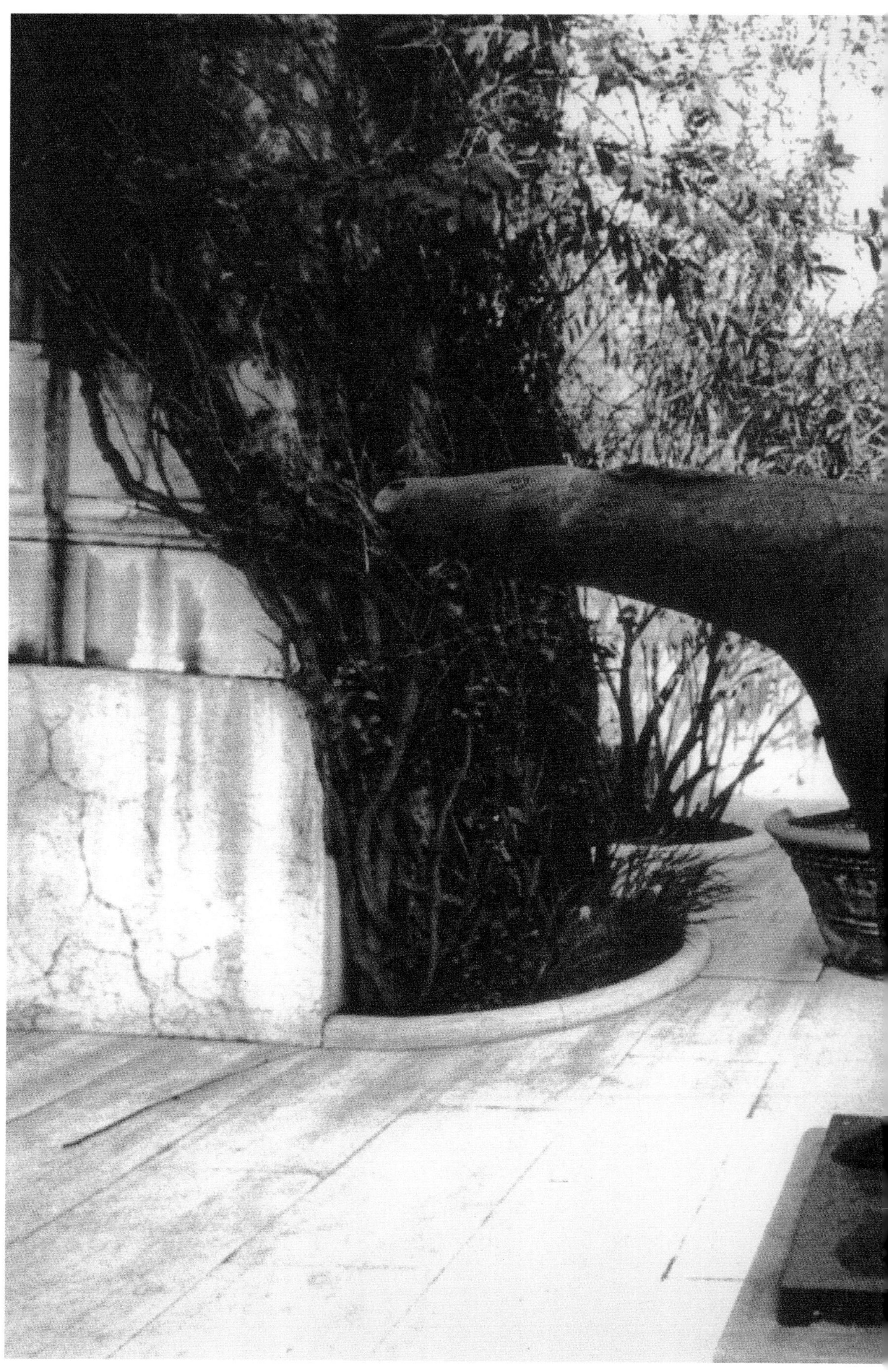

pp 76–79
*L'Angelo Della Città*
[The Angel of the City]
(1948) by Marino Marini.

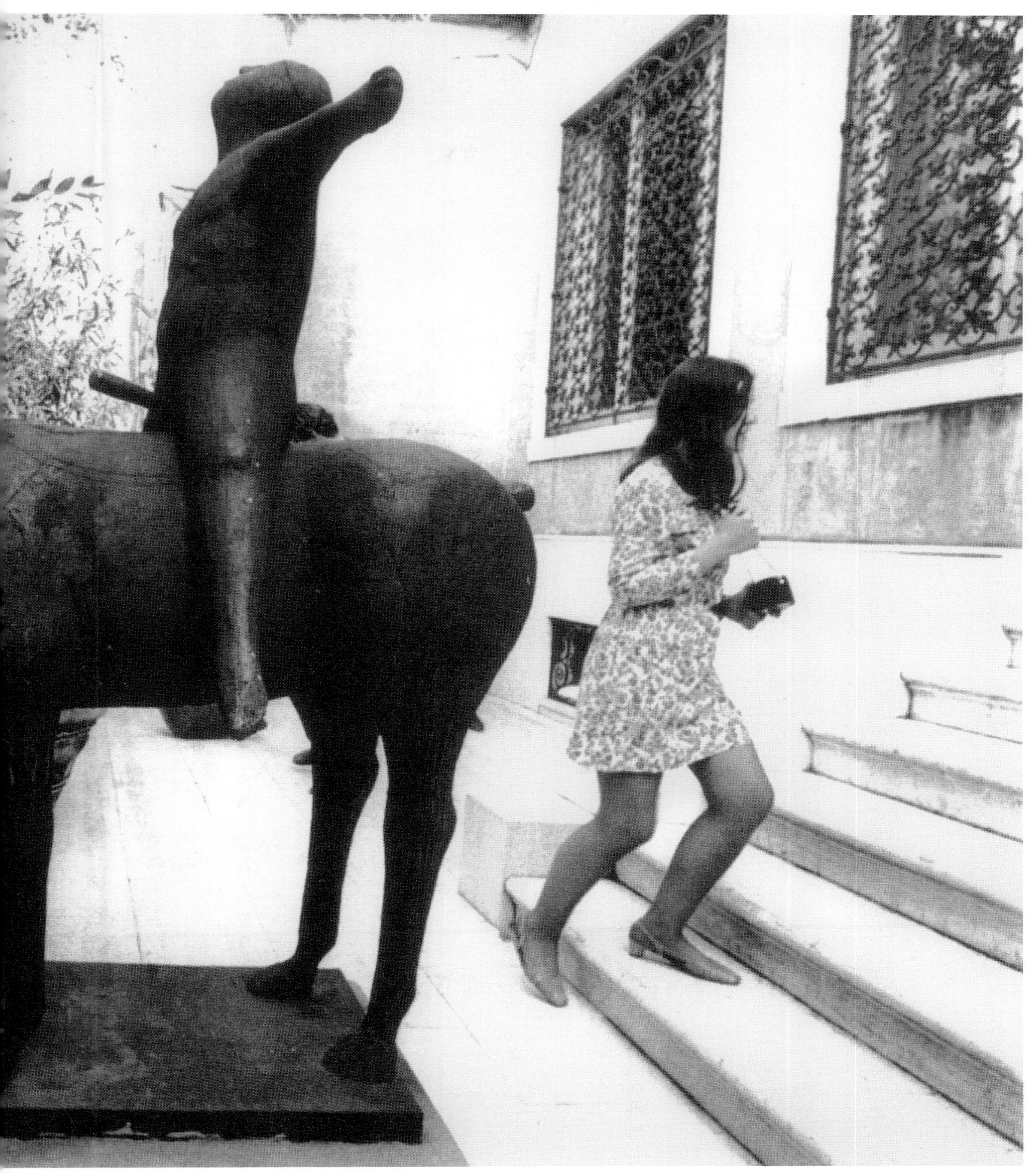

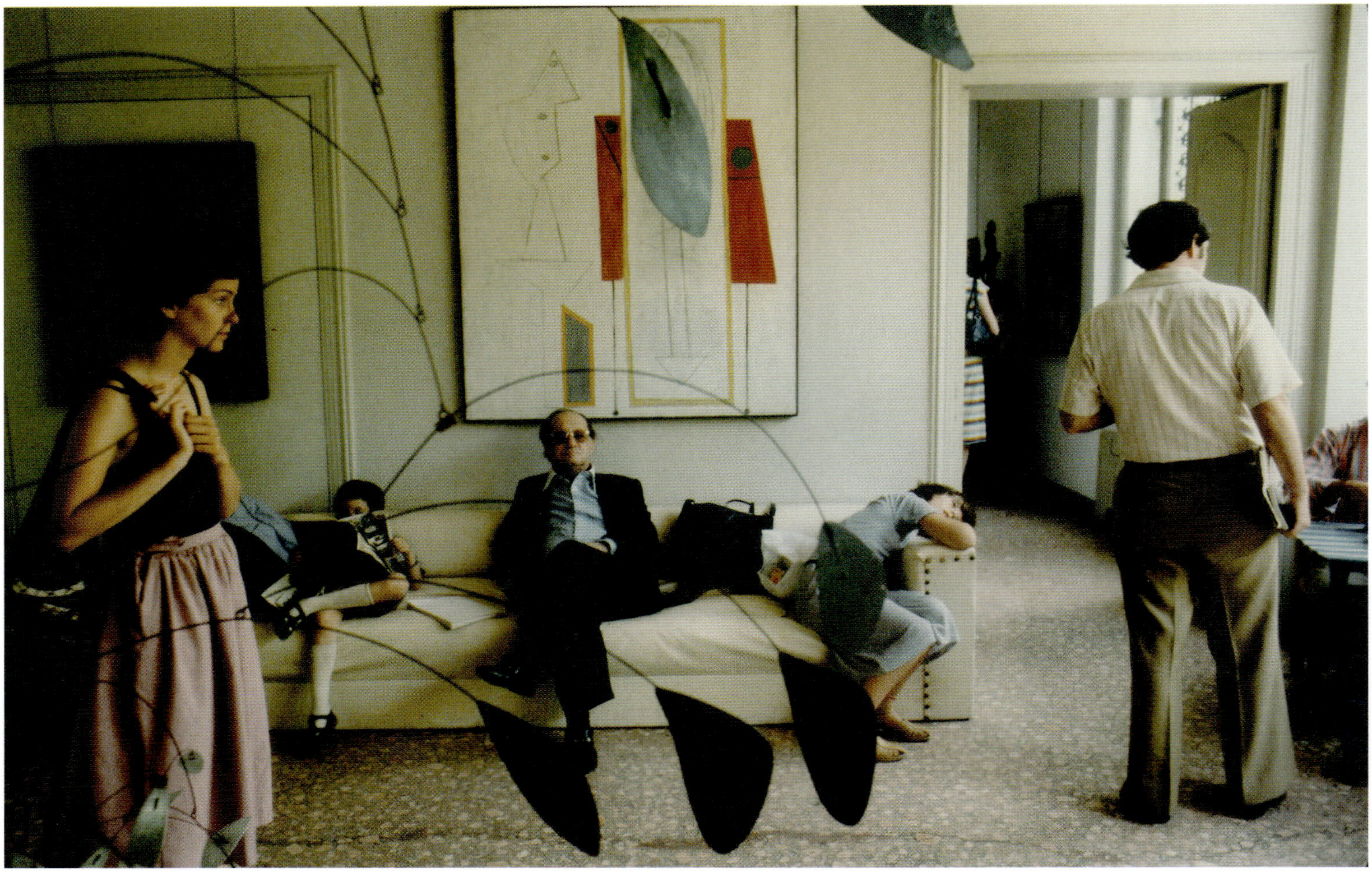

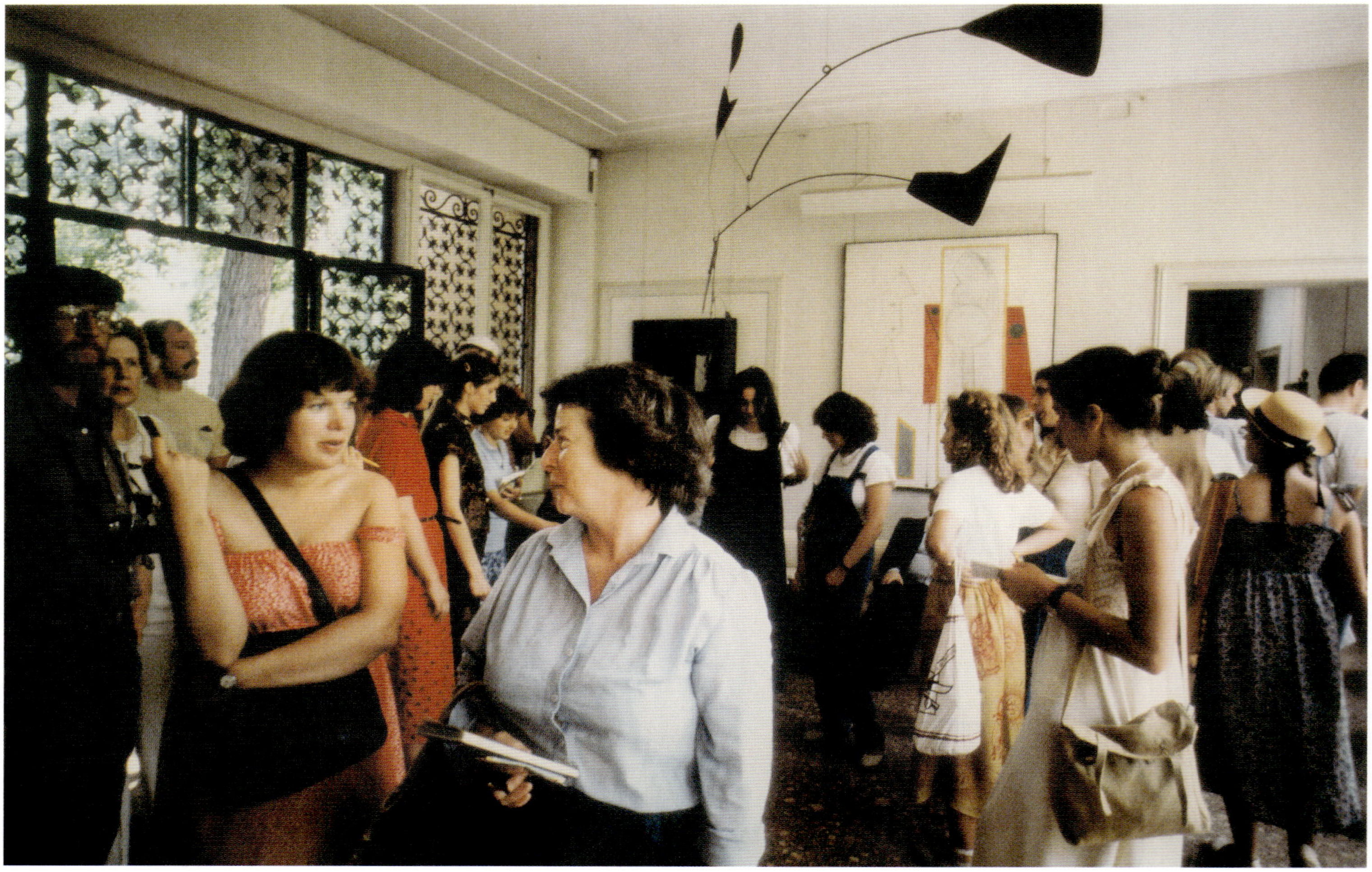

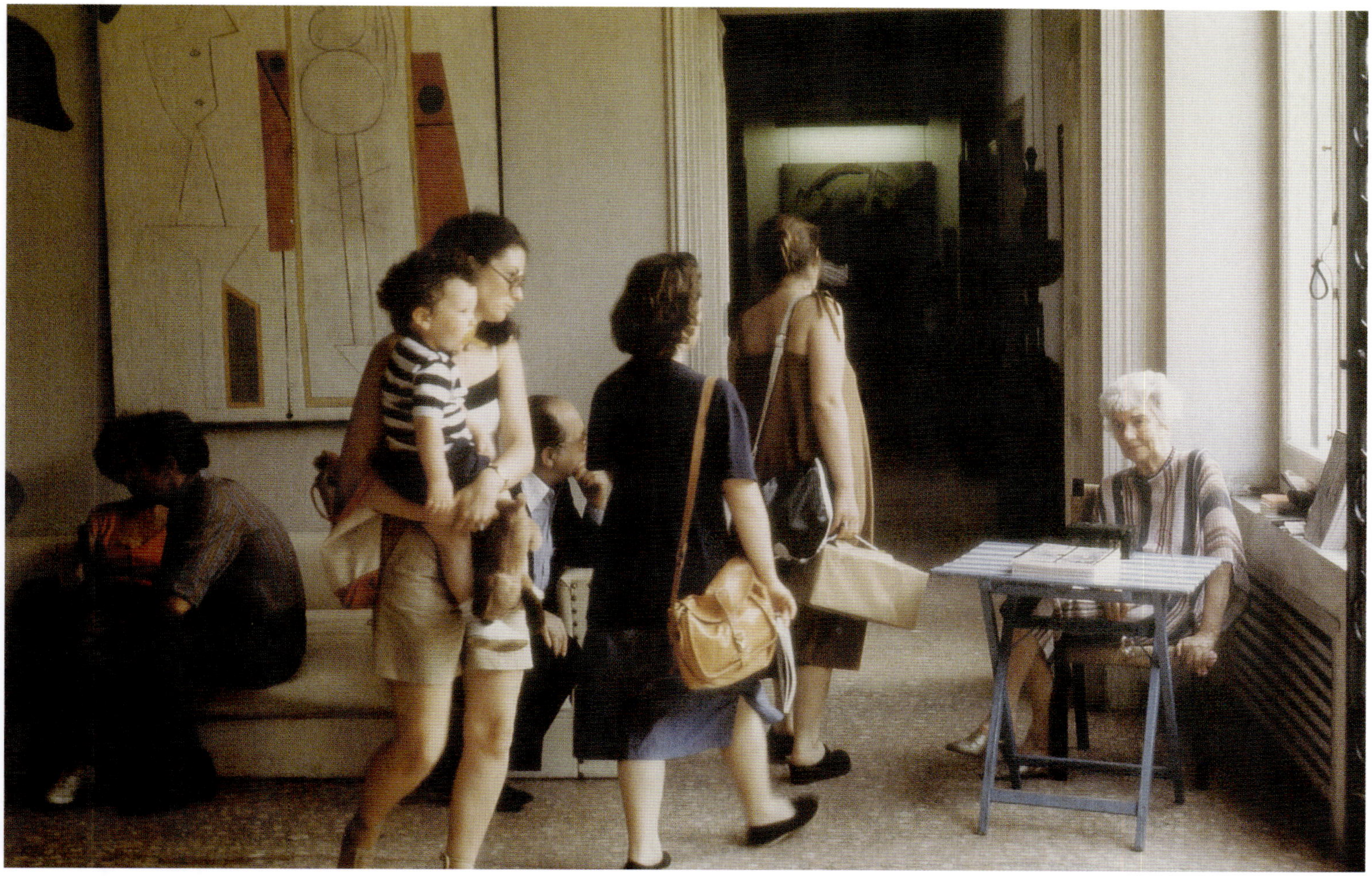

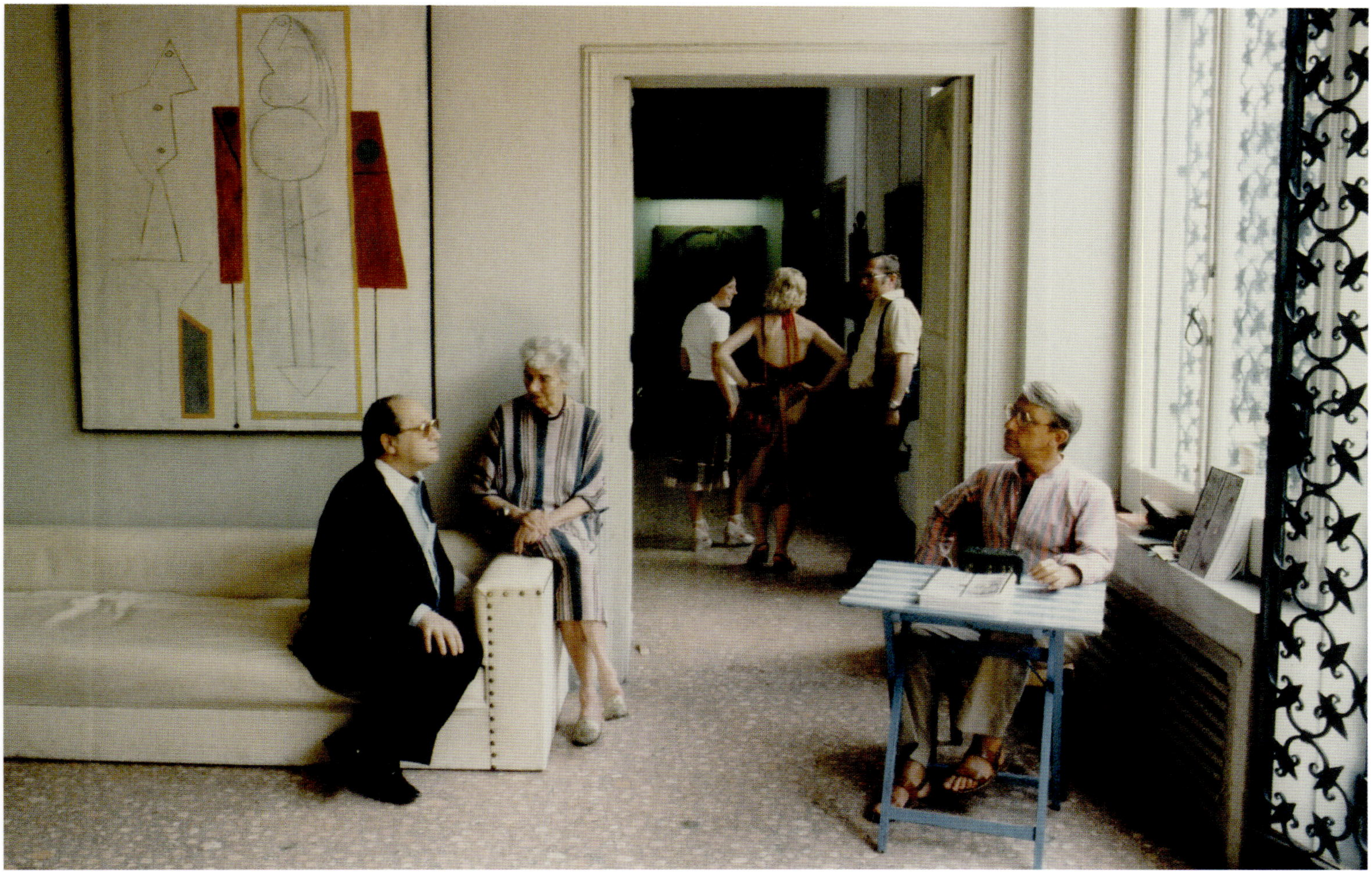

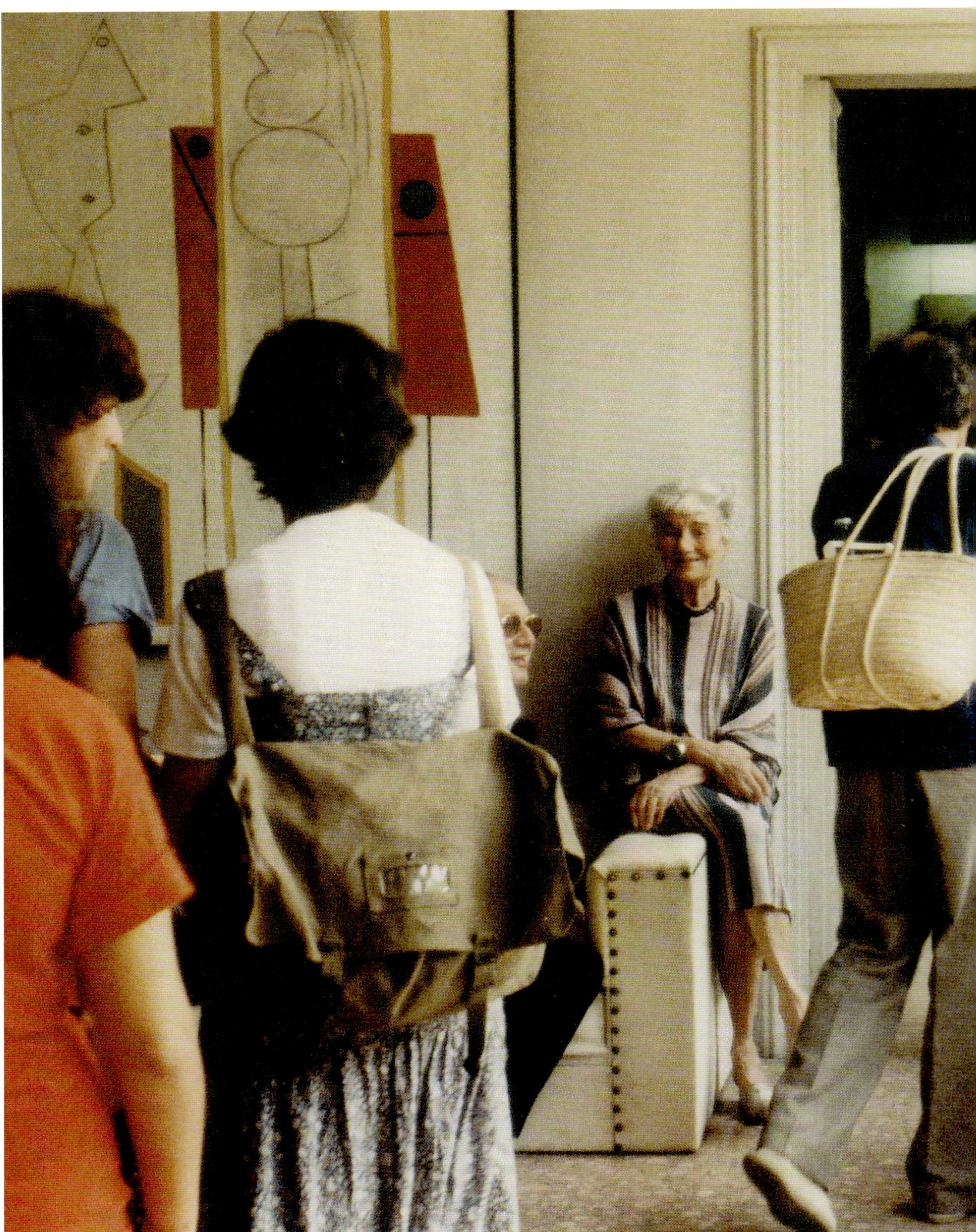

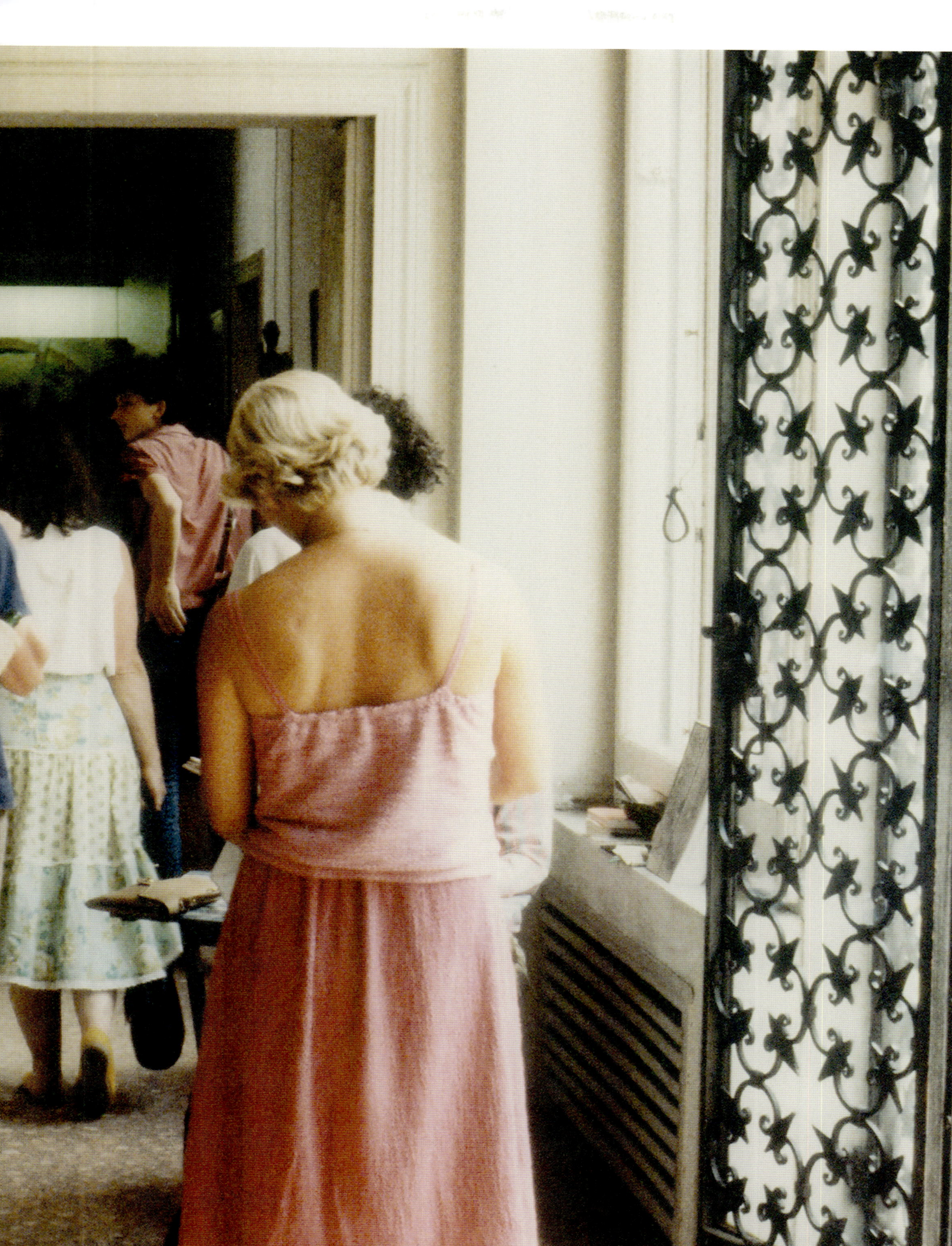

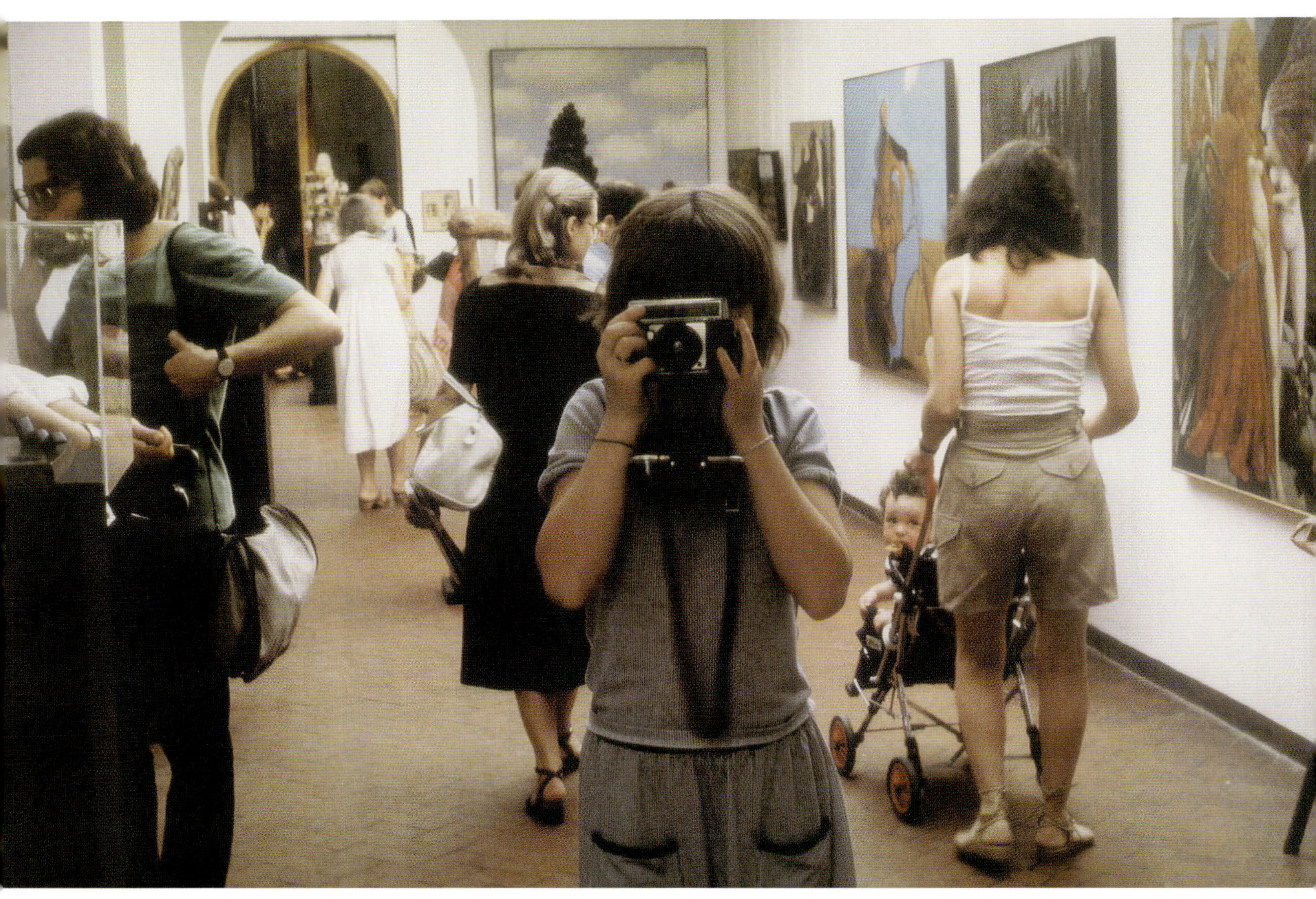



Top
Peggy's garden pavilion (barchessa) with surrealist works.

pp 80–83
During opening hours the visitors cluster in the entrance area. Peggy
alternates with John Hosbeen at the folding table at which the catalogues
are sold. Over the sofa is Pablo Picasso's *L'Atelier* [The Studio] (1928)

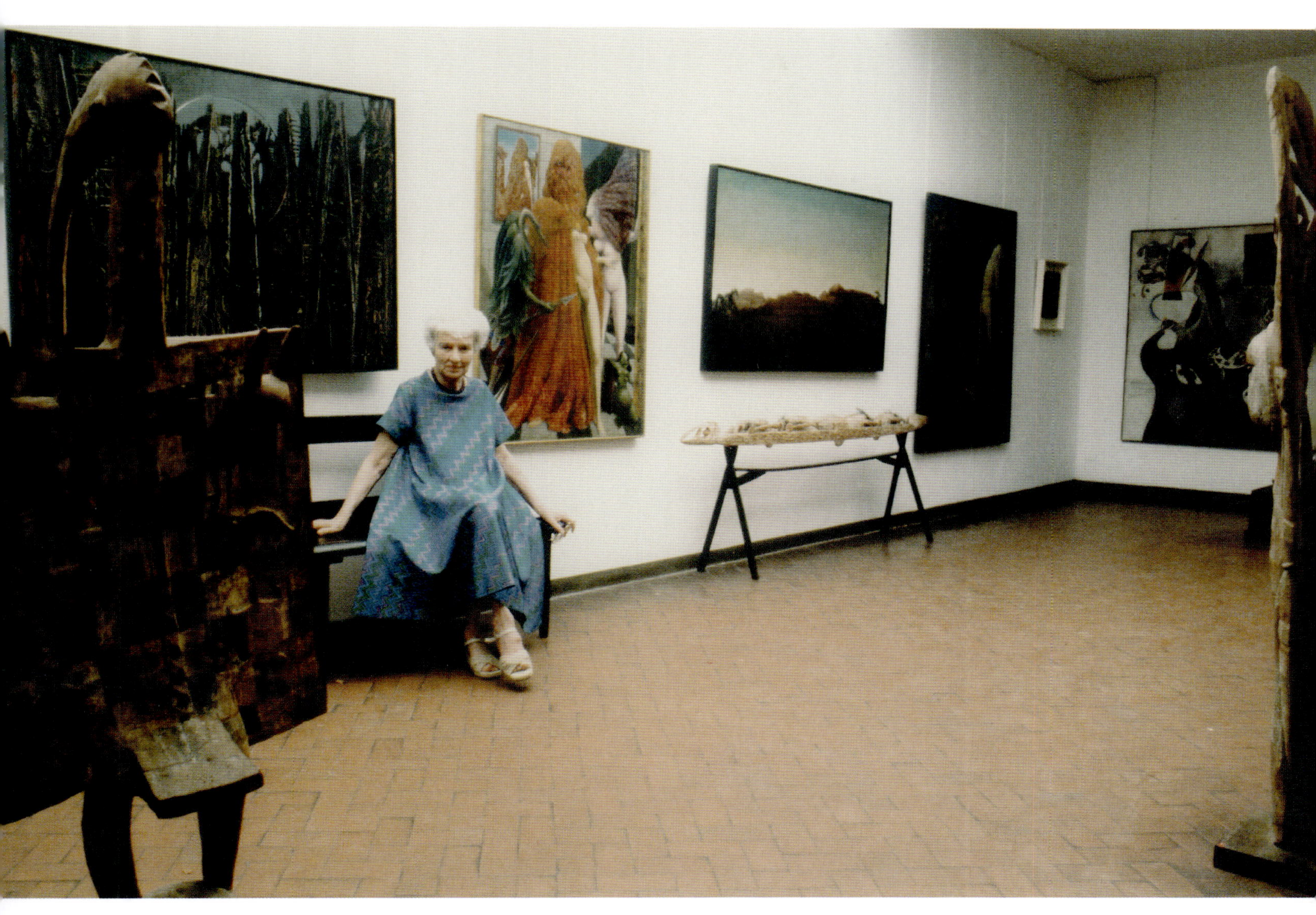

In the barchessa, surrounded by the
surrealist works from her collection.

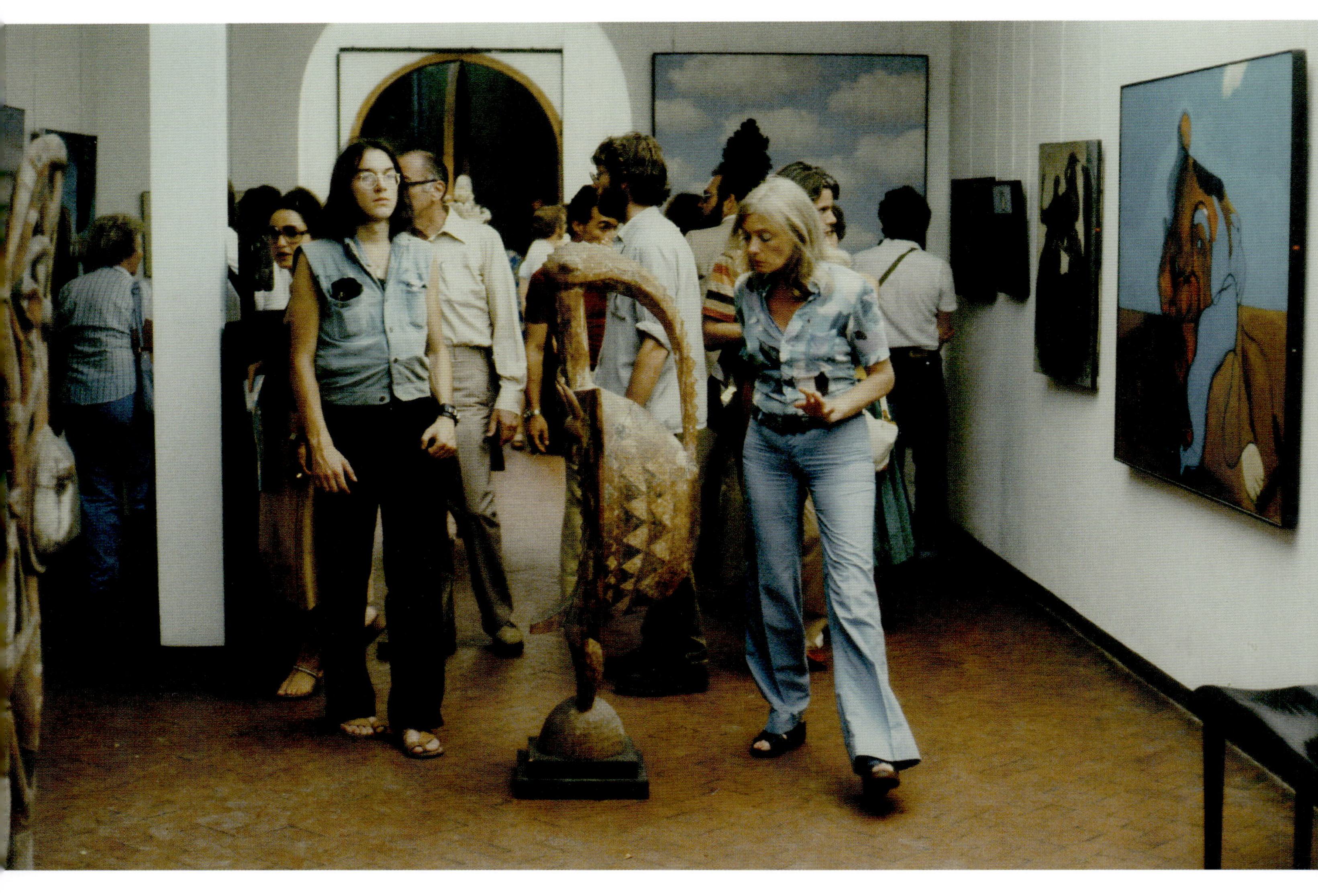

In Peggy's barchessa – paintings by René Magritte
and Max Ernst are to be seen on the walls.

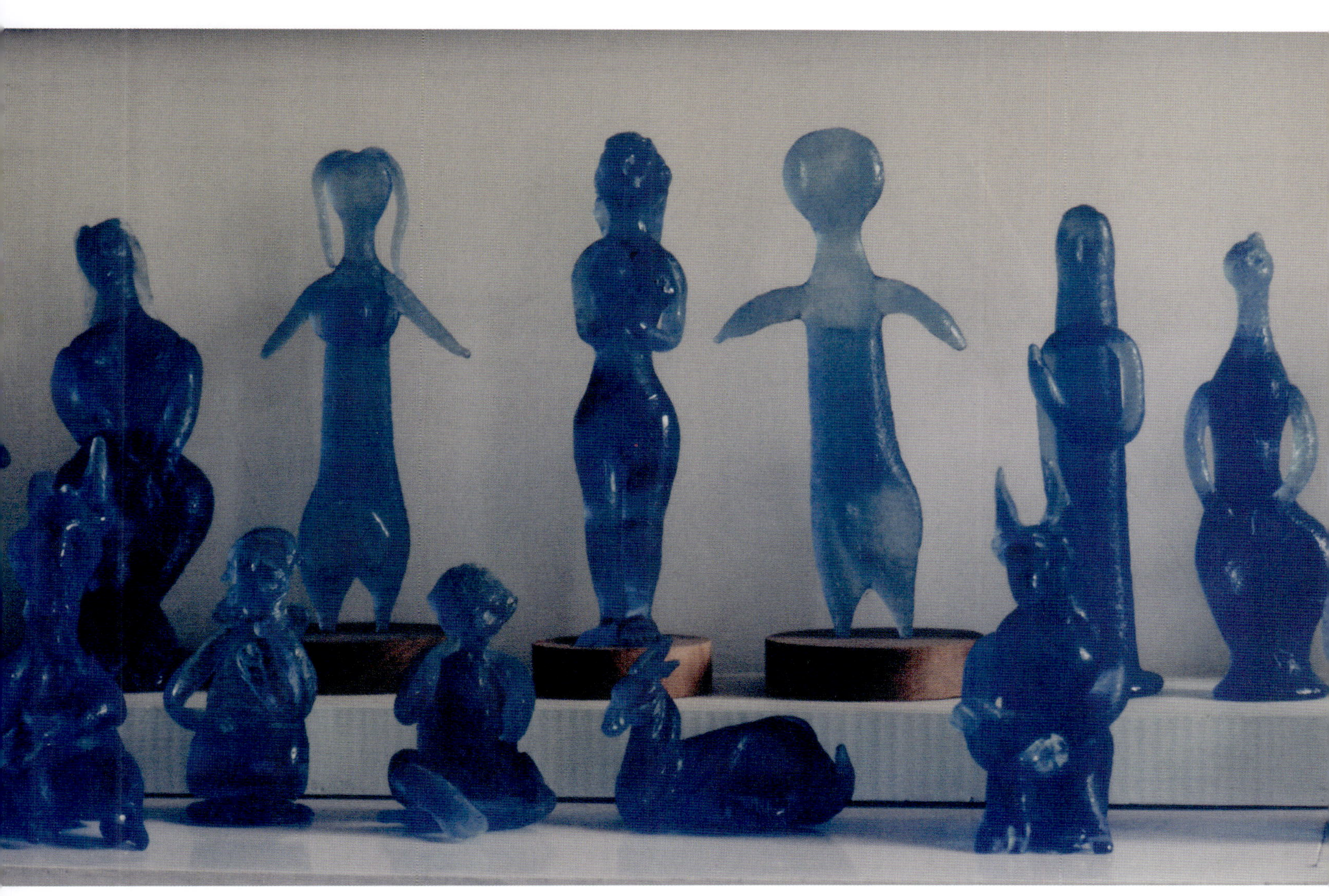

The blue glass figures by Egidio Costantini come from his
Venetian glasswork studio Fucina degli Angeli (Venice)
and are inspired by Pablo Picasso.

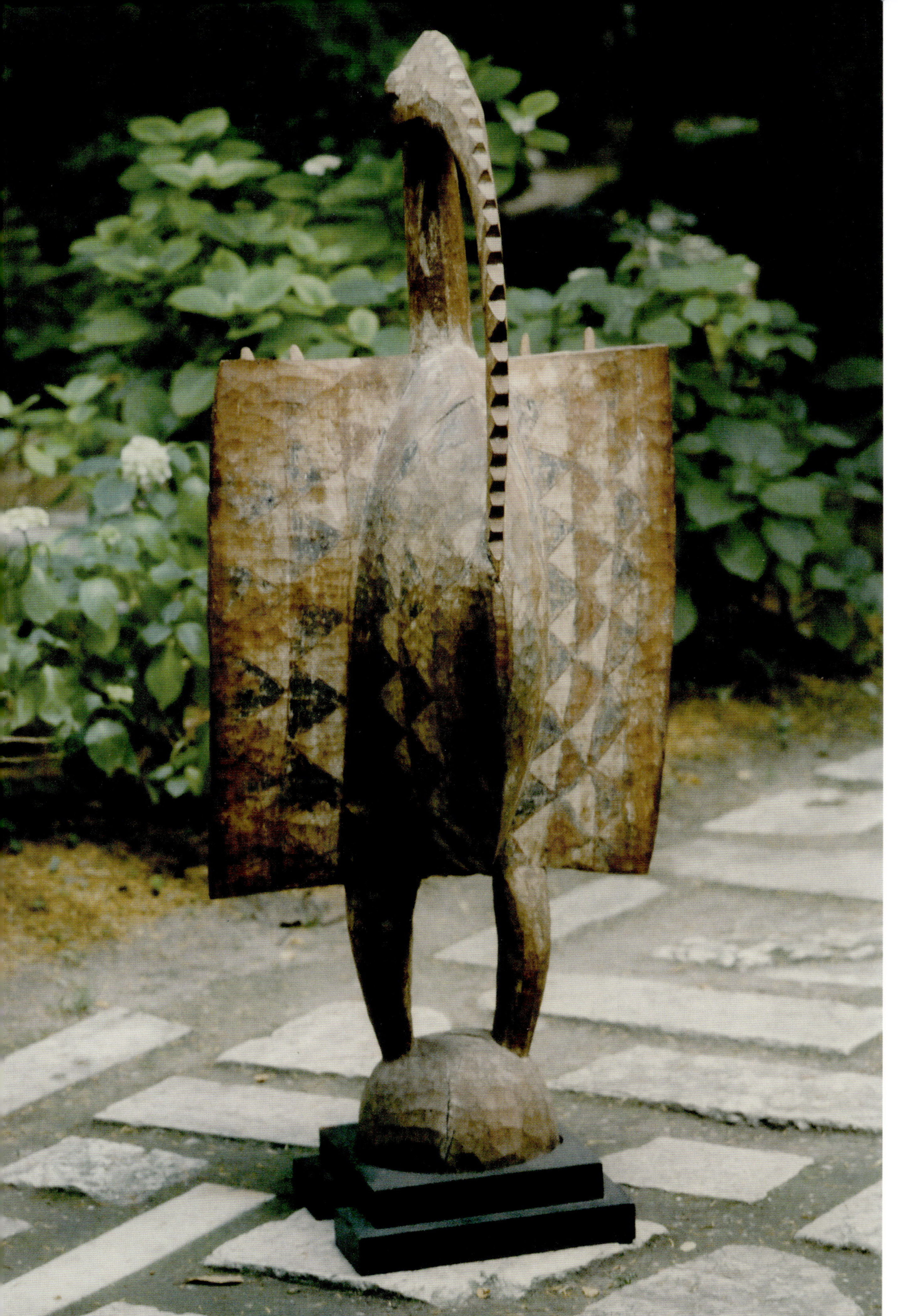

Mythical wooden bird of the Senufo people.

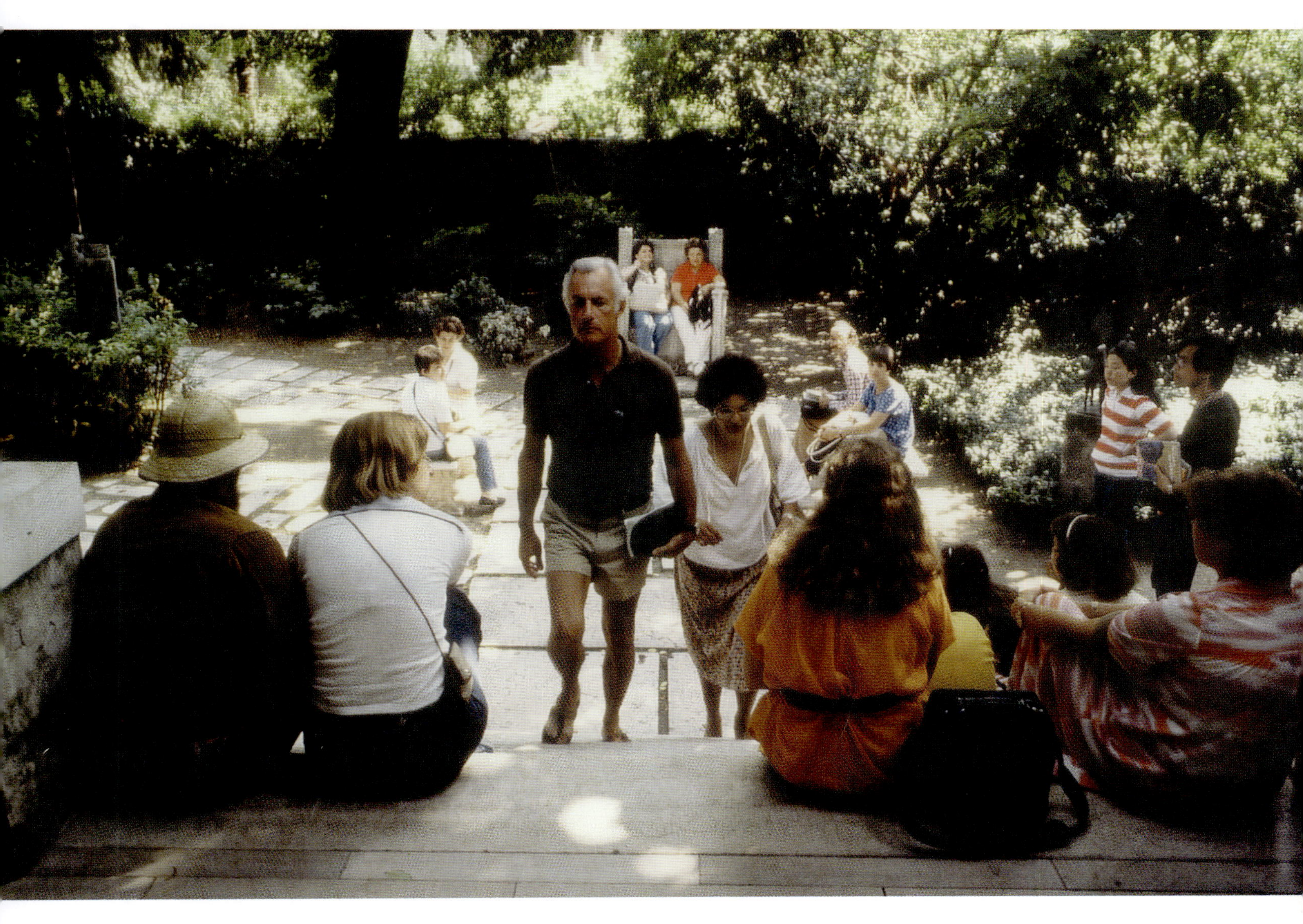

pp 90–91

Peggy with Germaine Richier's *La Tauromachie* [Bullfighting] (1953).

pp 92–95

Peggy in her Barchessa, with paintings by Giorgio de Chirico, Morris Hirshfield,
Joan Miró, Marc Chagall, Victor Brauner, Yves Tanguy and Max Ernst

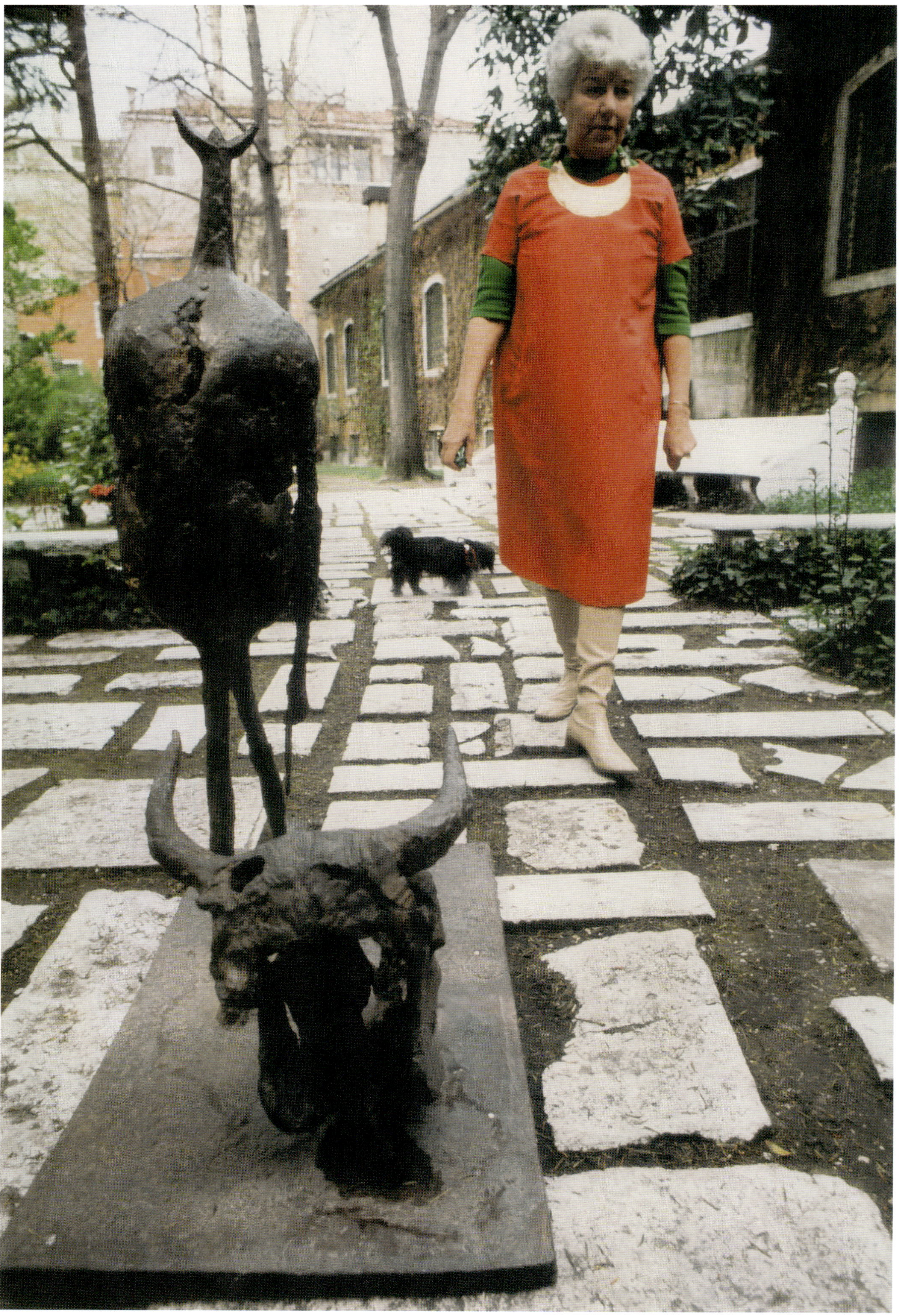

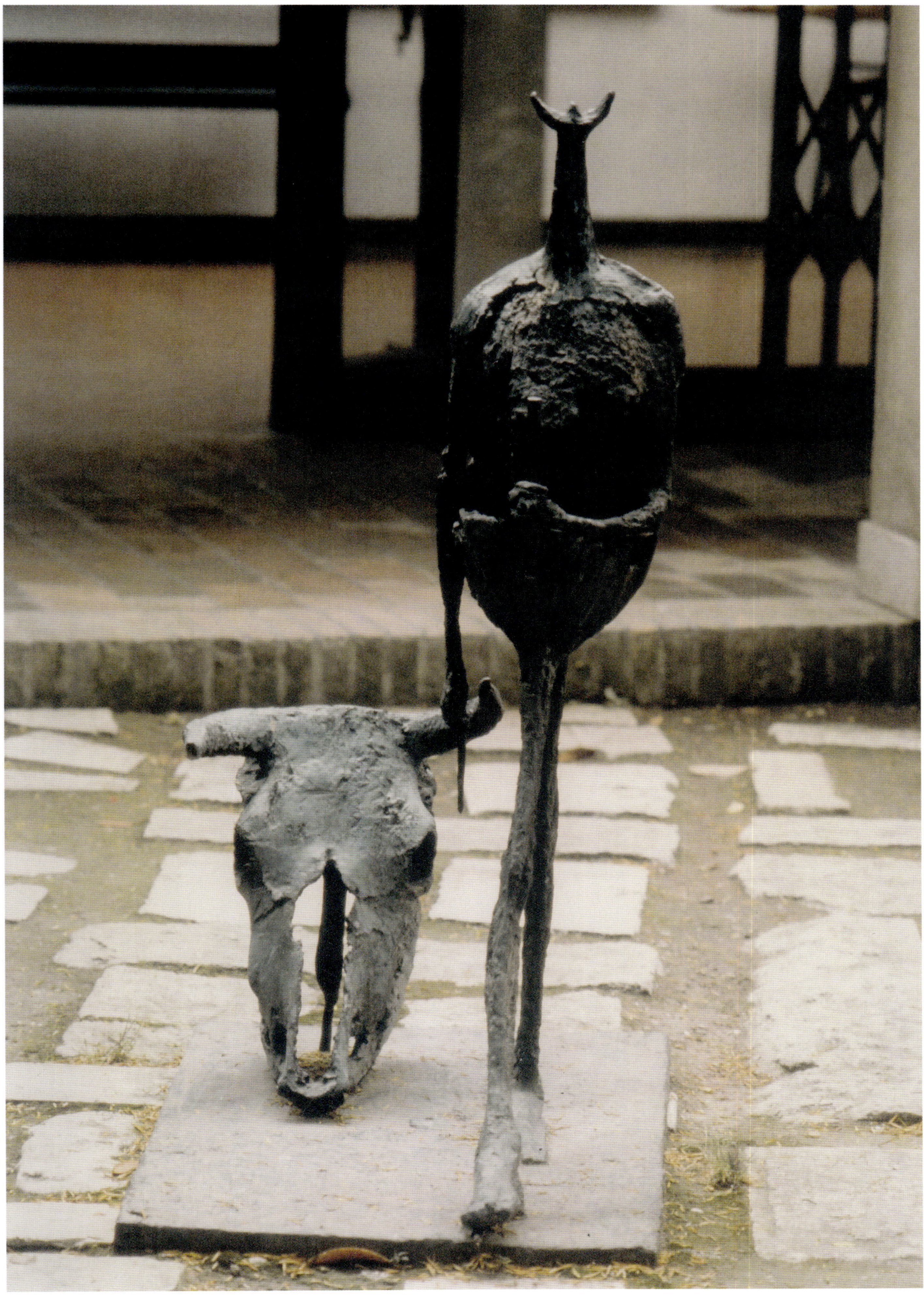

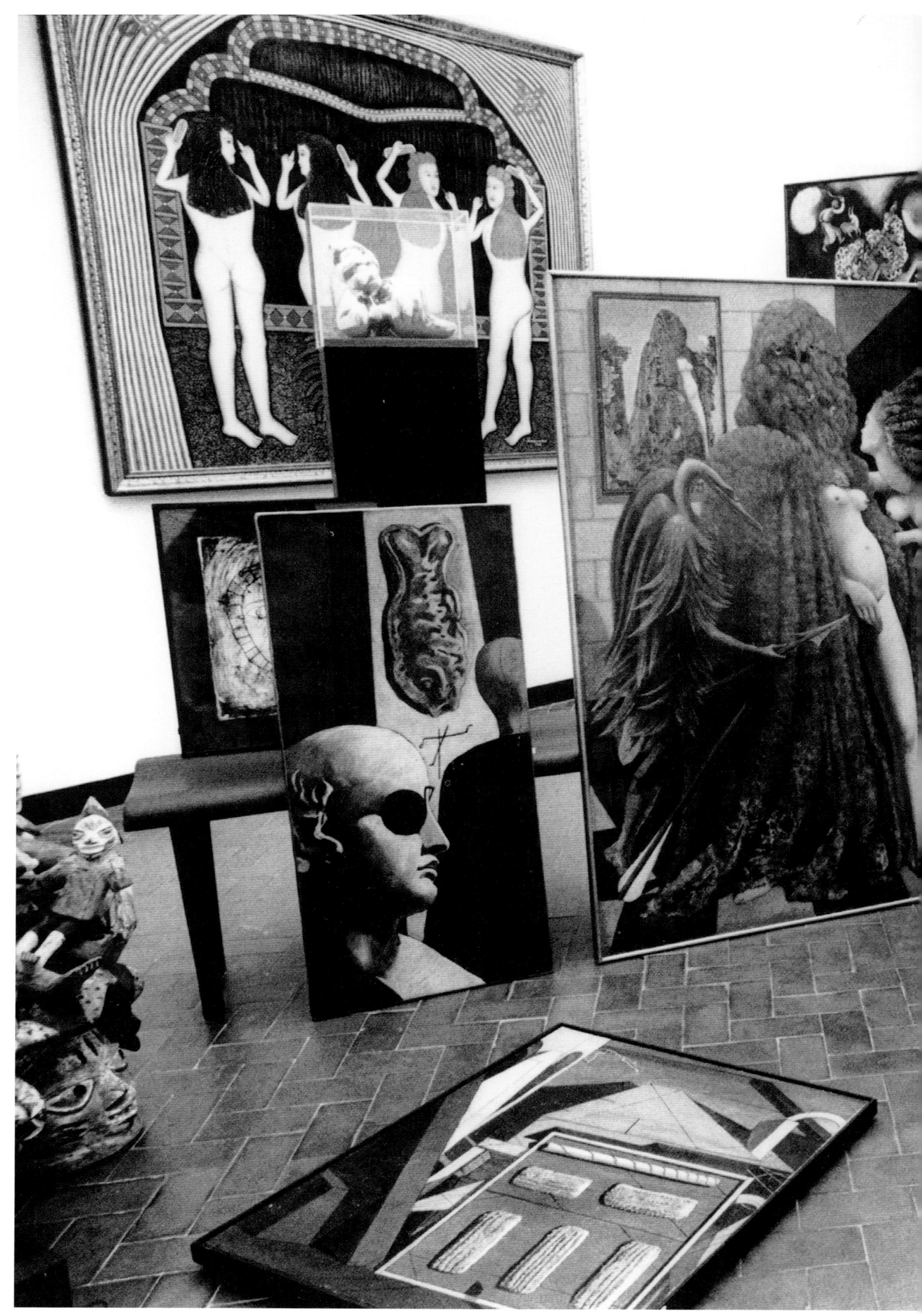

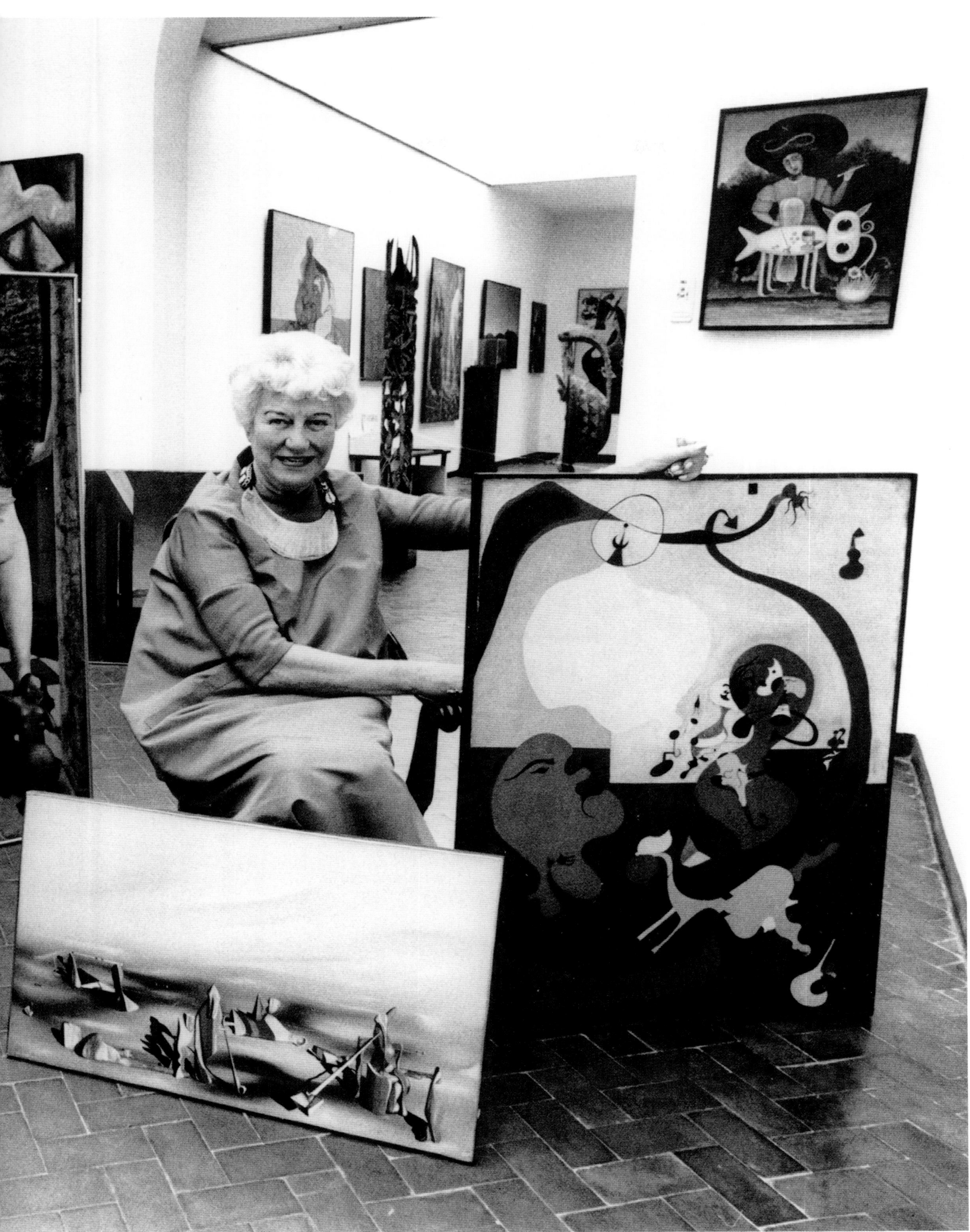

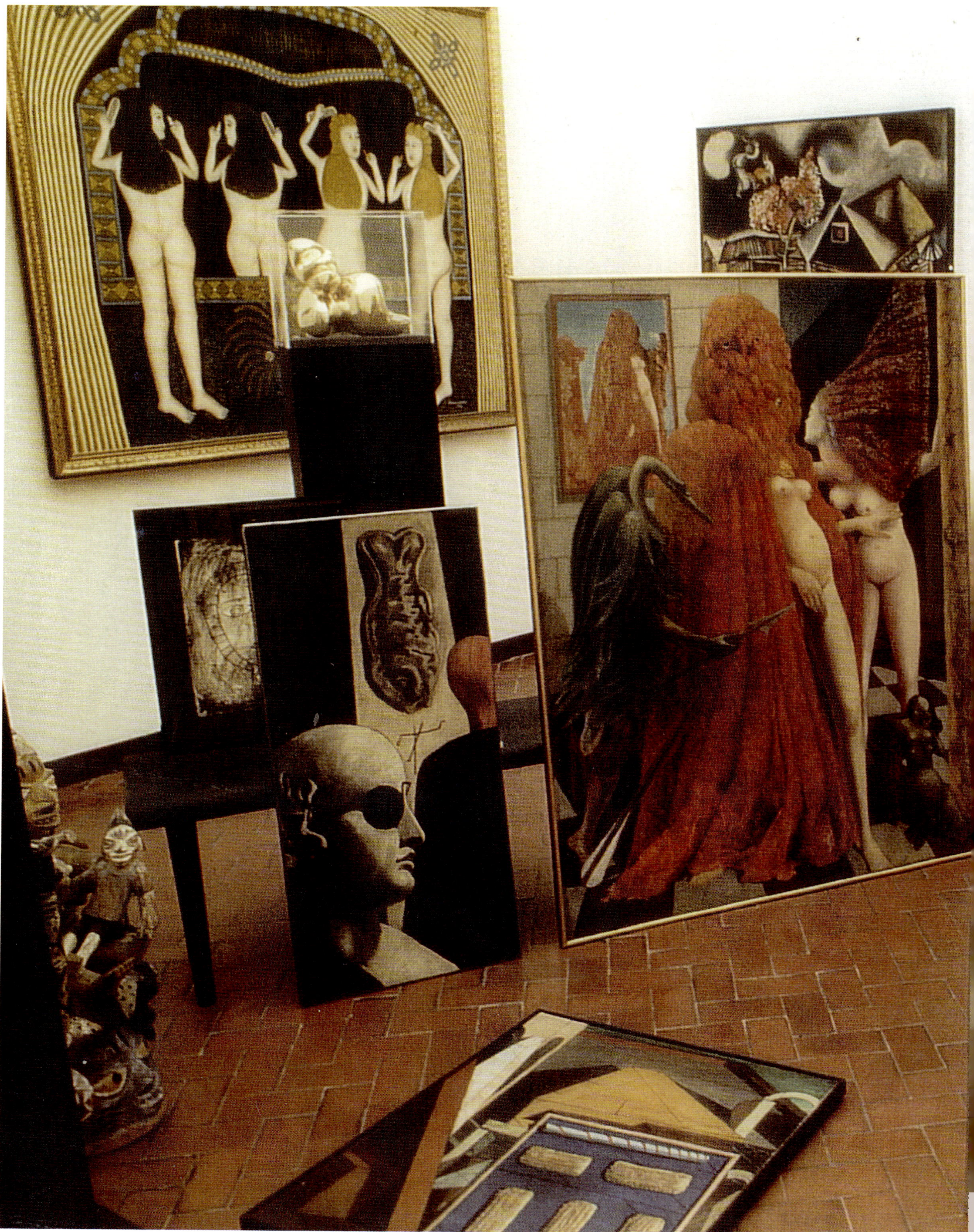

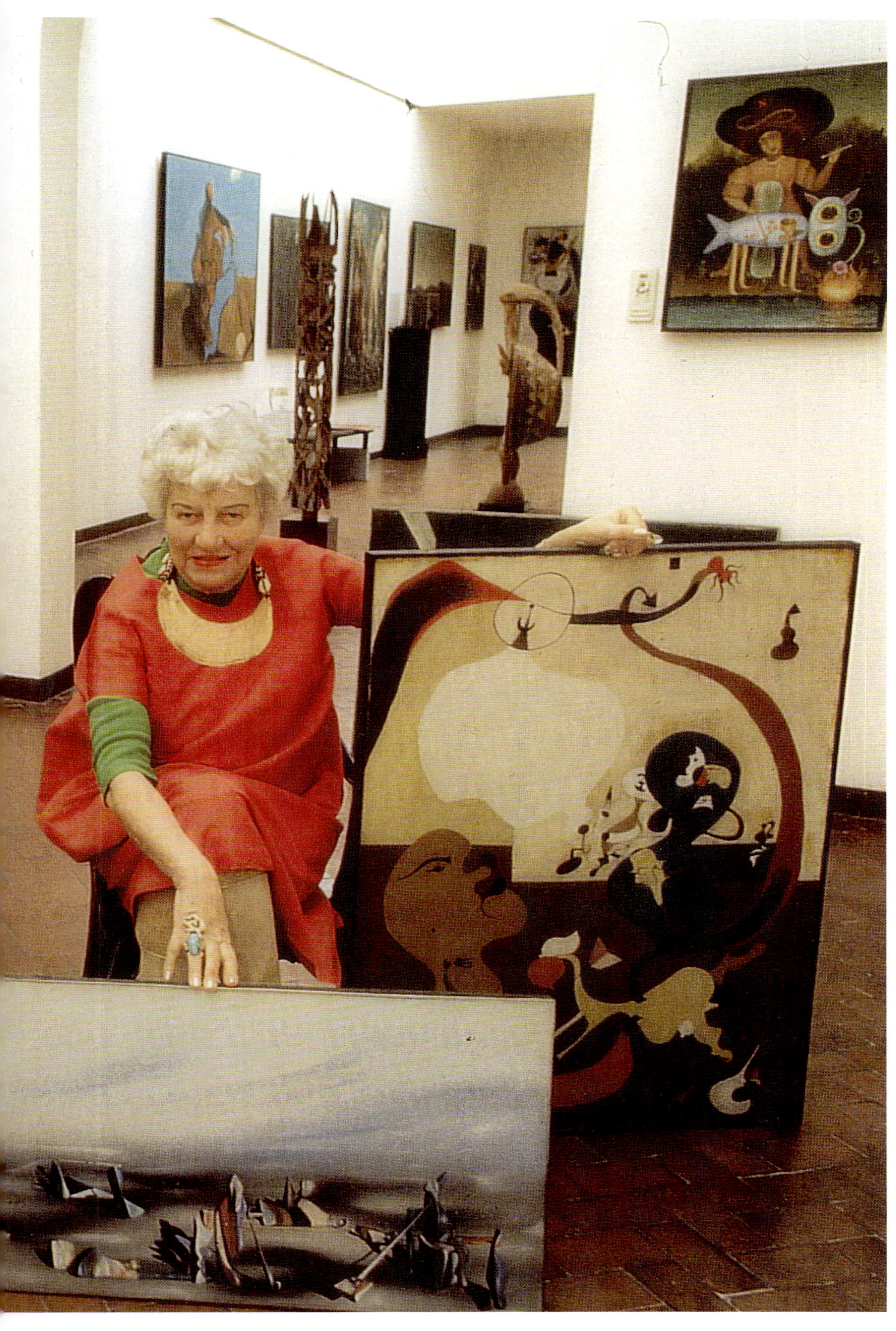

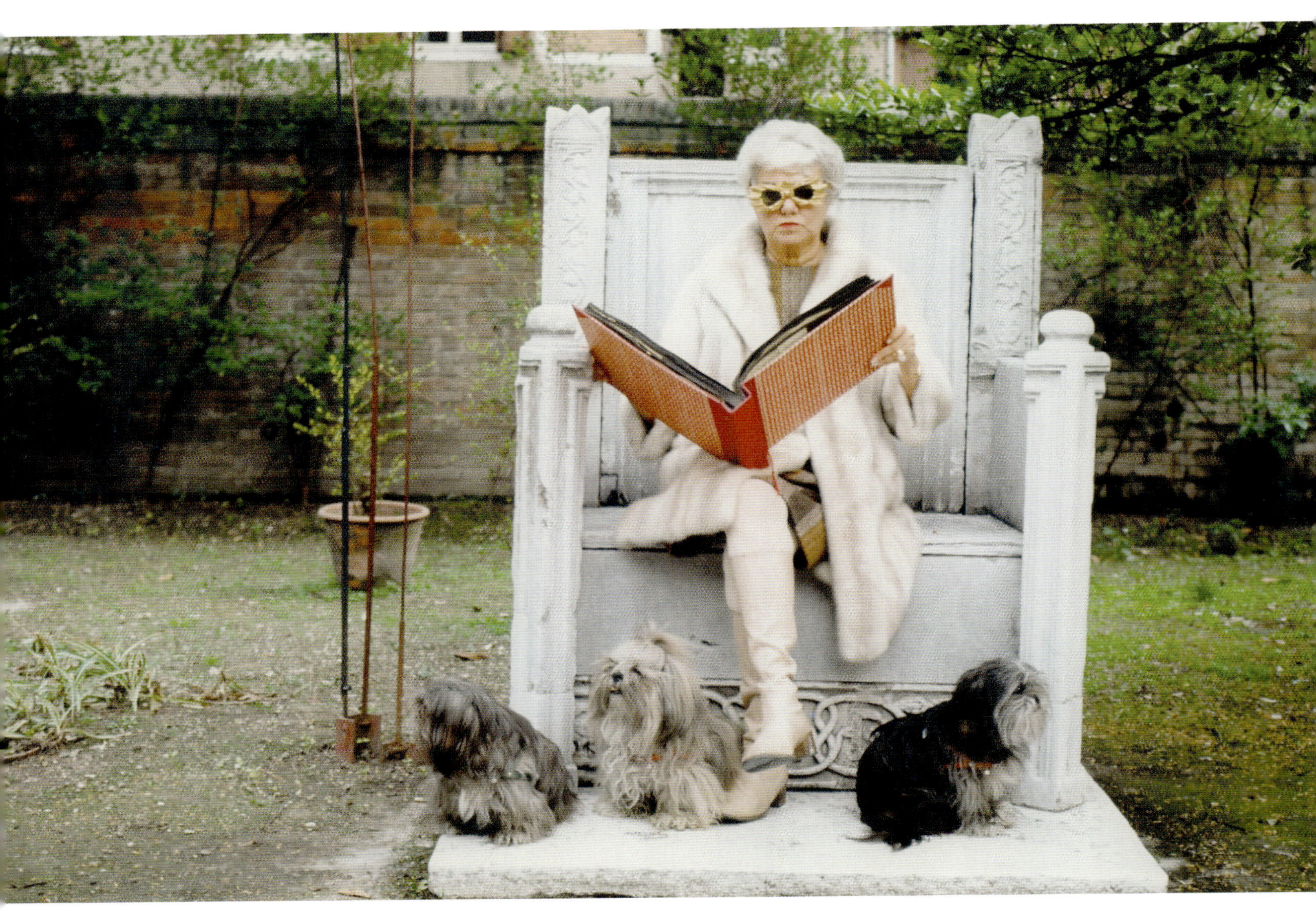

Peggy sitting on a Byzantine-style throne, looking at a photo album.
The iron rods to her left belong to Takis's terracotta figure *Signal* (1958).

Right
Alexander Archipenko's *La Boxe* [Boxing] (1935) is to be seen in the foreground.

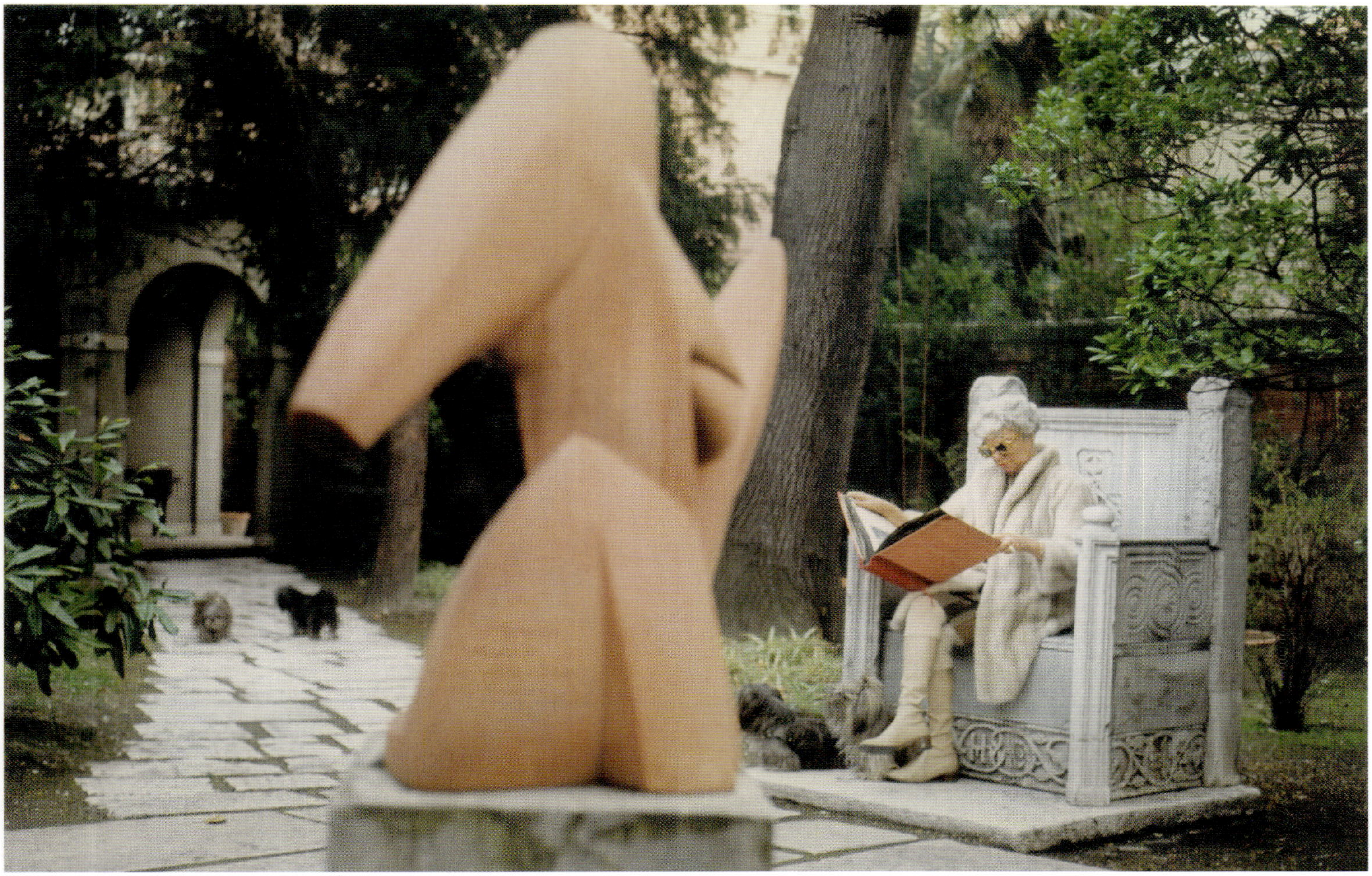

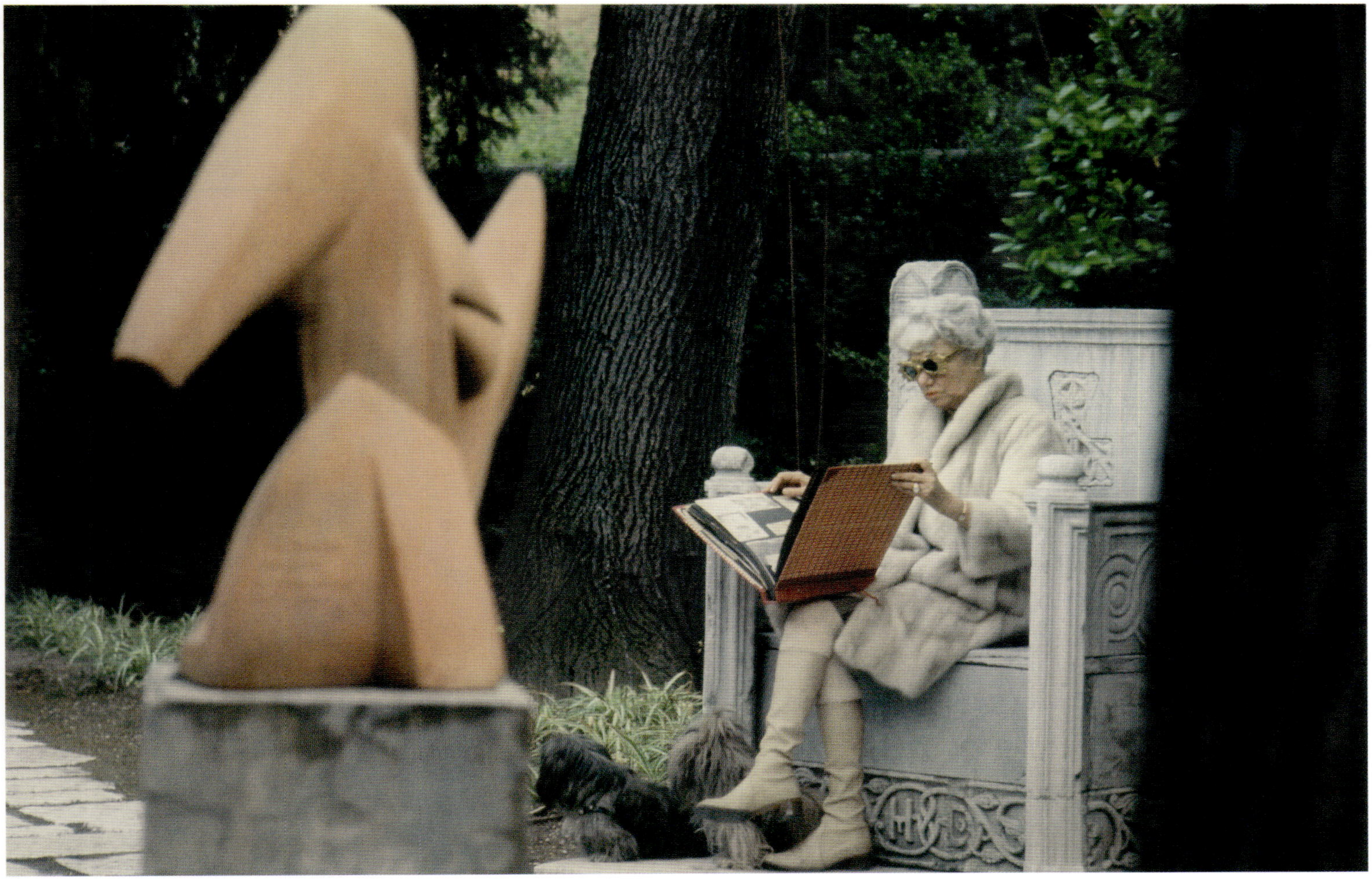

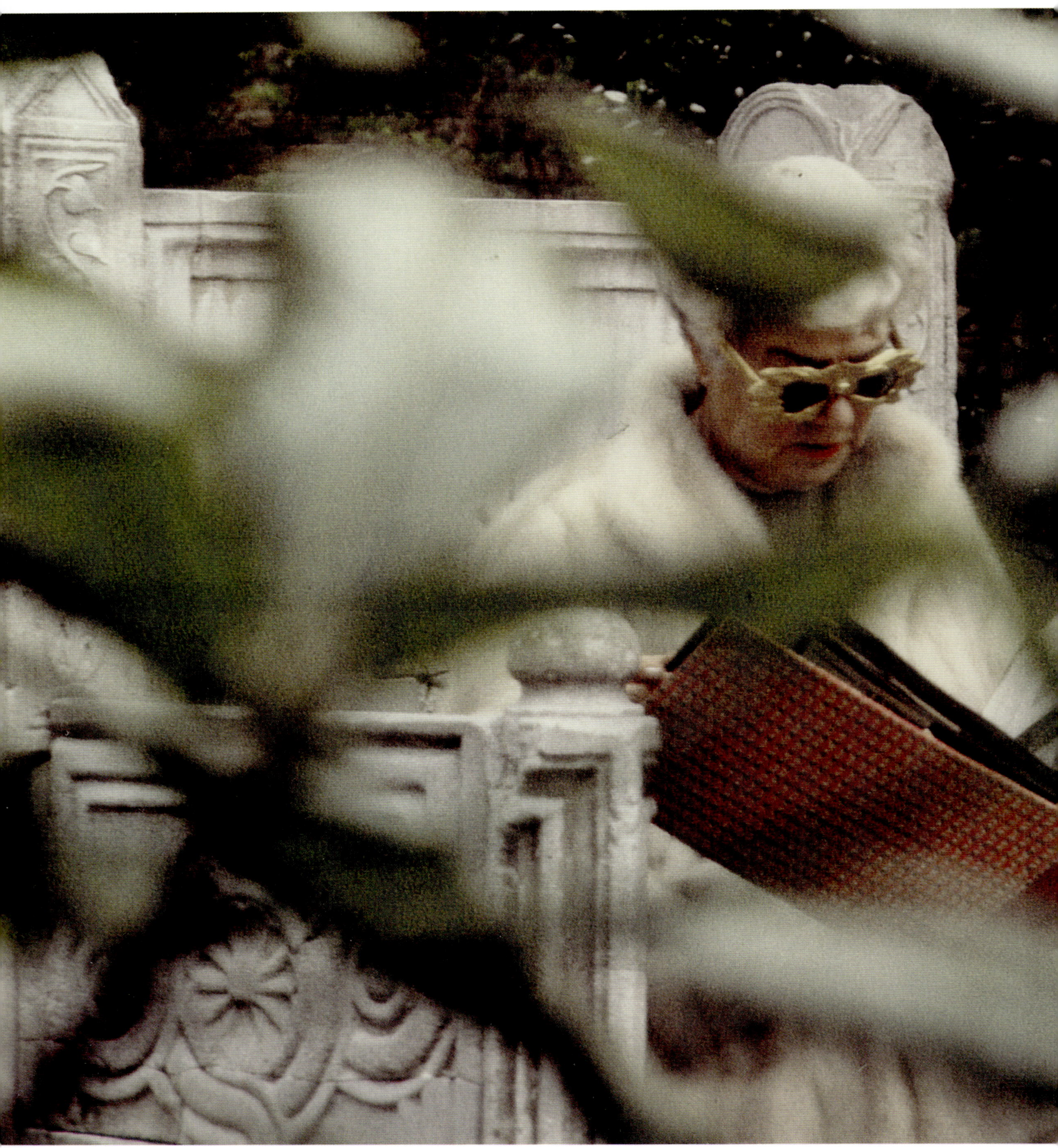

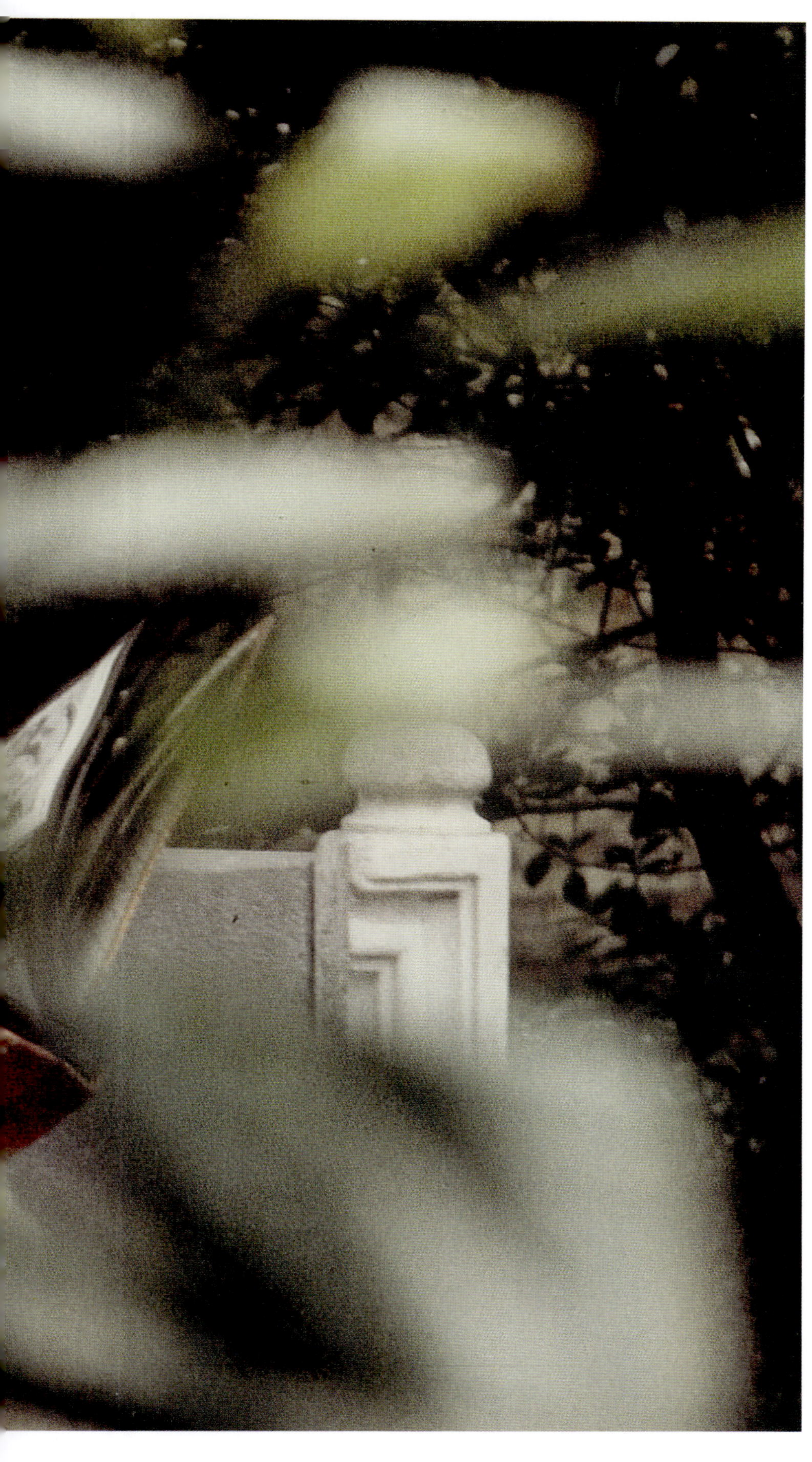

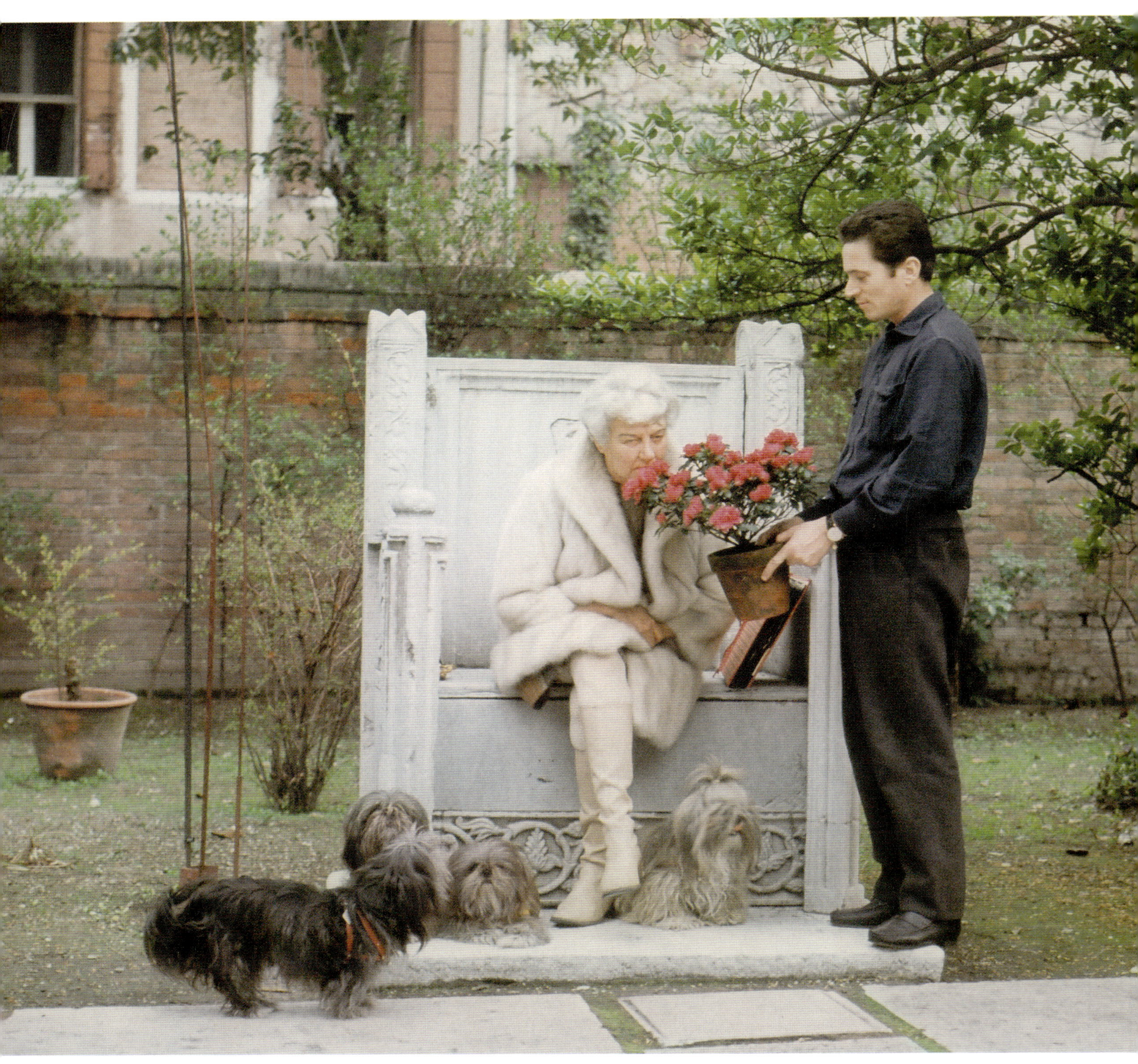

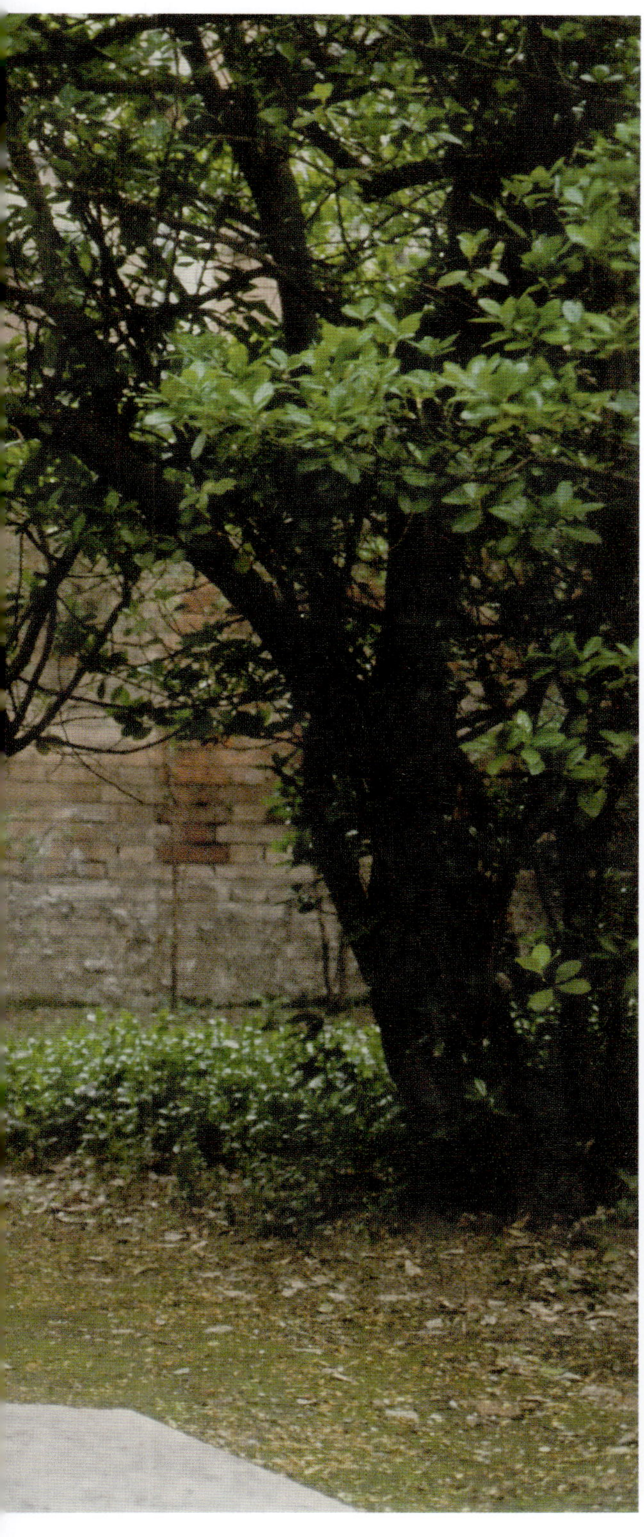

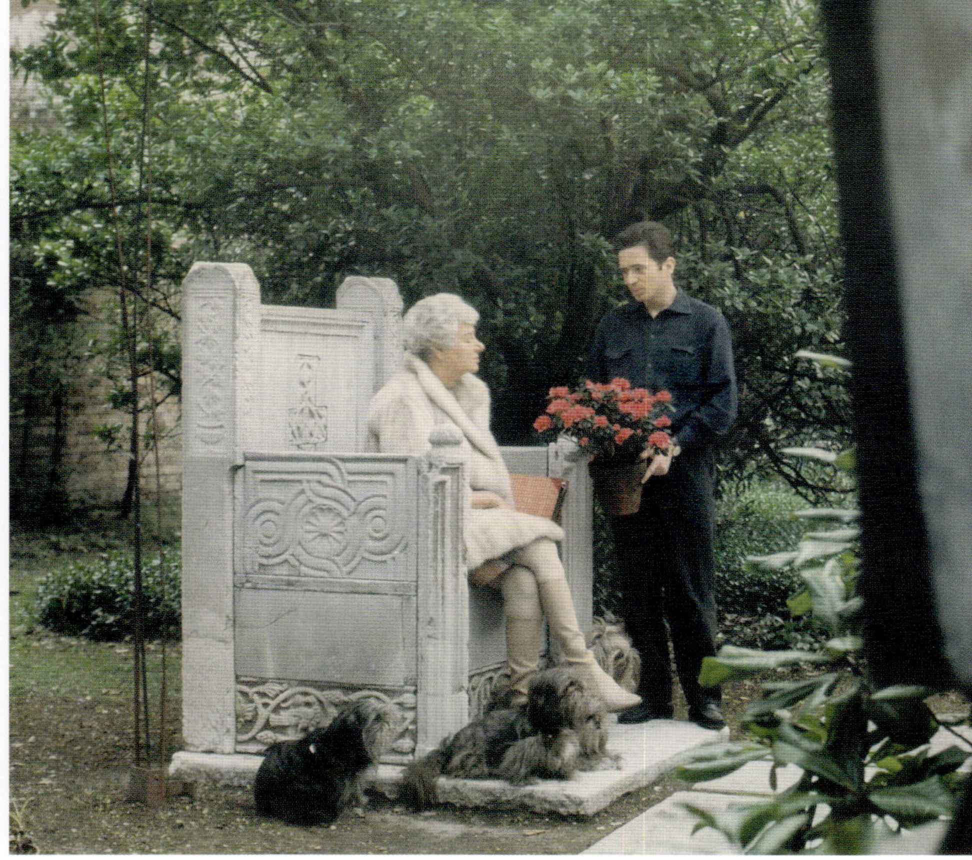

Left
A portrait of Pegeen Vail,
daughter of Peggy Guggenheim
and Laurence Vail.

Right
Passport photos of Peggy Guggenheim 1922–1974,
collaged by Stefan Moses.


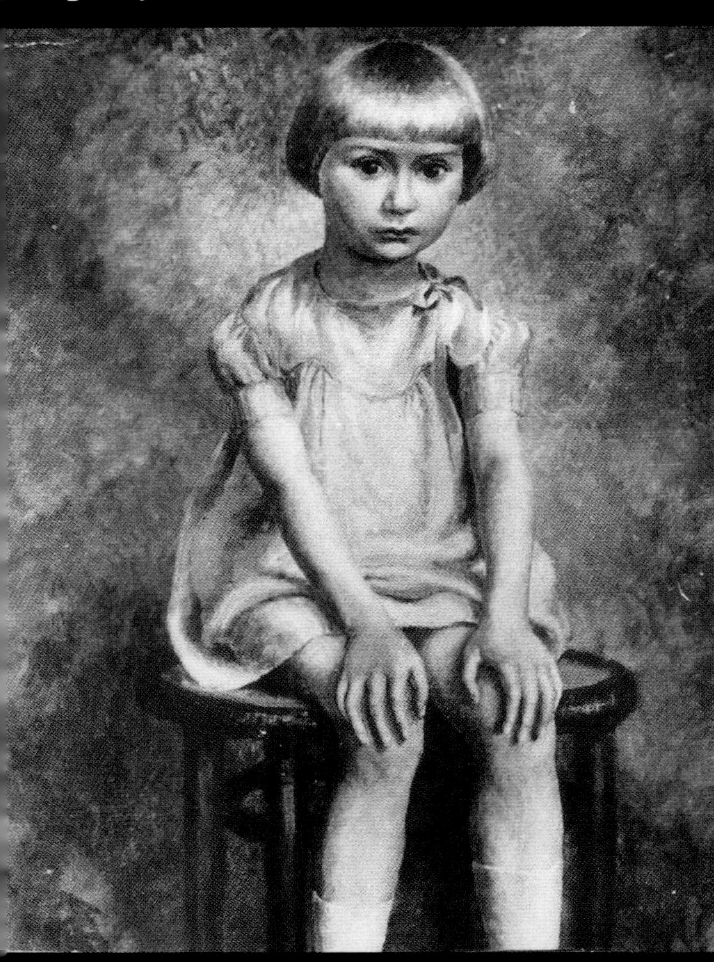

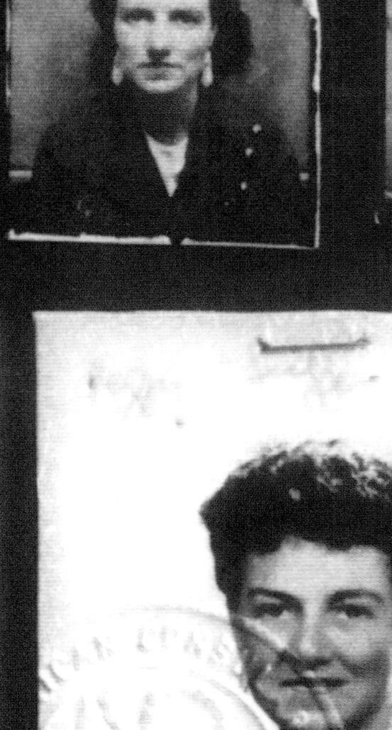

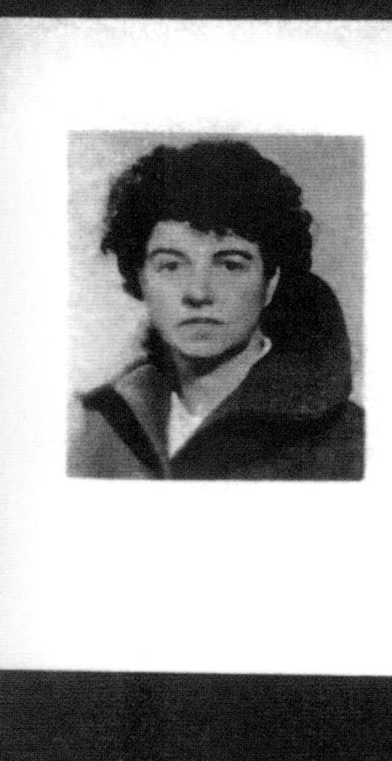

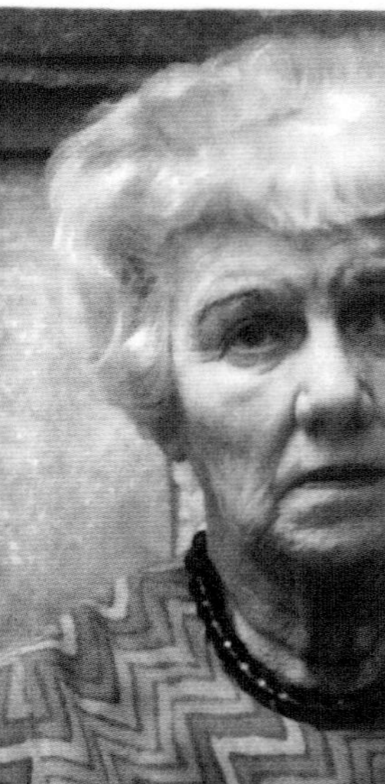


pp 104–105
Top row, first photo from the left
Pegeen Vail, daughter of Peggy Guggenheim
and Laurence Vail.
Top row, second photo from the left
Probably Sindbad Vail, the son of Peggy
Guggenheim and Laurence Vail.
Top row, third photo from the left
Peggy Guggenheim with Deborah Garman.
Top row, fourth photo from the left
Not Douglas Garman
Bottom row, fourth photo from the left
Peggy Guggenheim and Pegeen Vail.

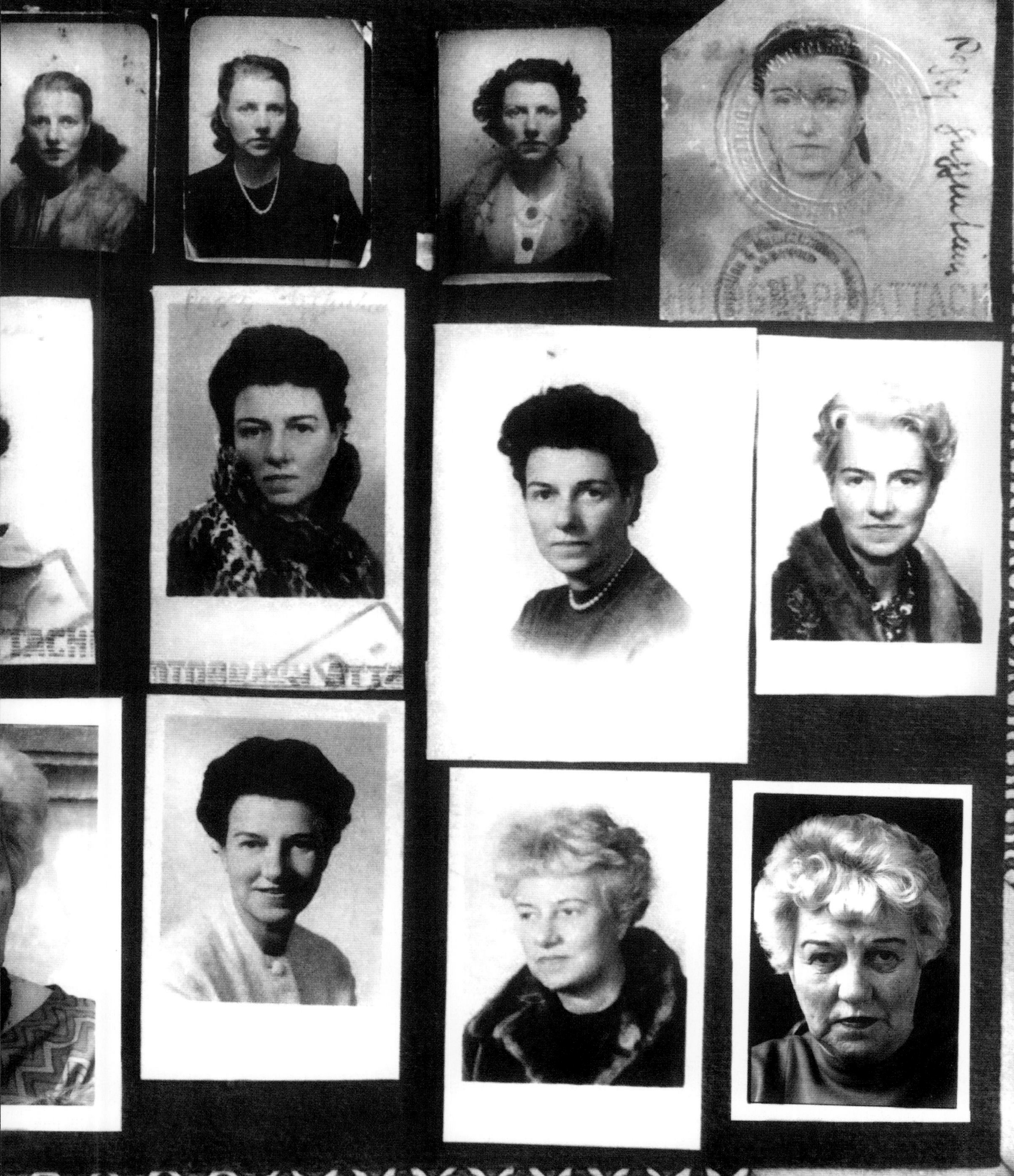

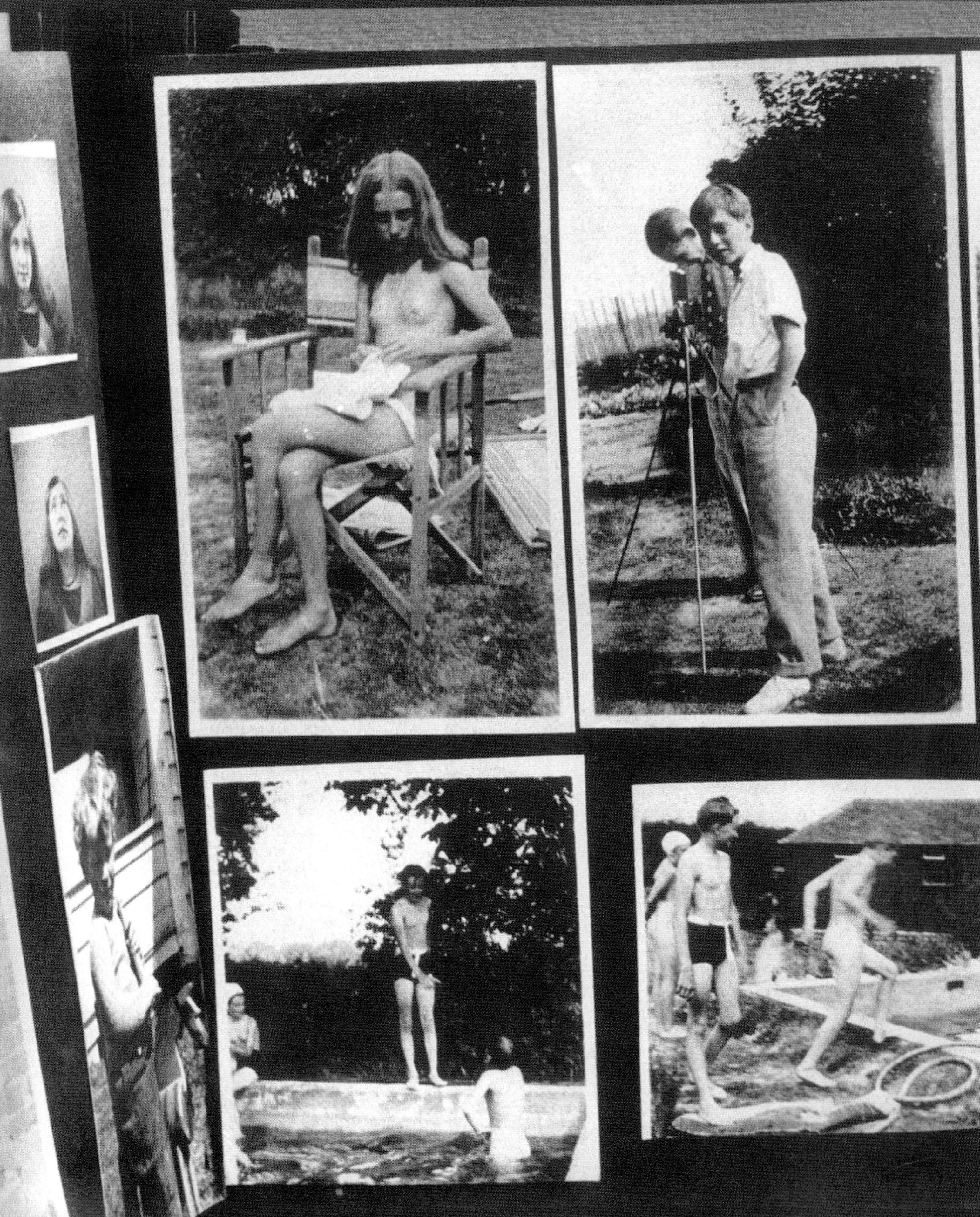

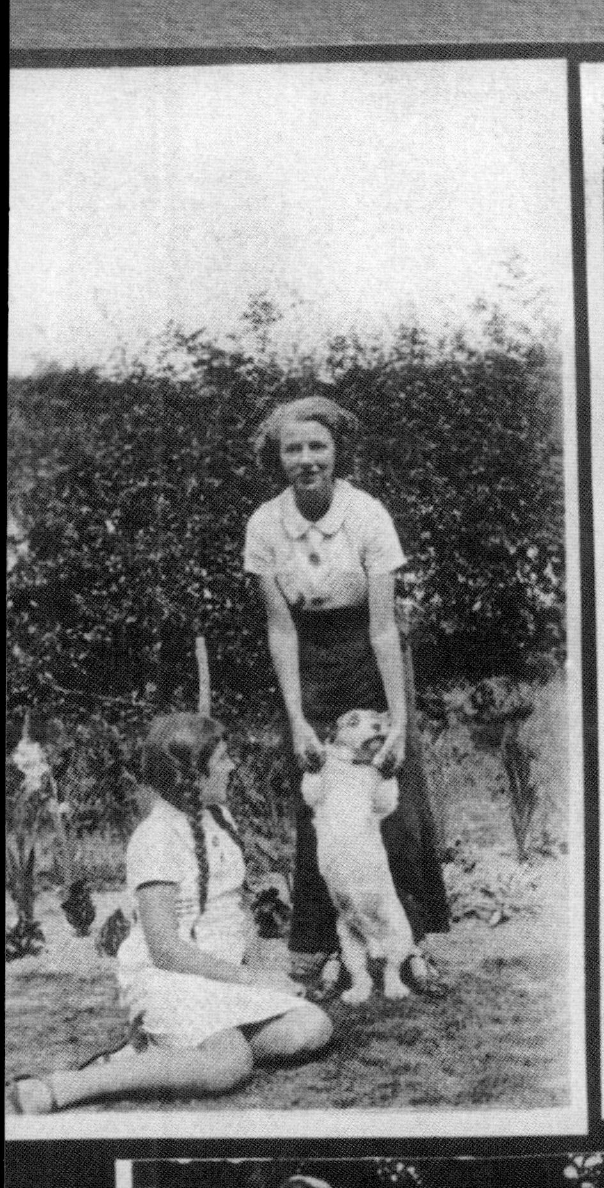

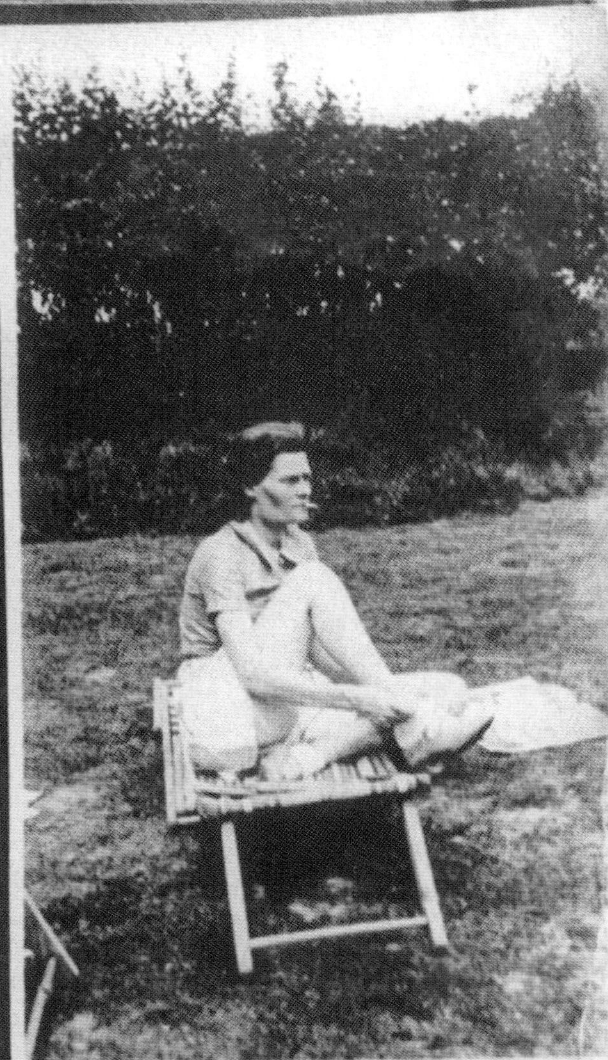

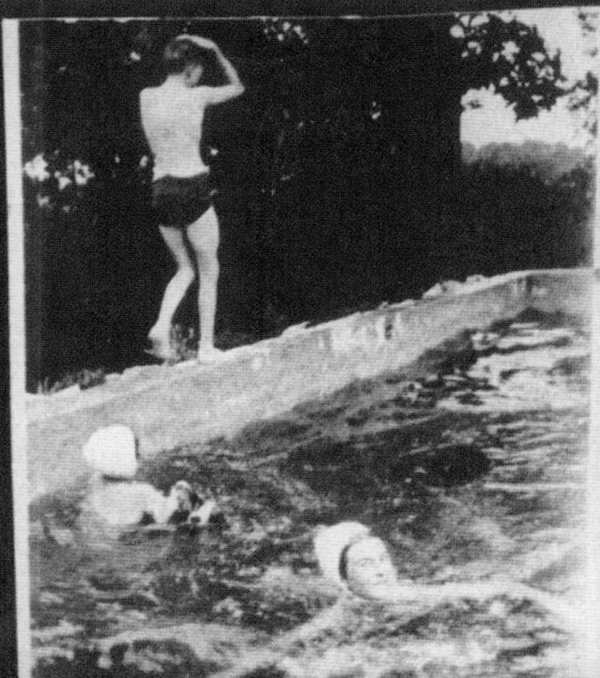

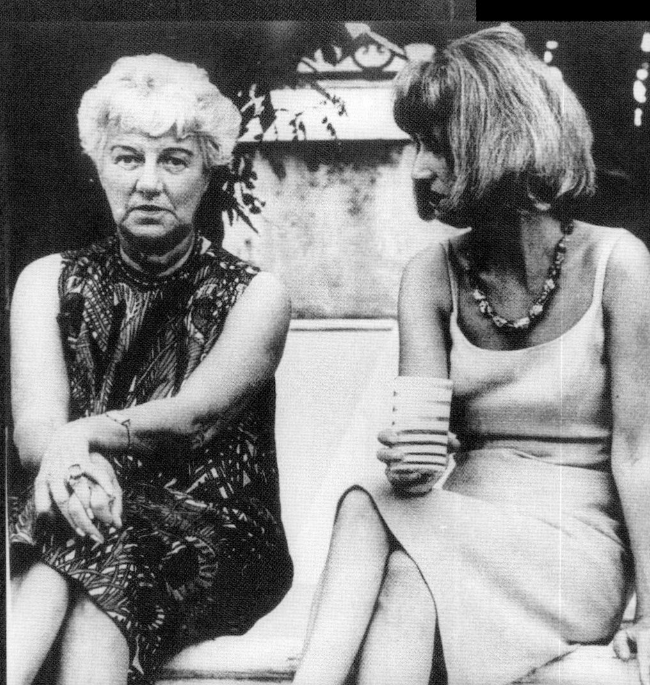

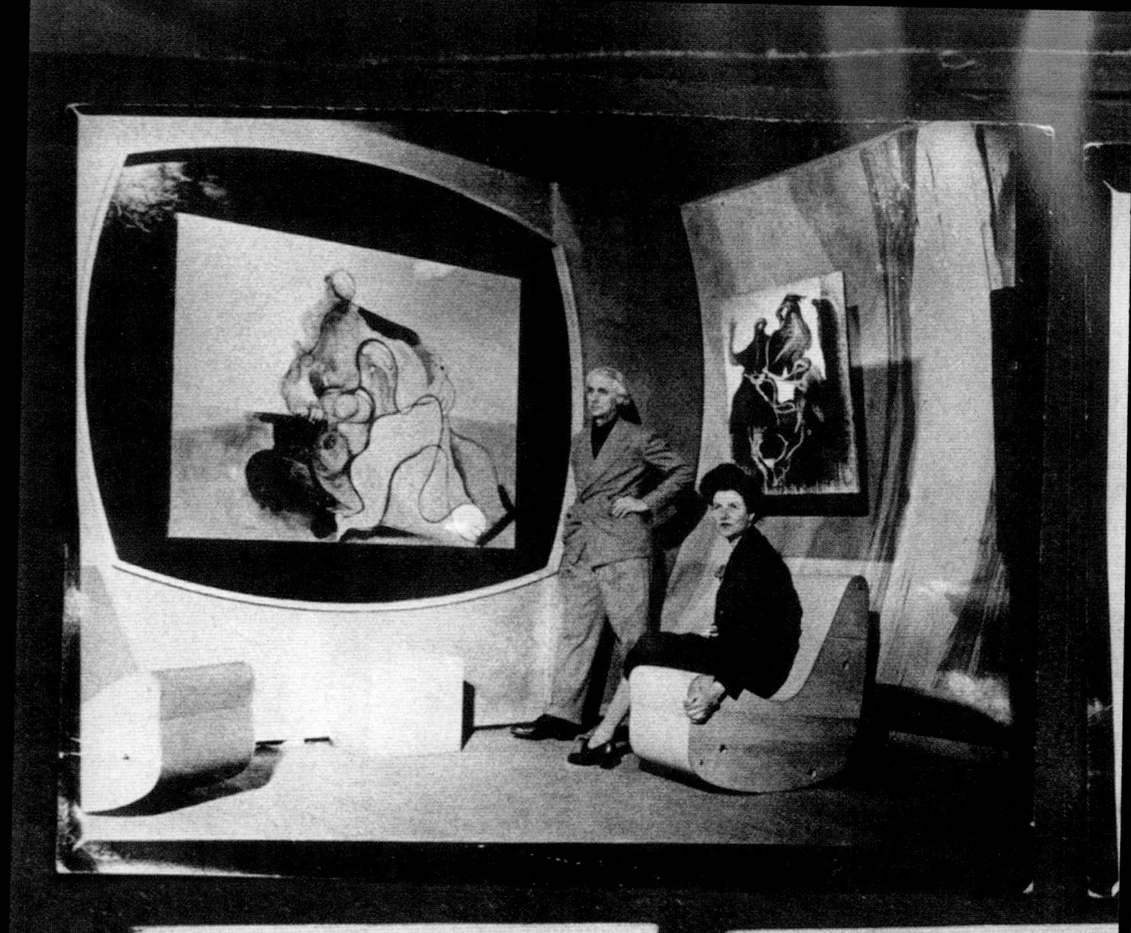

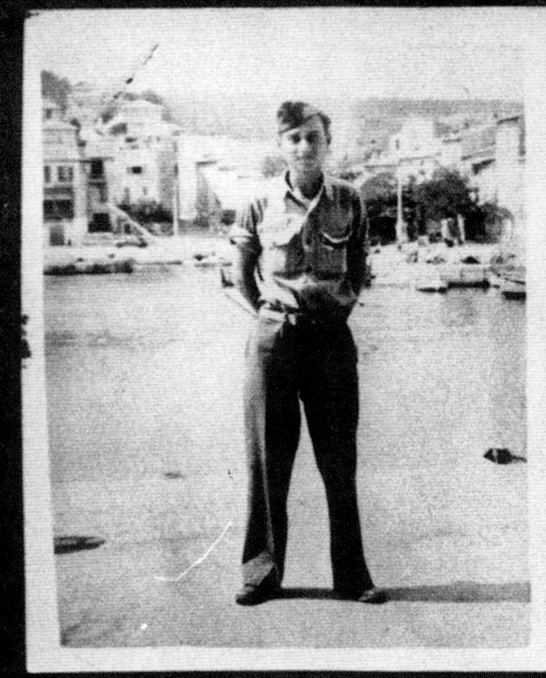

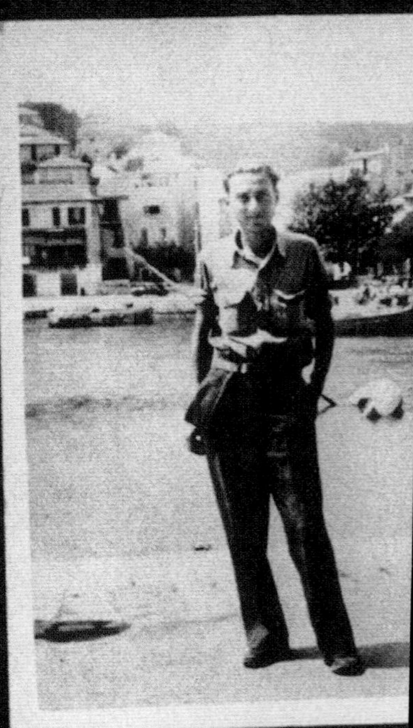

Top Left
Peggy Guggenheim and Max
Ernst in the surrealism gallery
'Art of This Century'.

Top Right
Peggy Guggenheim in front of
Max Ernst's *Der Wald*
[The Forest] in the 'Art of This
Century' gallery.

Bottom
The man in soldier's uniform is
Sindbad Vail. In the picture to
the right of this the older man
is Laurence Vail, together with
his third wife Jean Connolly and
their step-daughter Kathe Vail.
She is the second daughter
of Vail and Kay Boyle. The two
people at the bottom right are
of course Jackson Pollock and
his wife Lee Krasner.

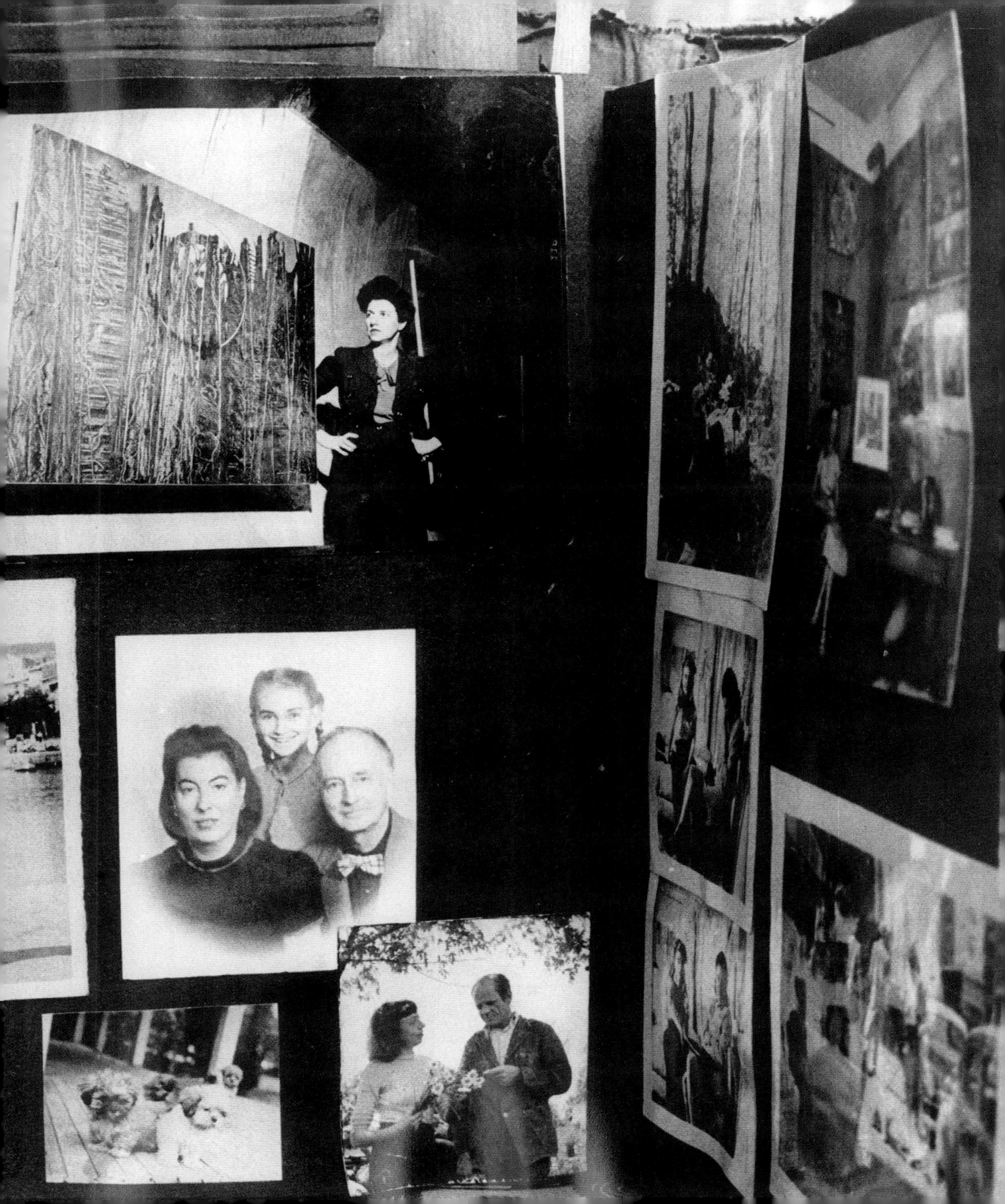

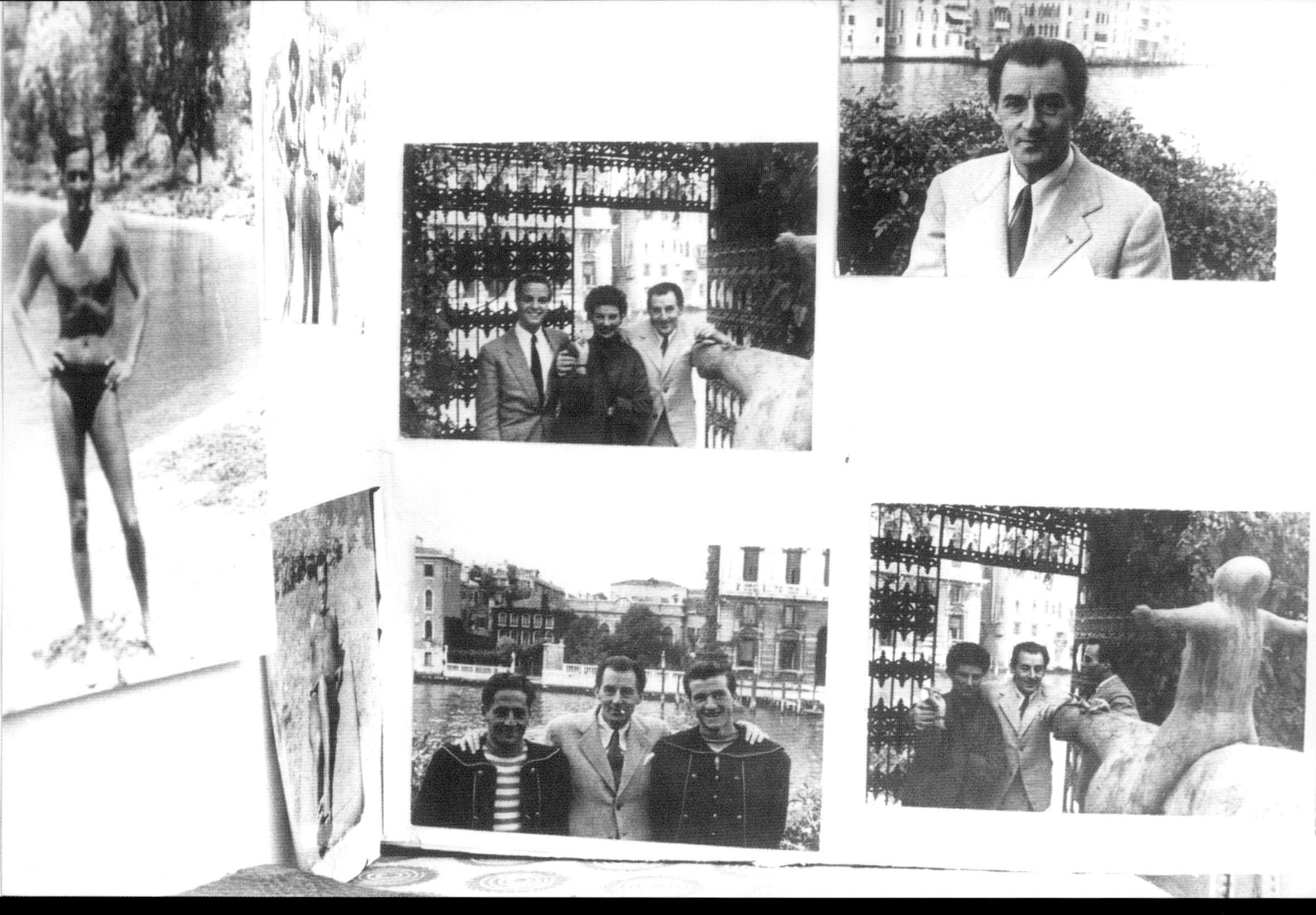

Photos of Raoul Gregorich in bathing trunks,
and looking dapper in a suit, with two gondoliers.

On the right-hand side Peggy is to be seen in a bikini,

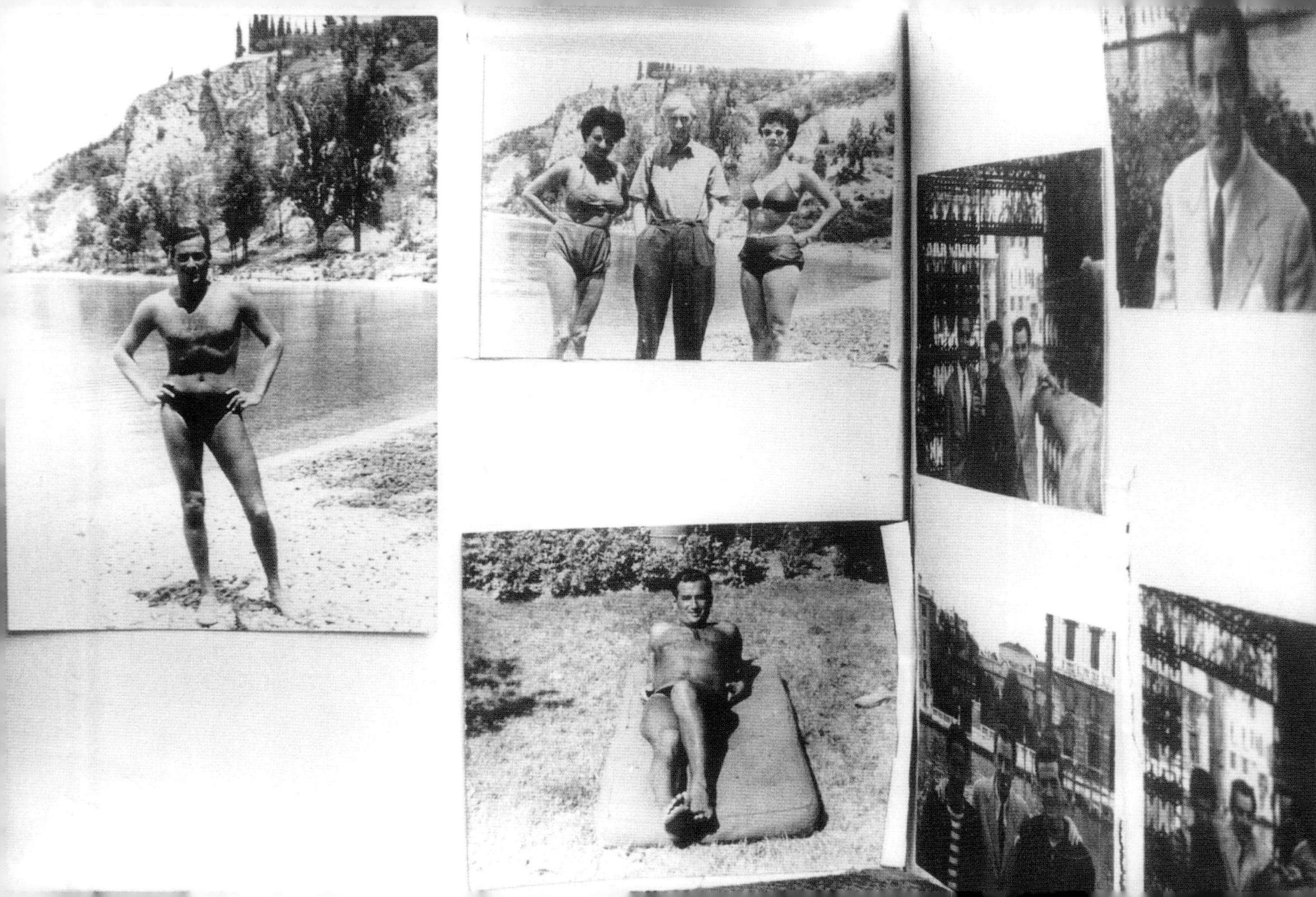

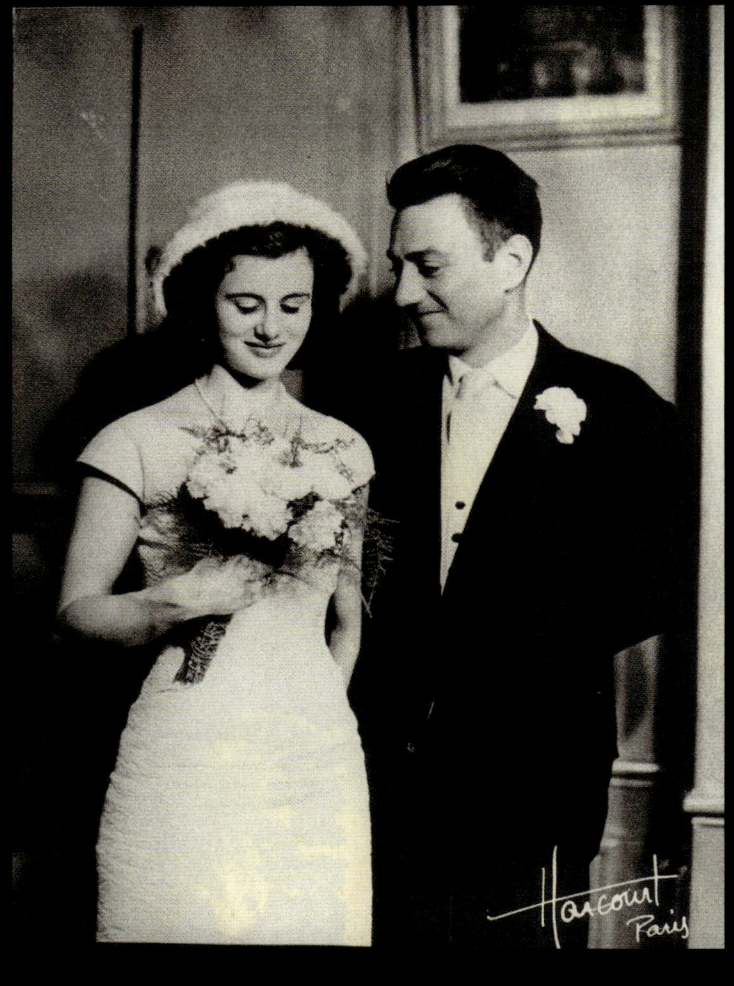


*Top left*
Sindbad Vail with his second wife
Peggy Angela Yeomans.

*Bottom left*
As the writing says: Peggy, Hazel and
Benita Guggenheim (in that order).

*Top right*
Peggy Guggenheim with Raoul Gregorich, 1951

*Bottom right*
Peggy Guggenheim with her son Sindbad
and Pegeen as a baby.

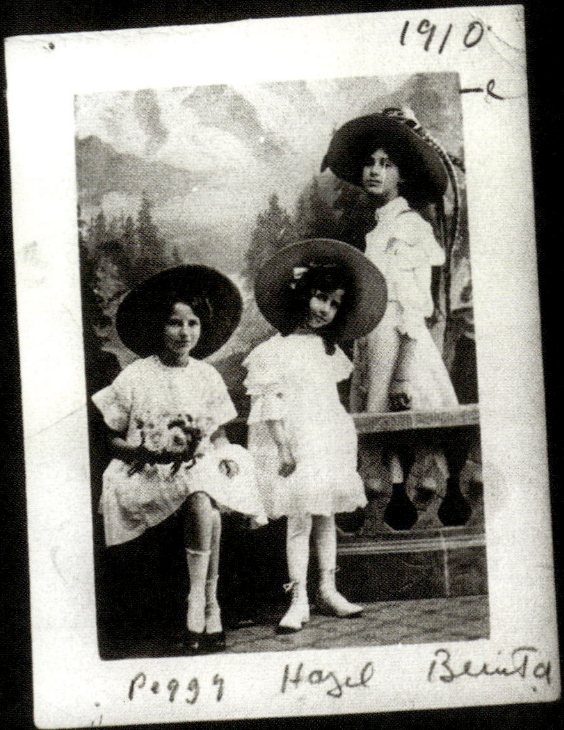

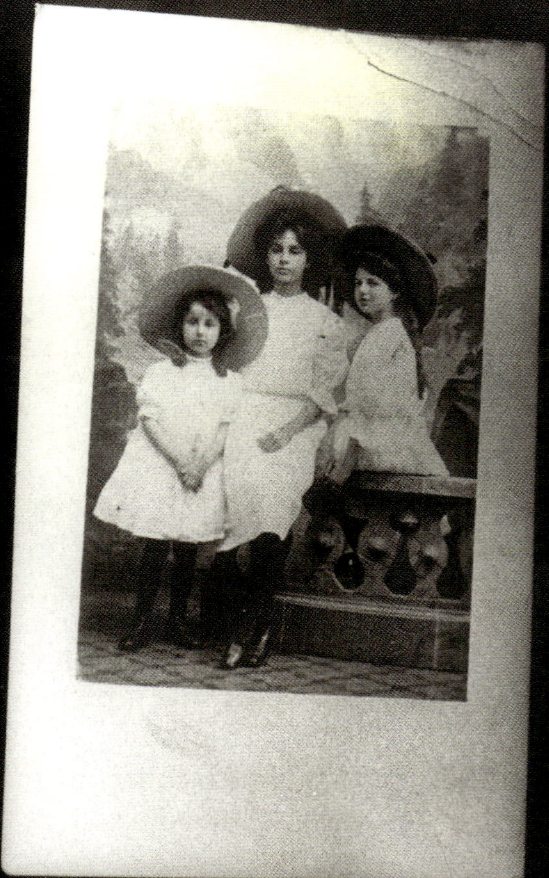

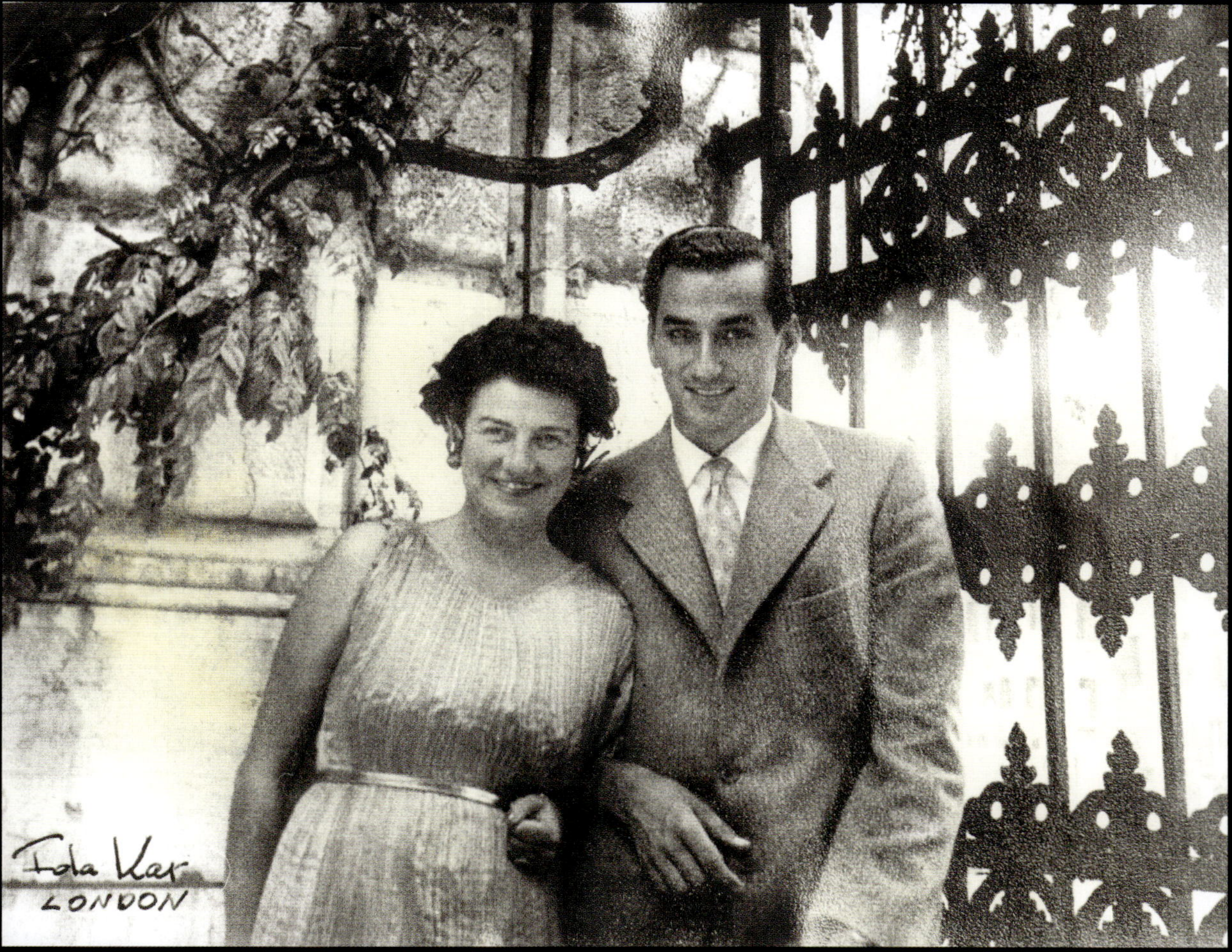

Ida Kar
LONDON

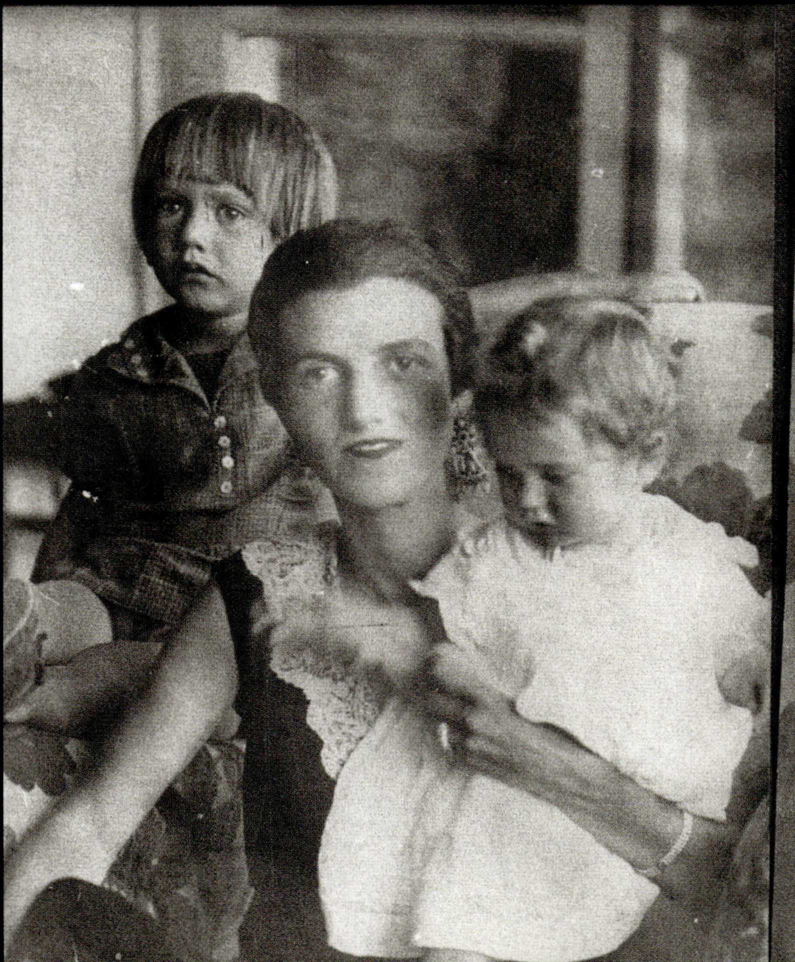

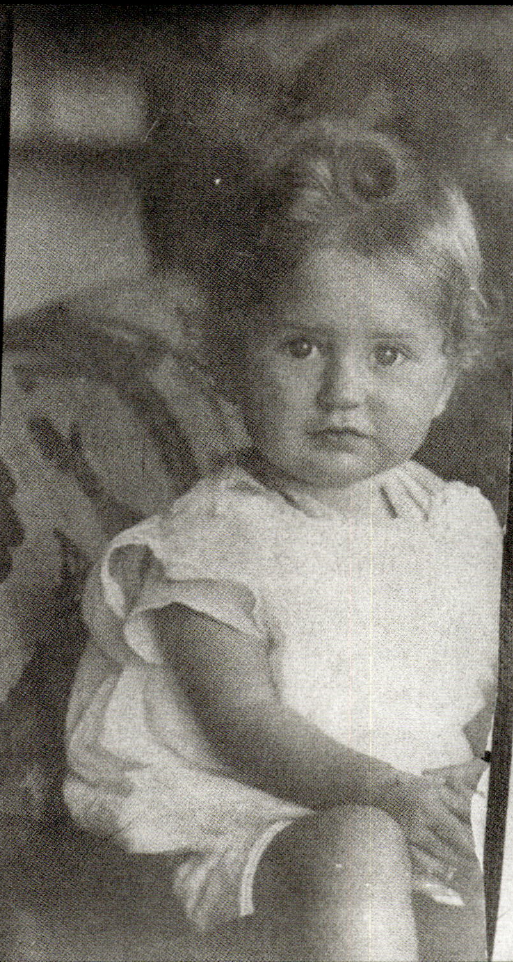

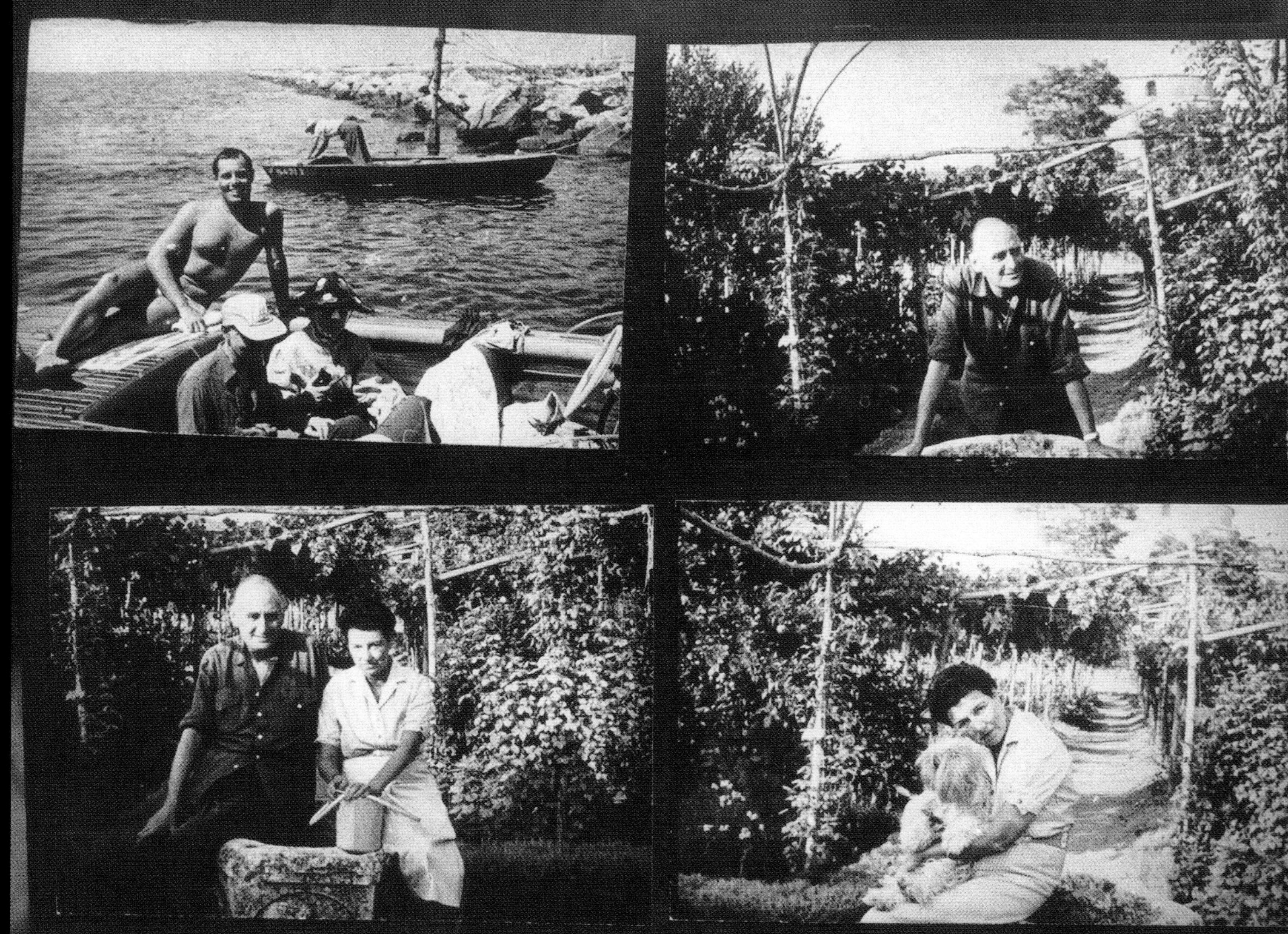

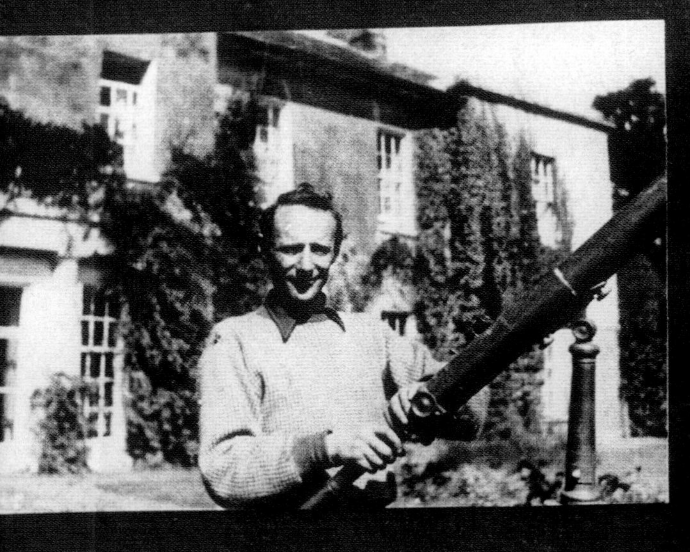

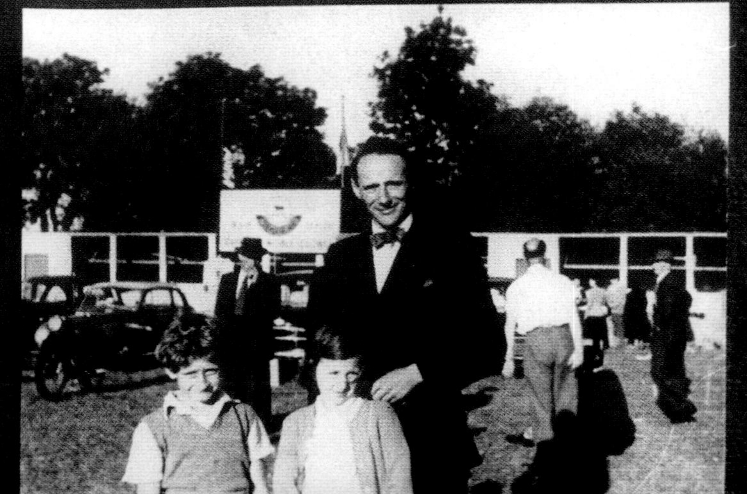

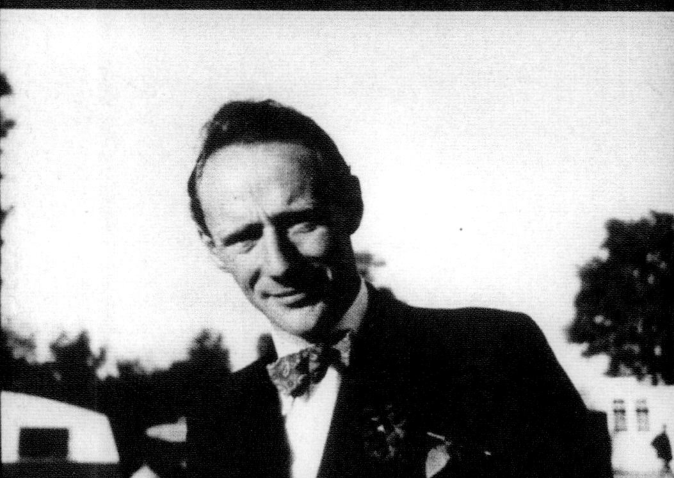

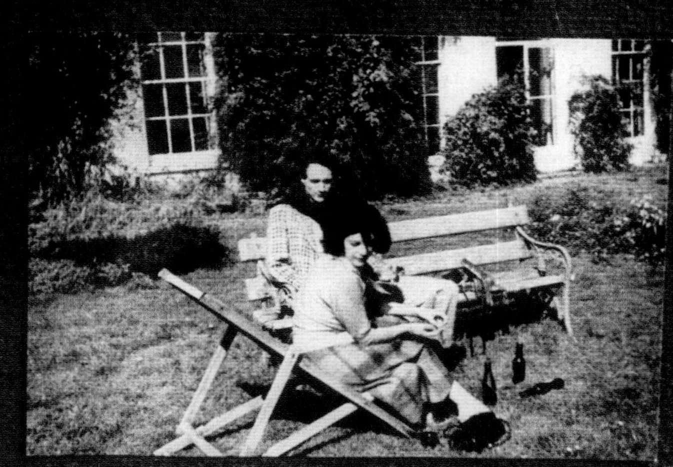

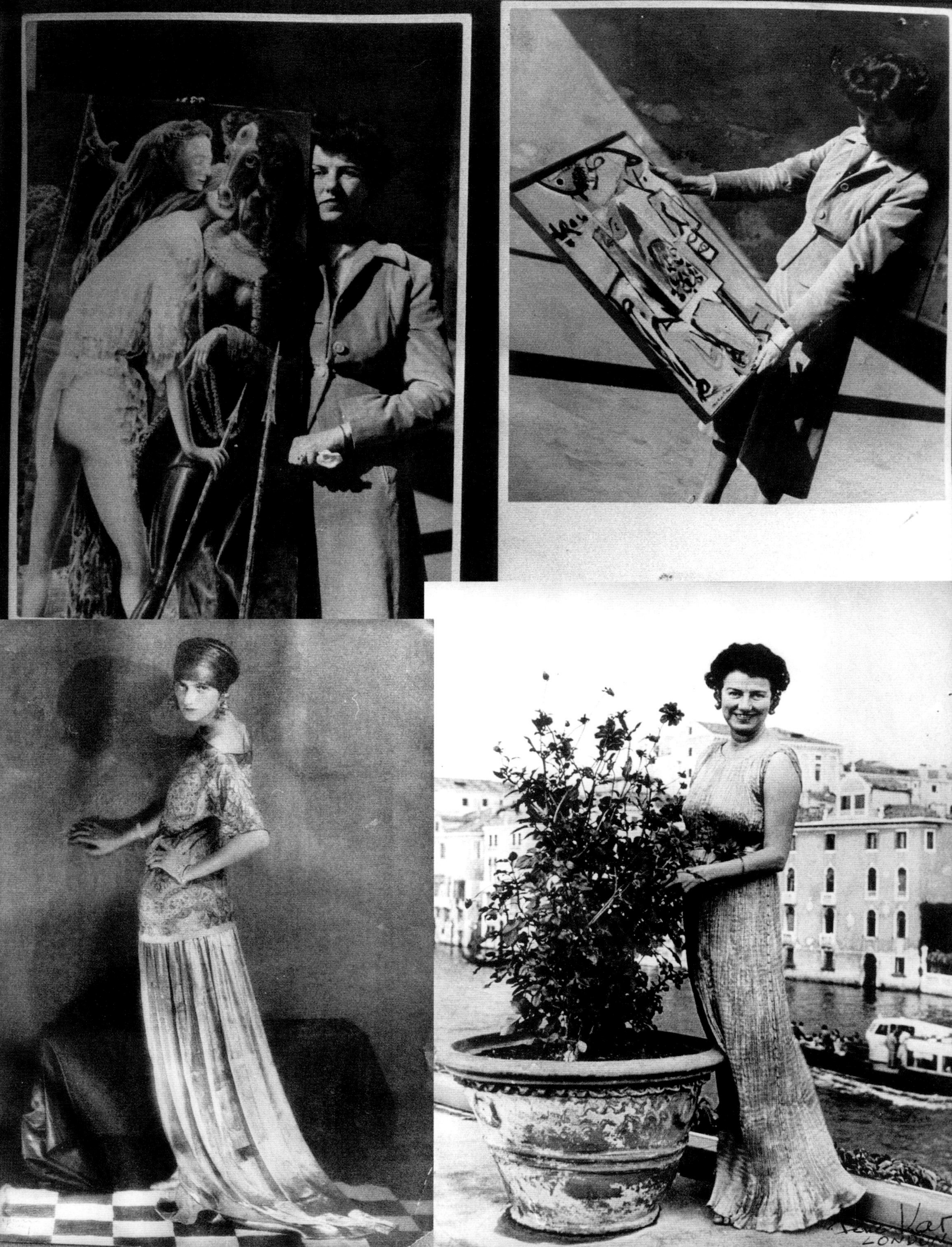

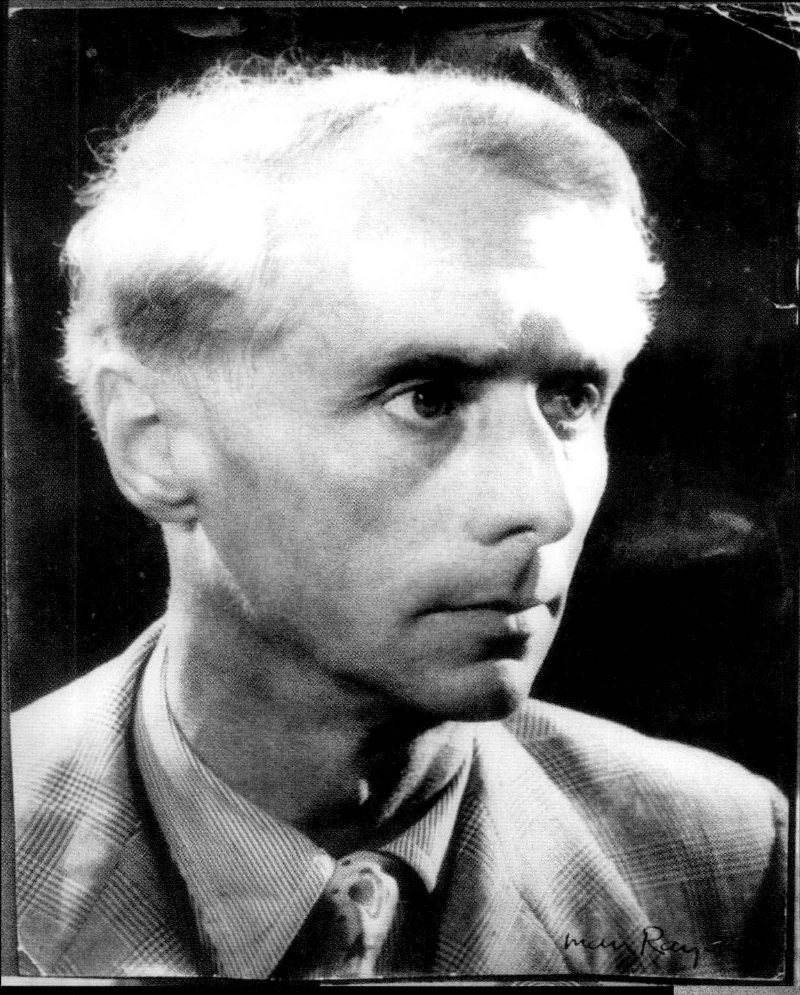

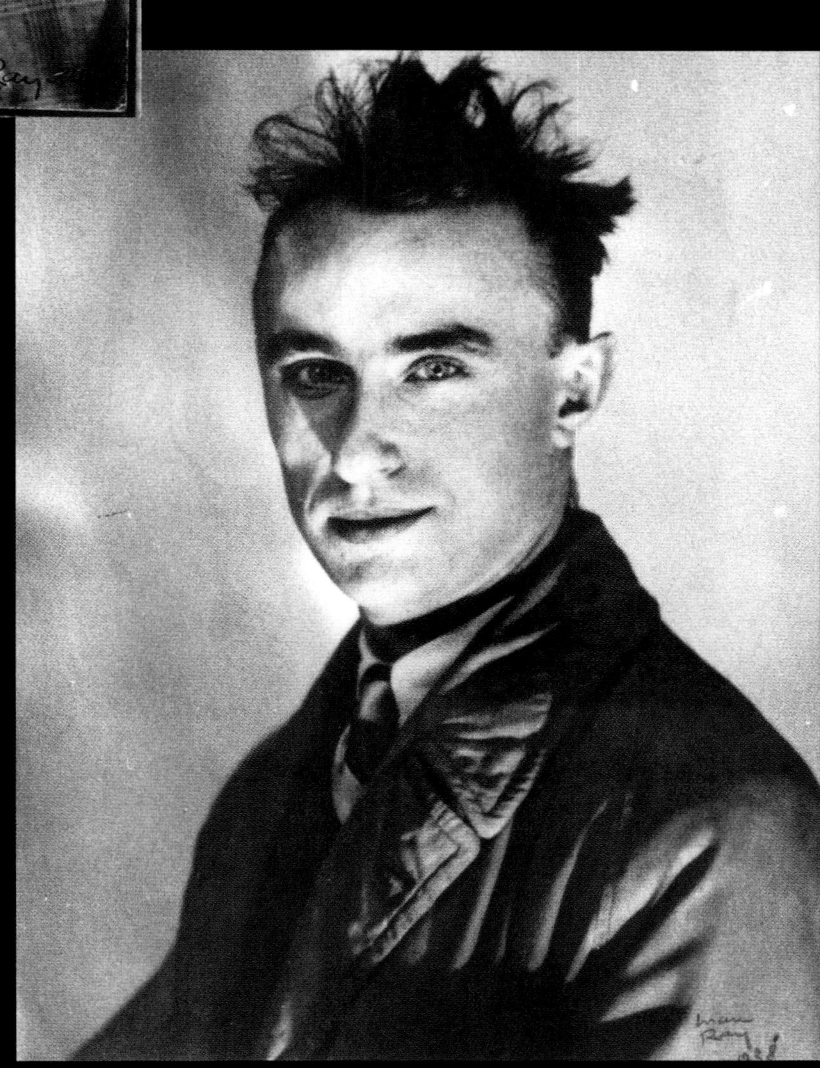


*Right*
*Top*
Max Ernst.

*Bottom*
Yves Tanguy.

*Left*
*Top, first and second photo from the left*
Peggy Guggenheim with Max Ernst's
Gegenpapst [Antipope], and Peggy
Guggenheim with an untitled painting
by Jackson Pollock.

*Bottom, first photo from the left*
Peggy Guggenheim, photographed
by Man Ray, c. 1925.

*Bottom, second photo from the left*
Peggy Guggenheim, 1951, in her golden
Delphos dress by Mariano Fortuny.

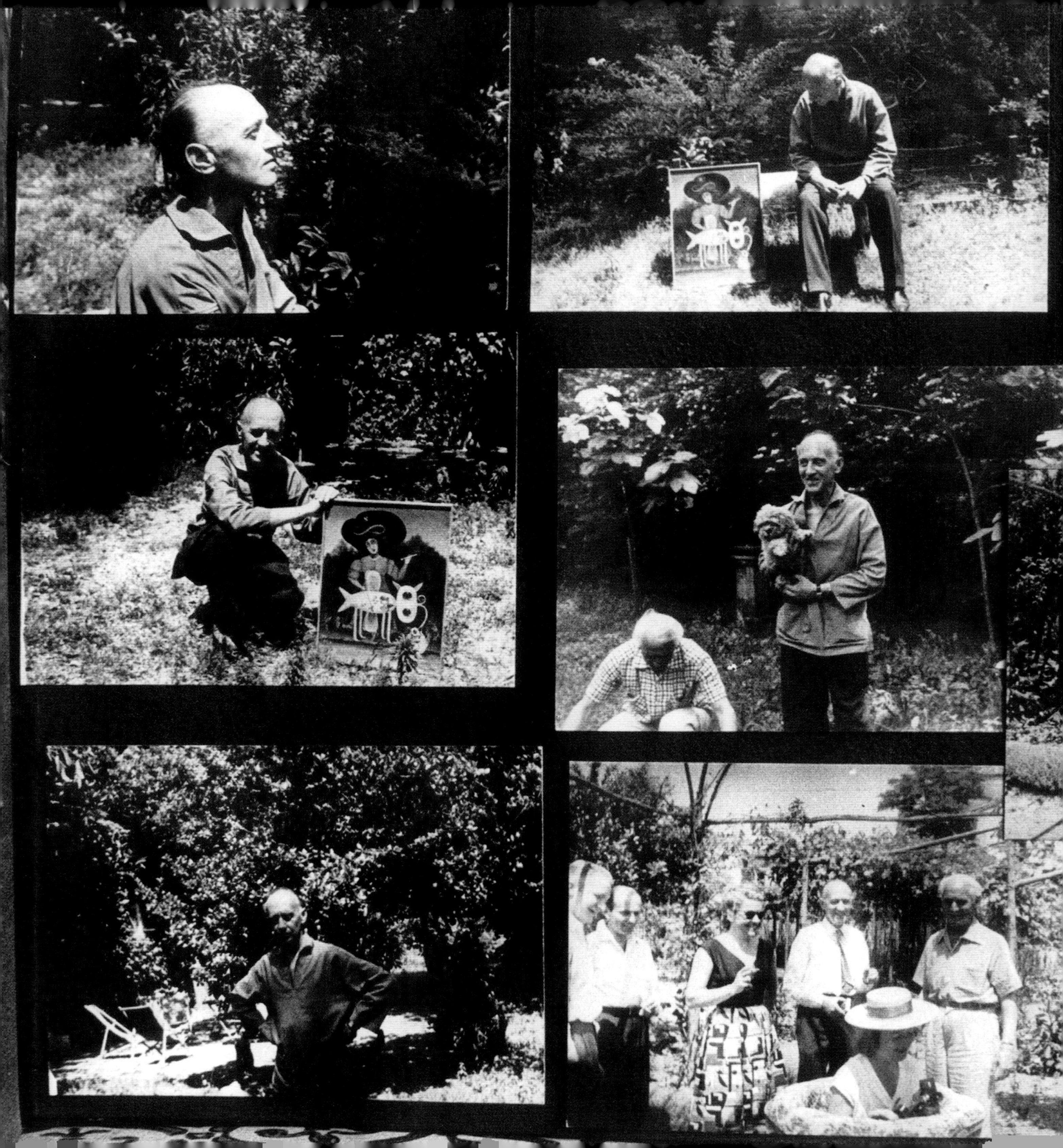

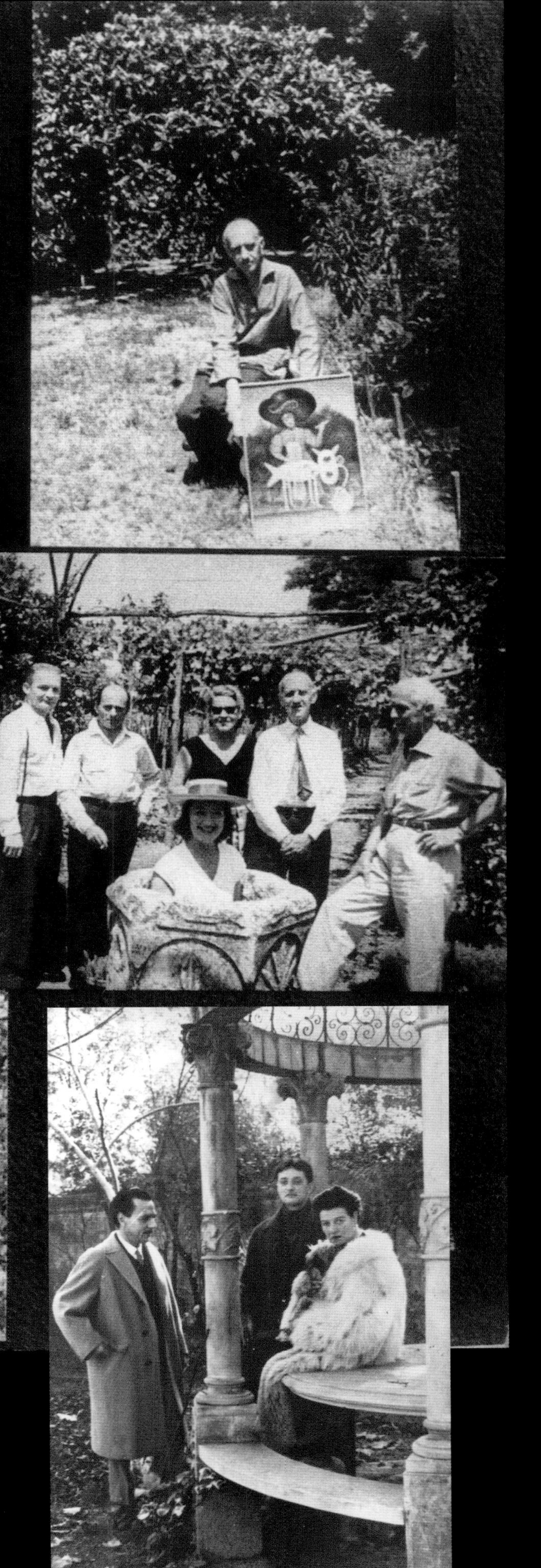

Most of the photos here show Victor Brauner.
In the group pictures Max Ernst is also to be s[een]
and Dorothea Tanning is sitting on the founta[in]

Bottom right
Edmondo Bacci, Tancredi Parmeggiani and Pe[ggy]
Guggenheim in the garden of Palazzo Venier d[ei]

*Left*
Max Ernst


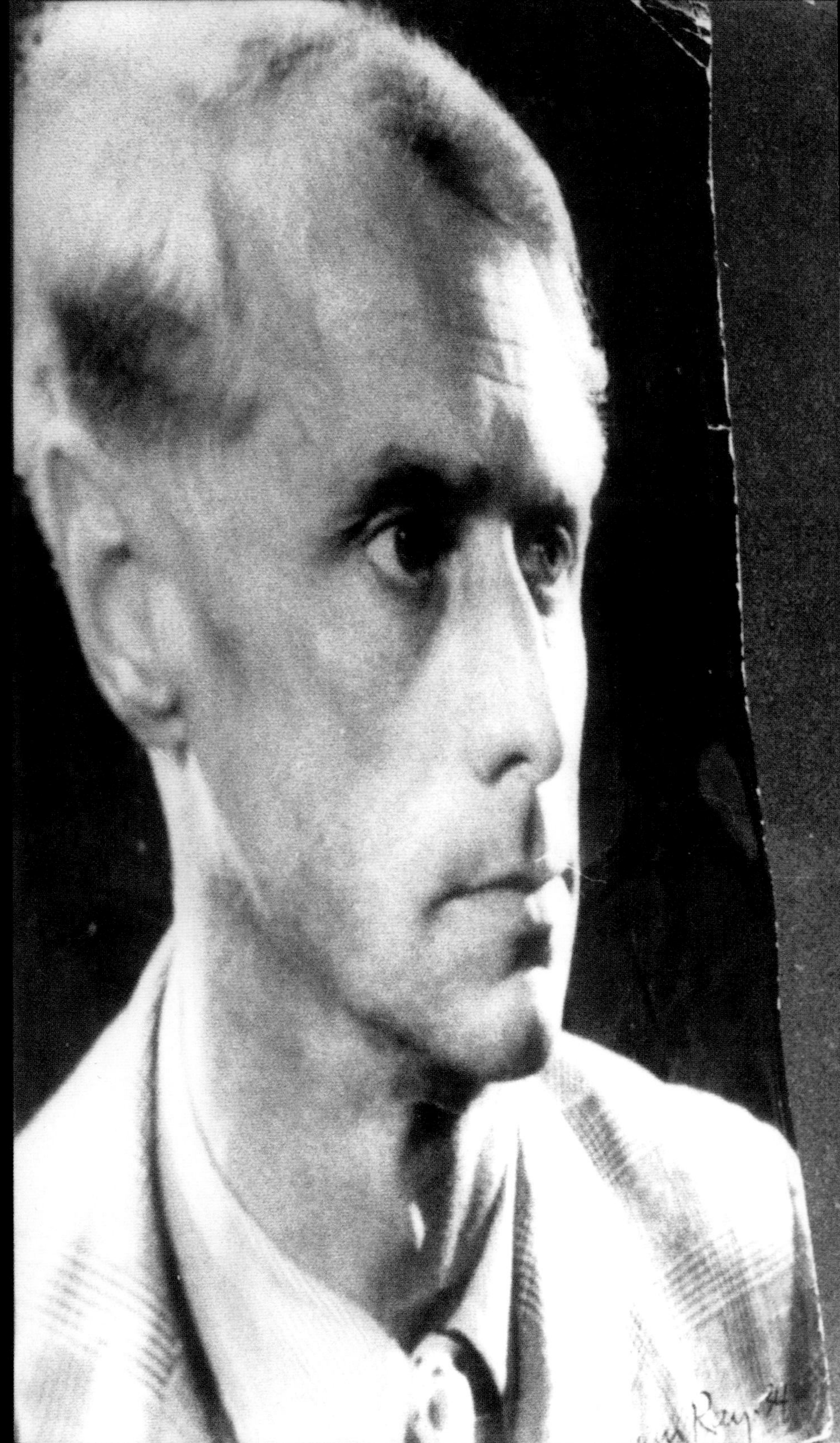


*Right*
*Top left*
*From left to right:* Pegeen Vail,
Peggy Guggenheim, unknown friend,
Max Ernst.

*Top right*
*Standing: Unknown man, Max Ernst,*
*Peggy Guggenheim.*
*Seated: Unknown woman,*
*Roberto Matta, Pegeen Vail.*

*Bottom left*
Peggy Guggenheim and Max Ernst at
Hazel McKinley's in California, 1941.

*Bottom right*
Max Ernst, Marc Chagall and
Peggy Guggenheim, 1942.

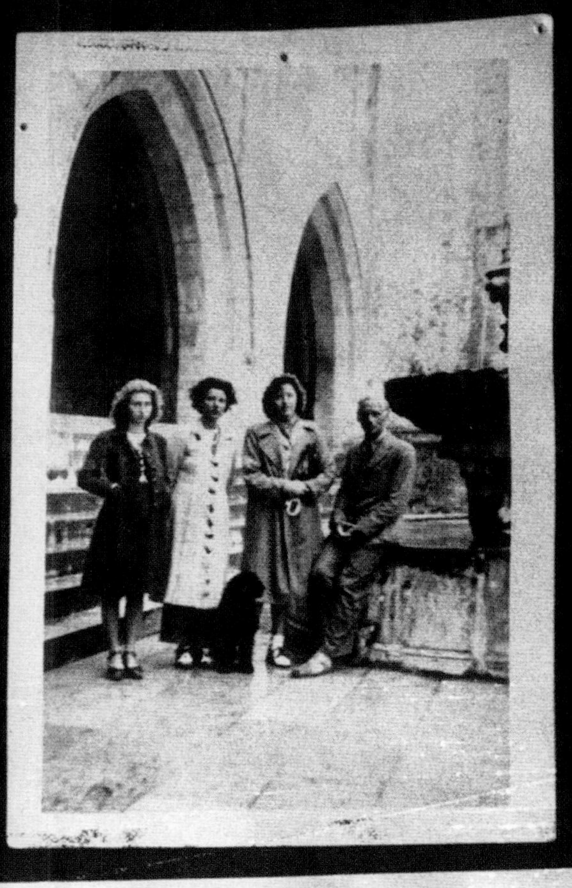
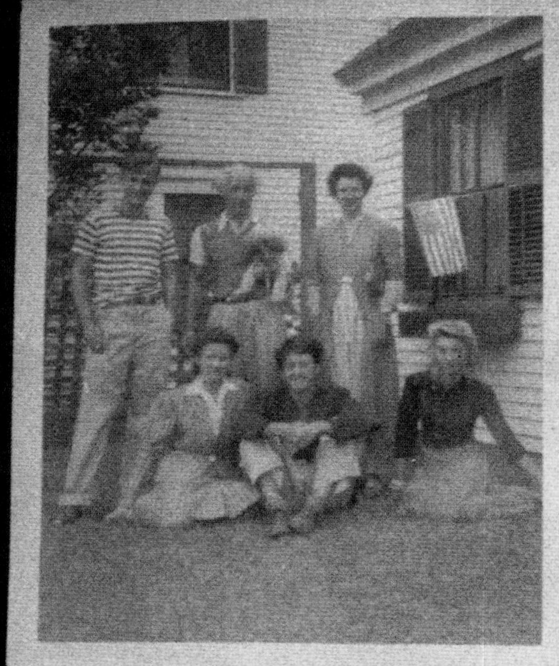
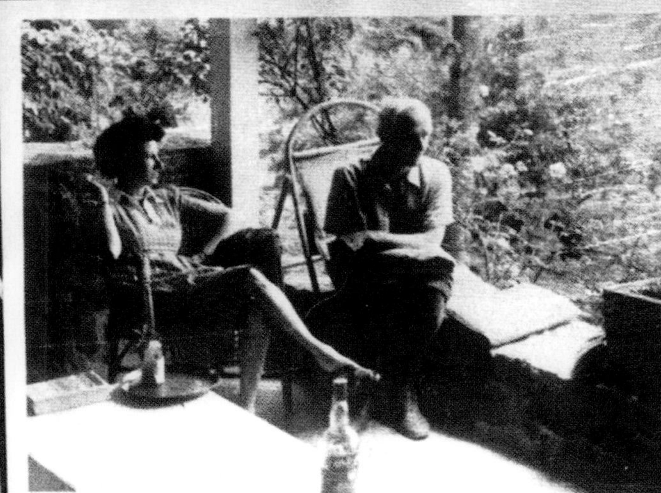
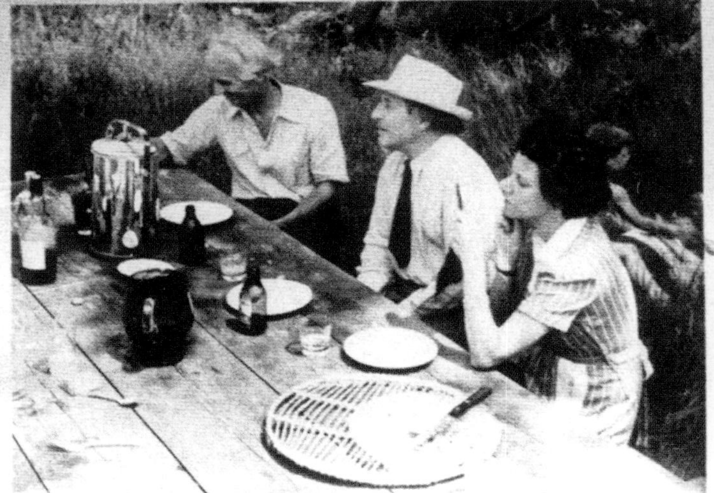

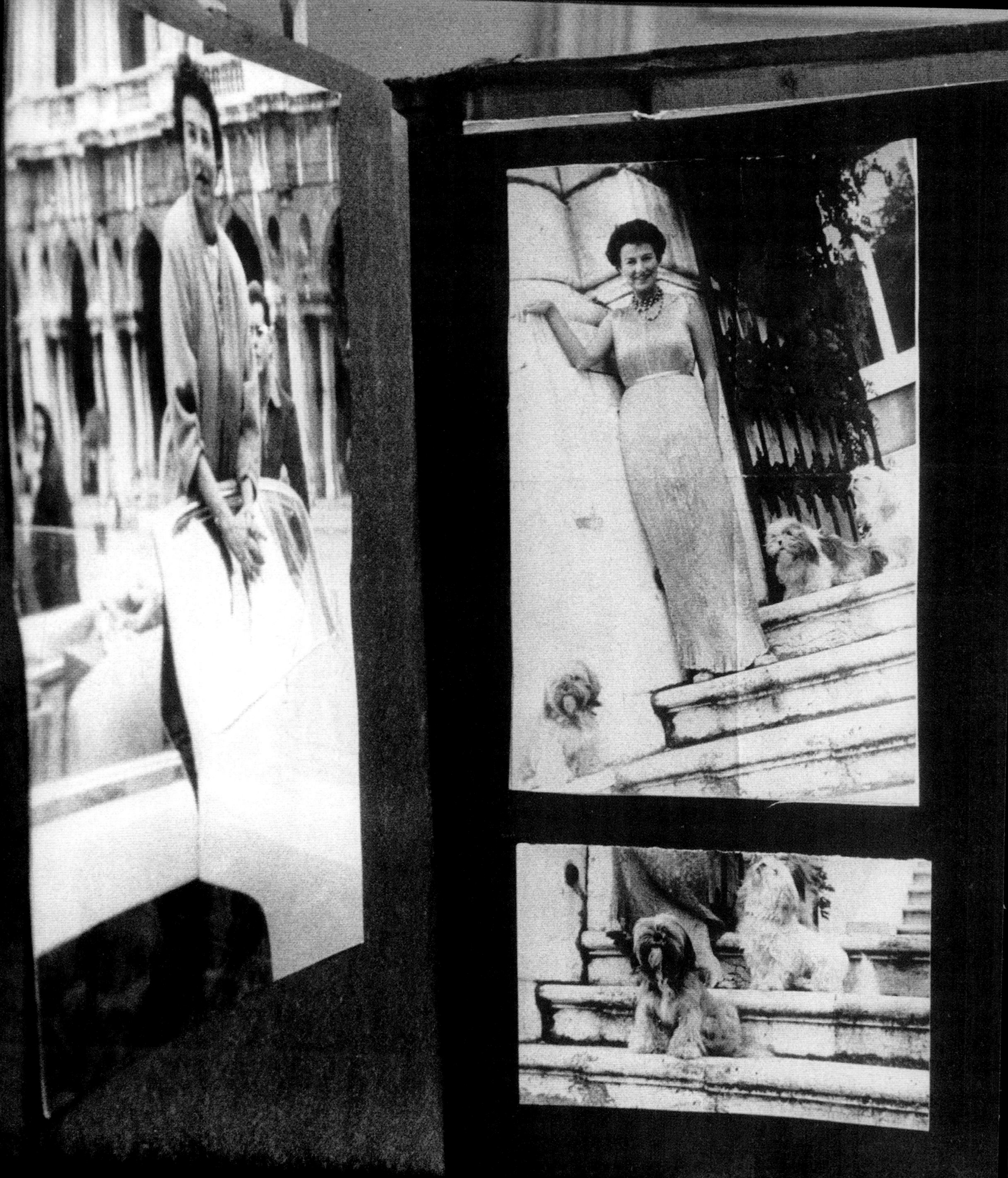

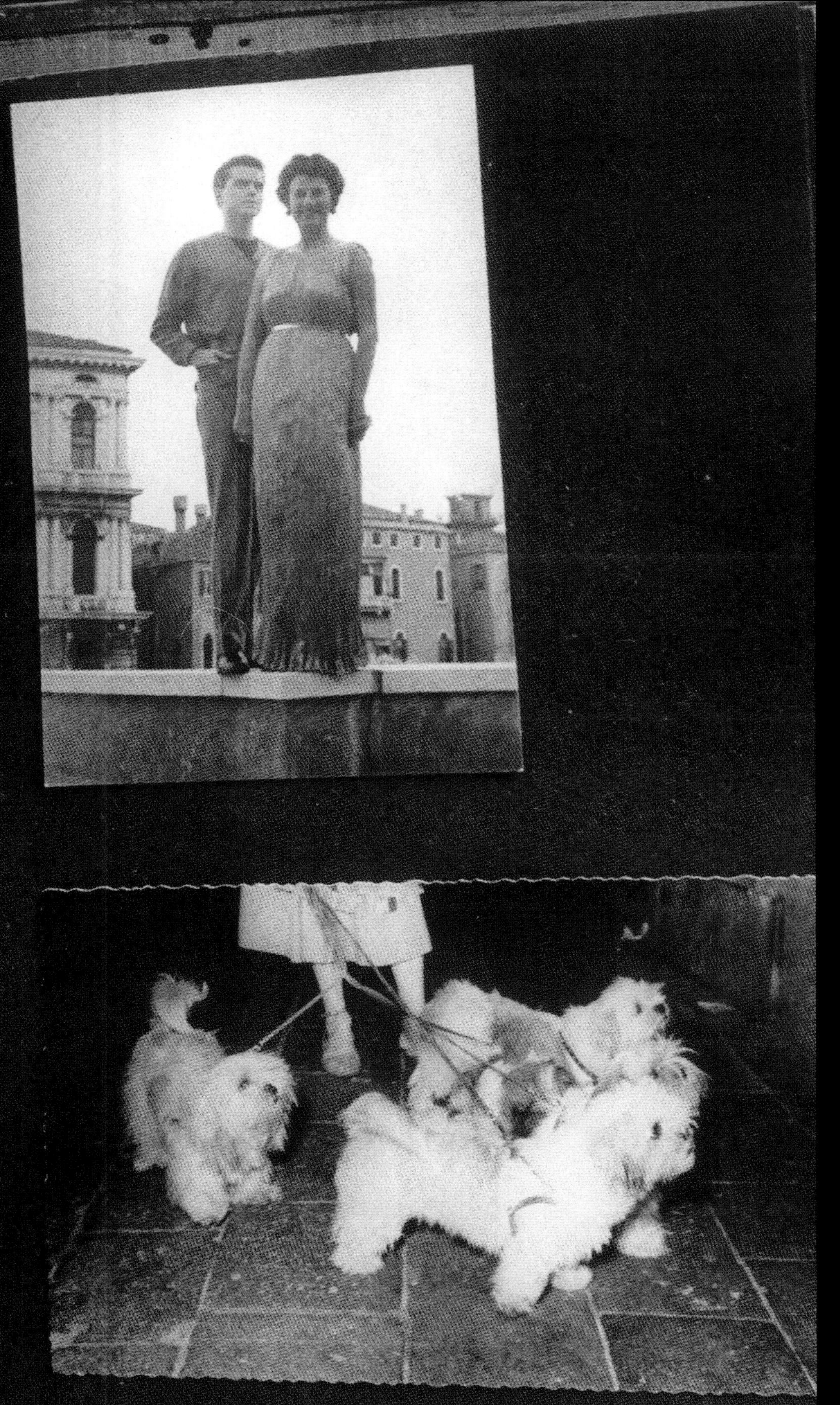

Peggy Guggenheim,
photographed by Ida Kar (1951),
and Peggy Guggenheim with
Roloff Beny, evidently also 1951.

Max Ernst,
Marc Chagall and
Peggy Guggenheim,
1942.

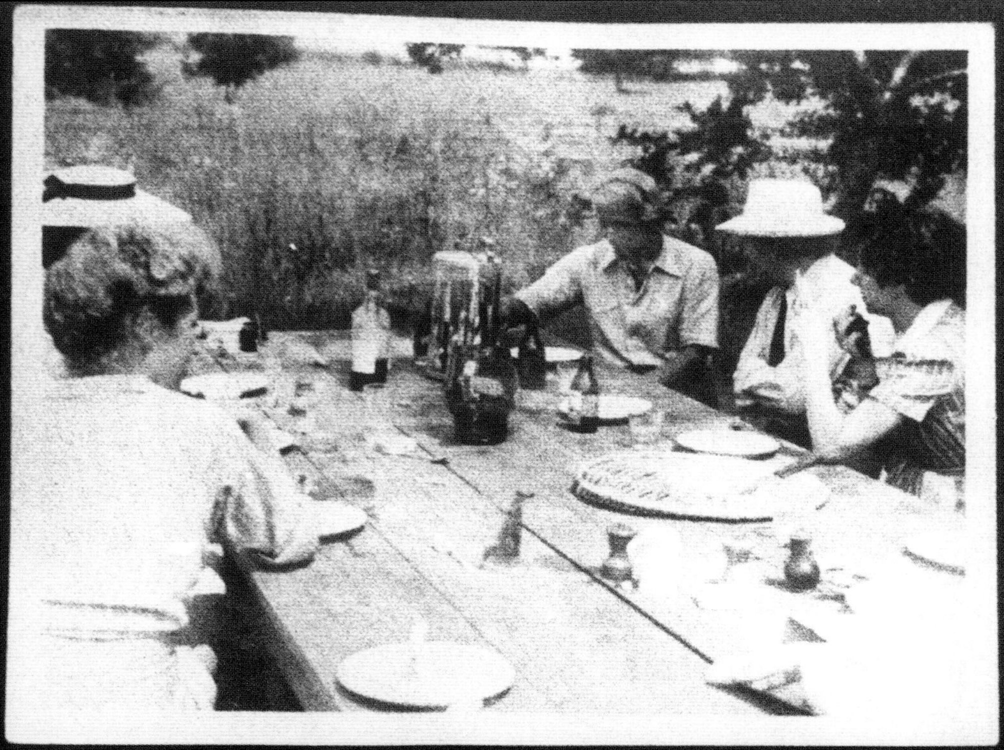

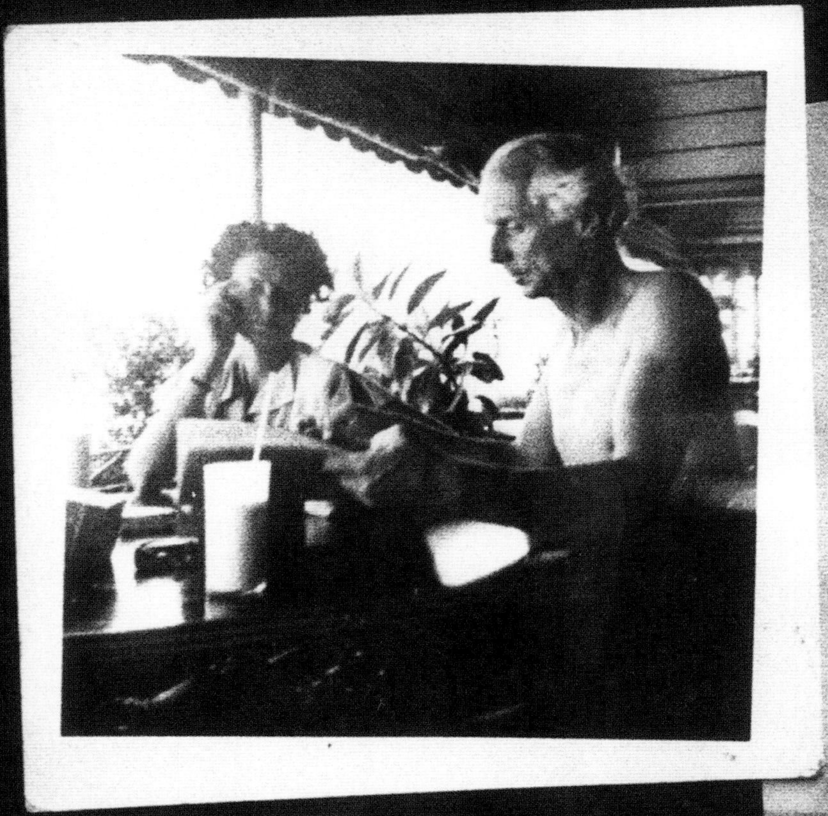

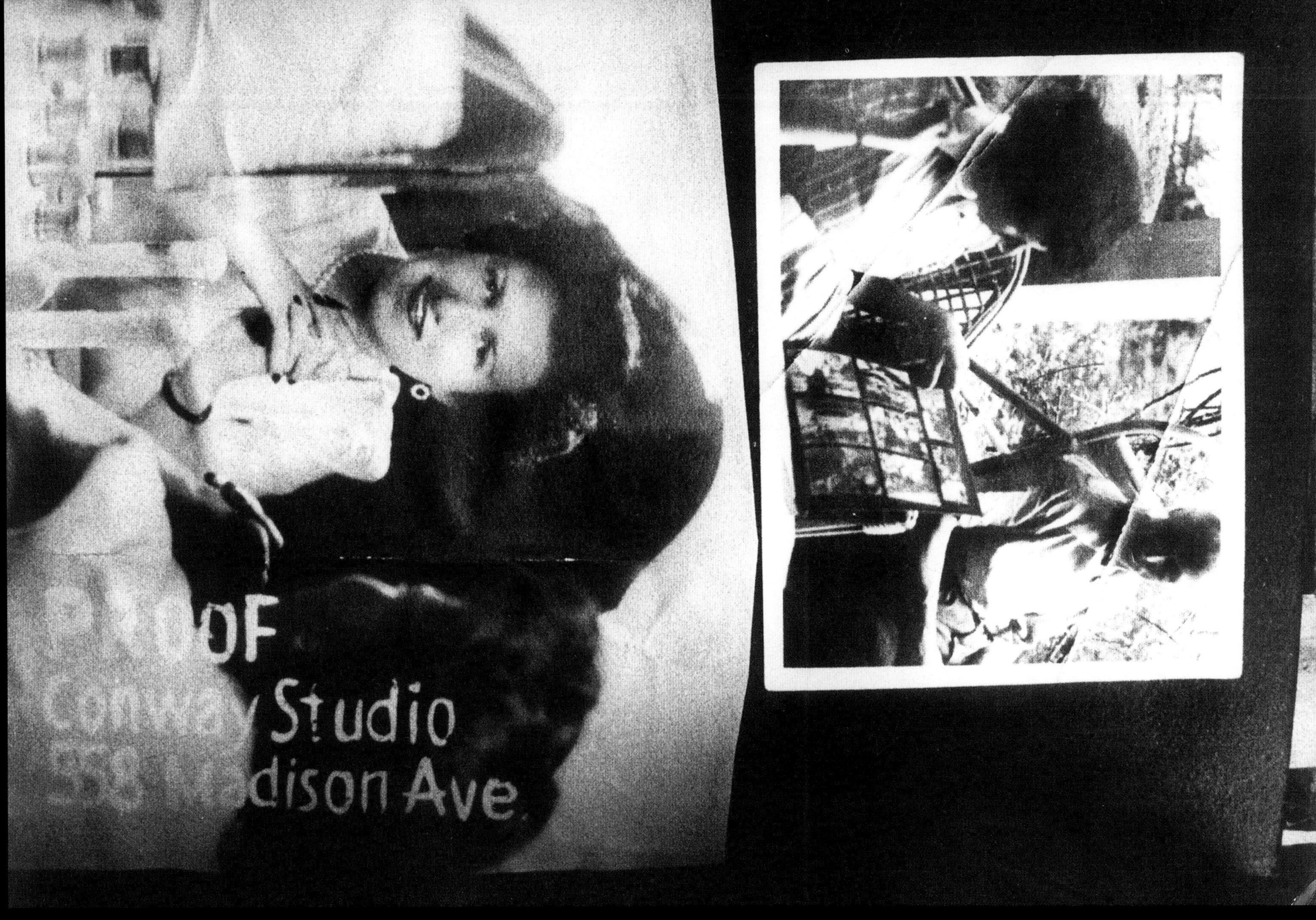
PROOF
Conway Studio
558 Madison Ave.

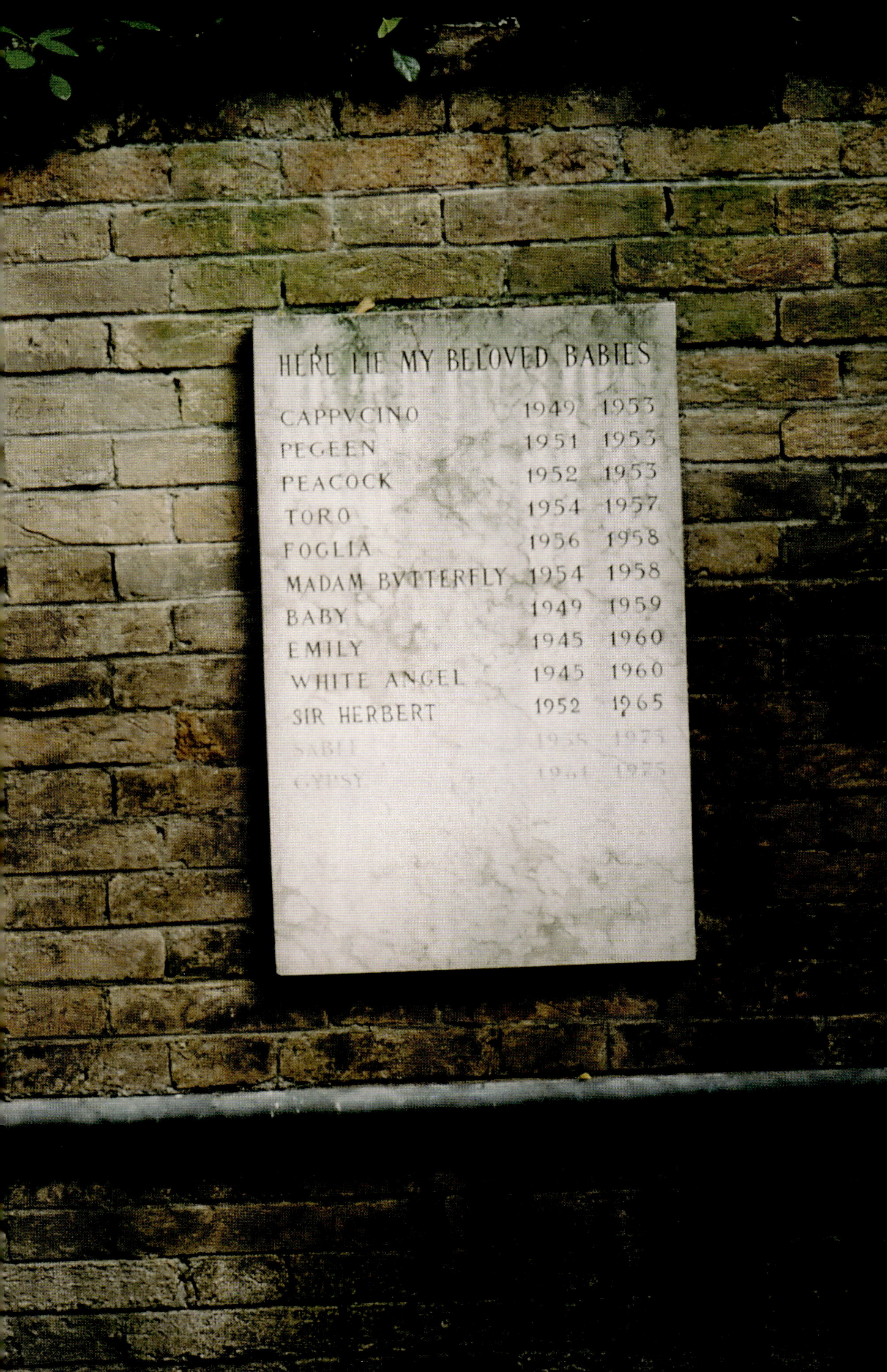
HERE LIE MY BELOVED BABIES
CAPPVCINO        1949  1953
PEGEEN           1951  1953
PEACOCK          1952  1953
TORO             1954  1957
FOGLIA           1956  1958
MADAM BVTTERFLY  1954  1958
BABY             1949  1959
EMILY            1945  1960
WHITE ANGEL      1945  1960
SIR HERBERT      1952  1965
SABLE            1955  1973
GYPSY            1961  1975

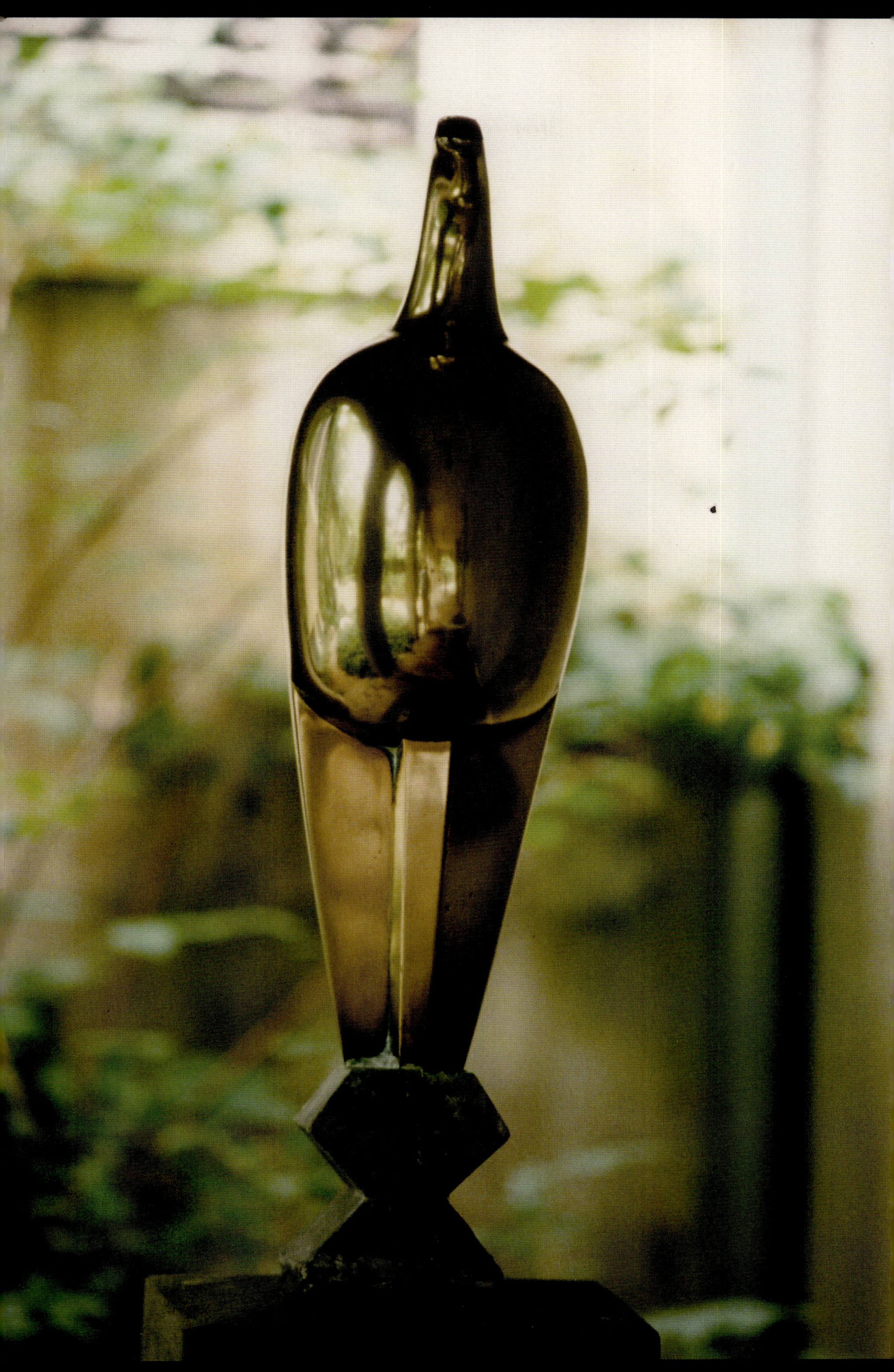

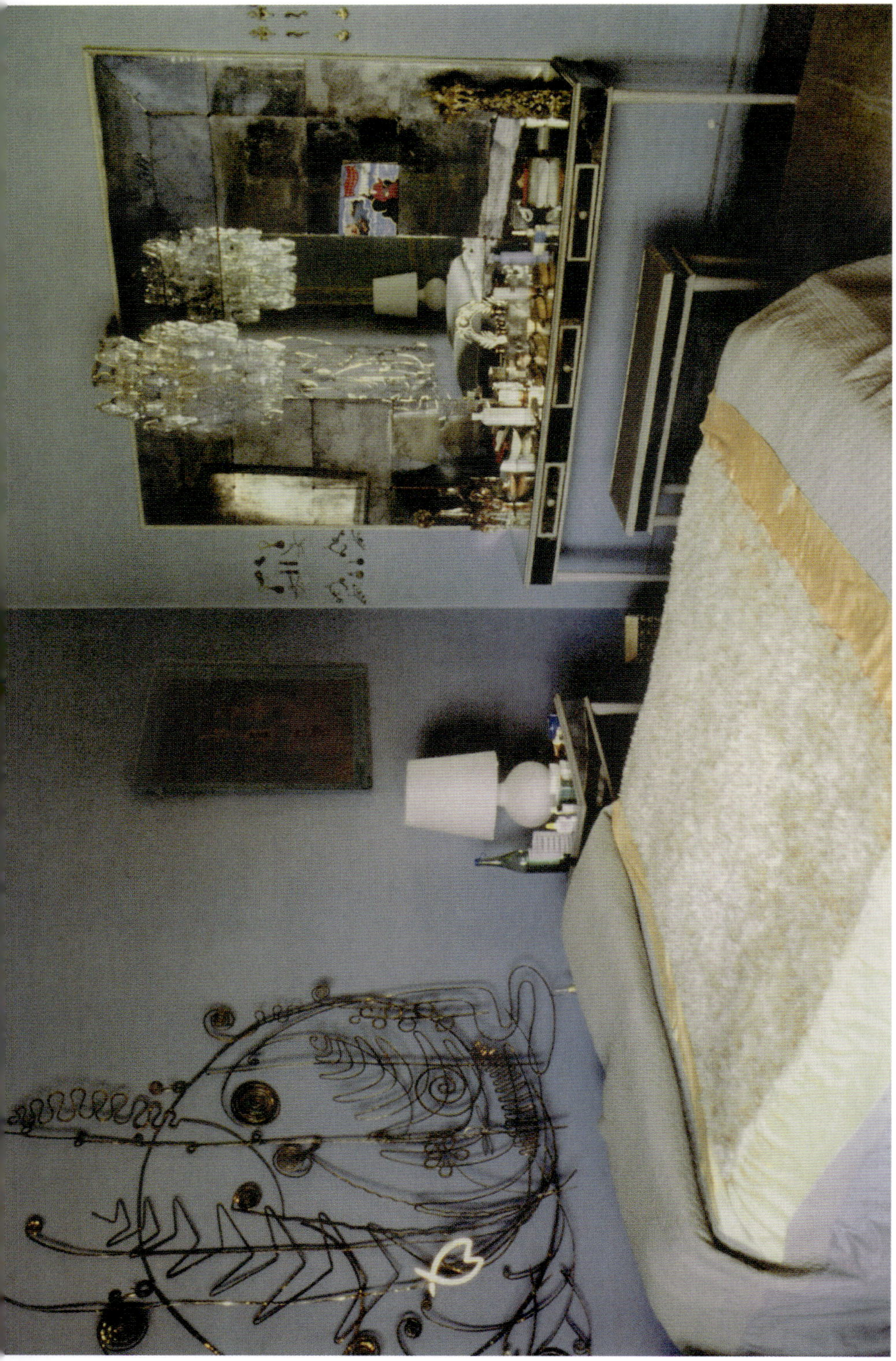

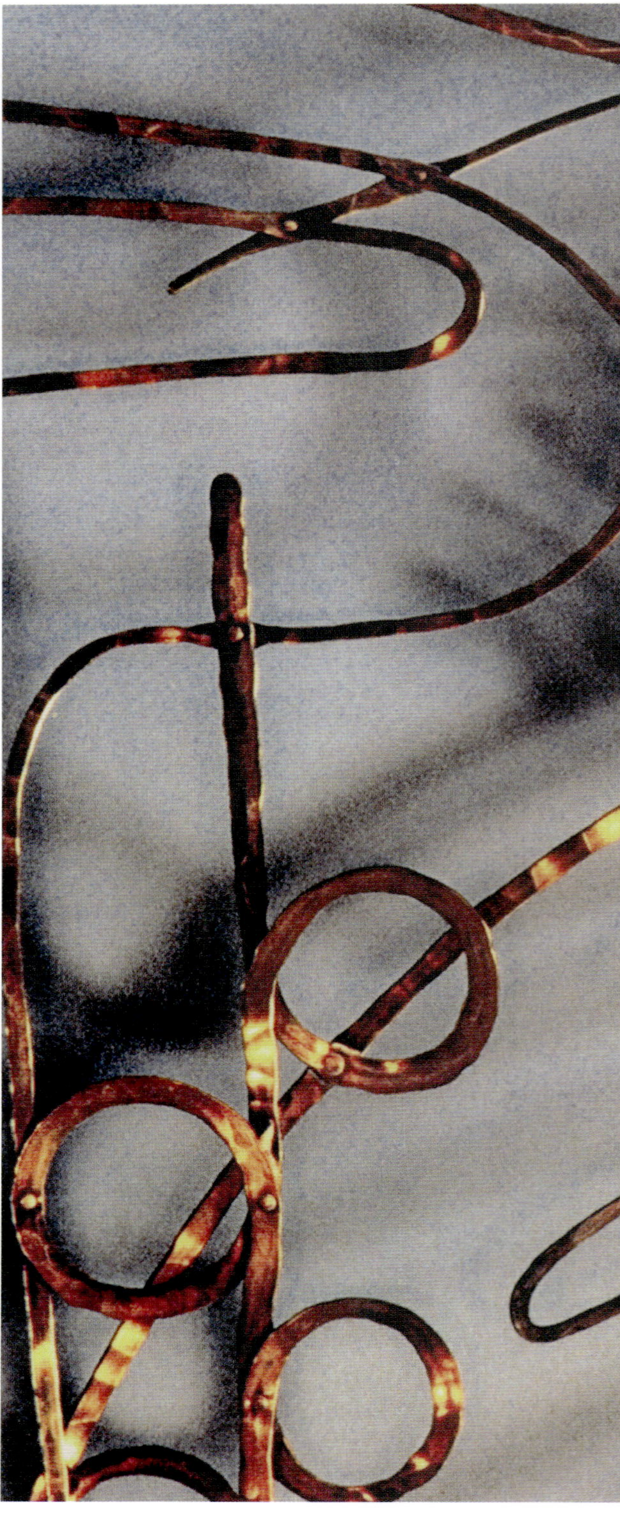

Peggy Guggenheim's turquoise bedroom. The bed's 'headboard' is by Alexander Calder (1945/46)
and the lamps were made by Carlo Scarpa for Venini.
The painting on the wall, showing Peggy and her sister Benita, was created by Franz von Lenbach.
Peggy's earrings, including pairs by Alexander Calder and Yves Tanguy, are hanging on the wall.

Right
Detail of the 'headboard'.

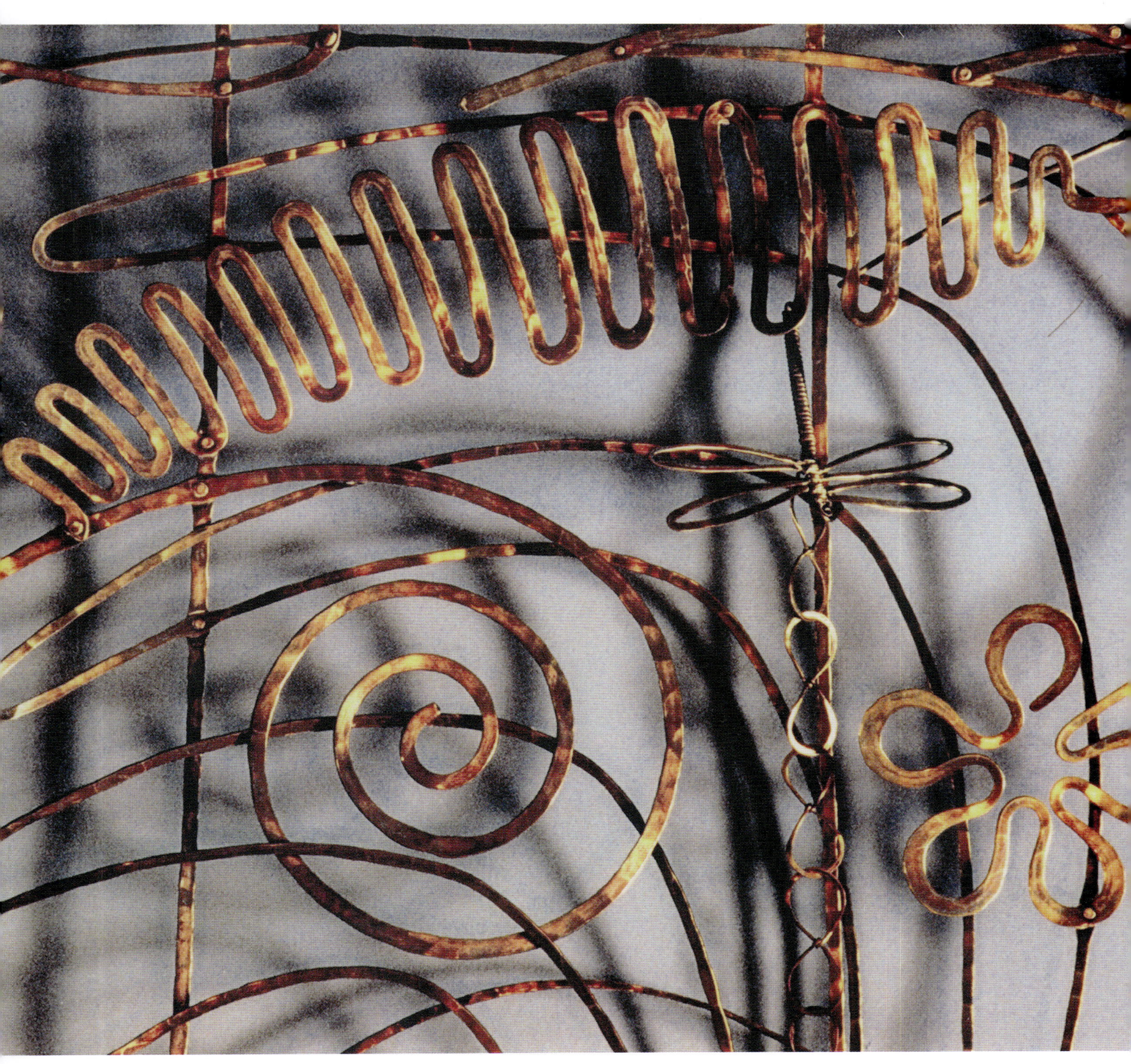

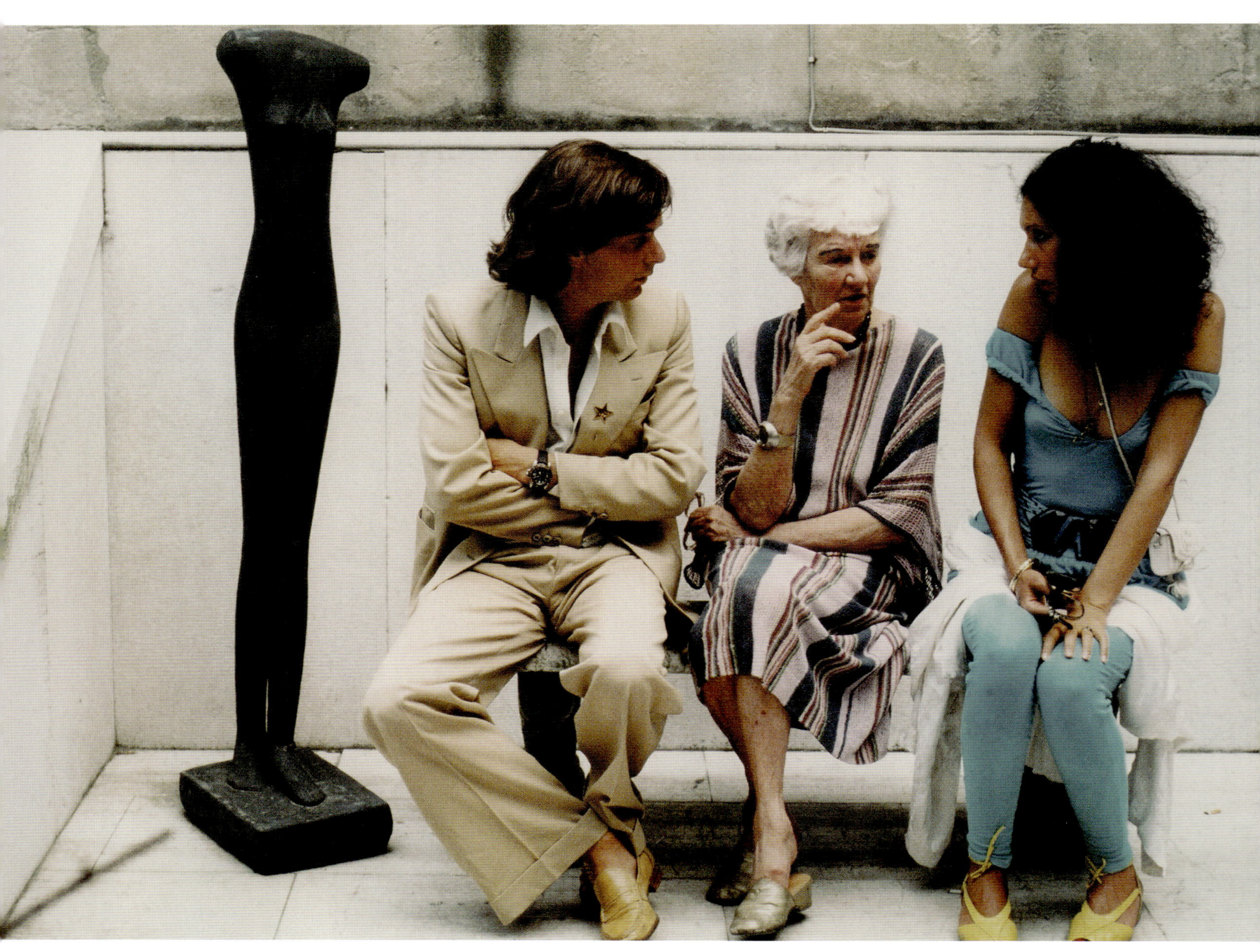

Peggy with her grandson Nicolas Hélion and his wife
Dolly. The bronze sculpture is Alberto Giacometti's
*Gehende Frau* [Walking Woman] (1936).

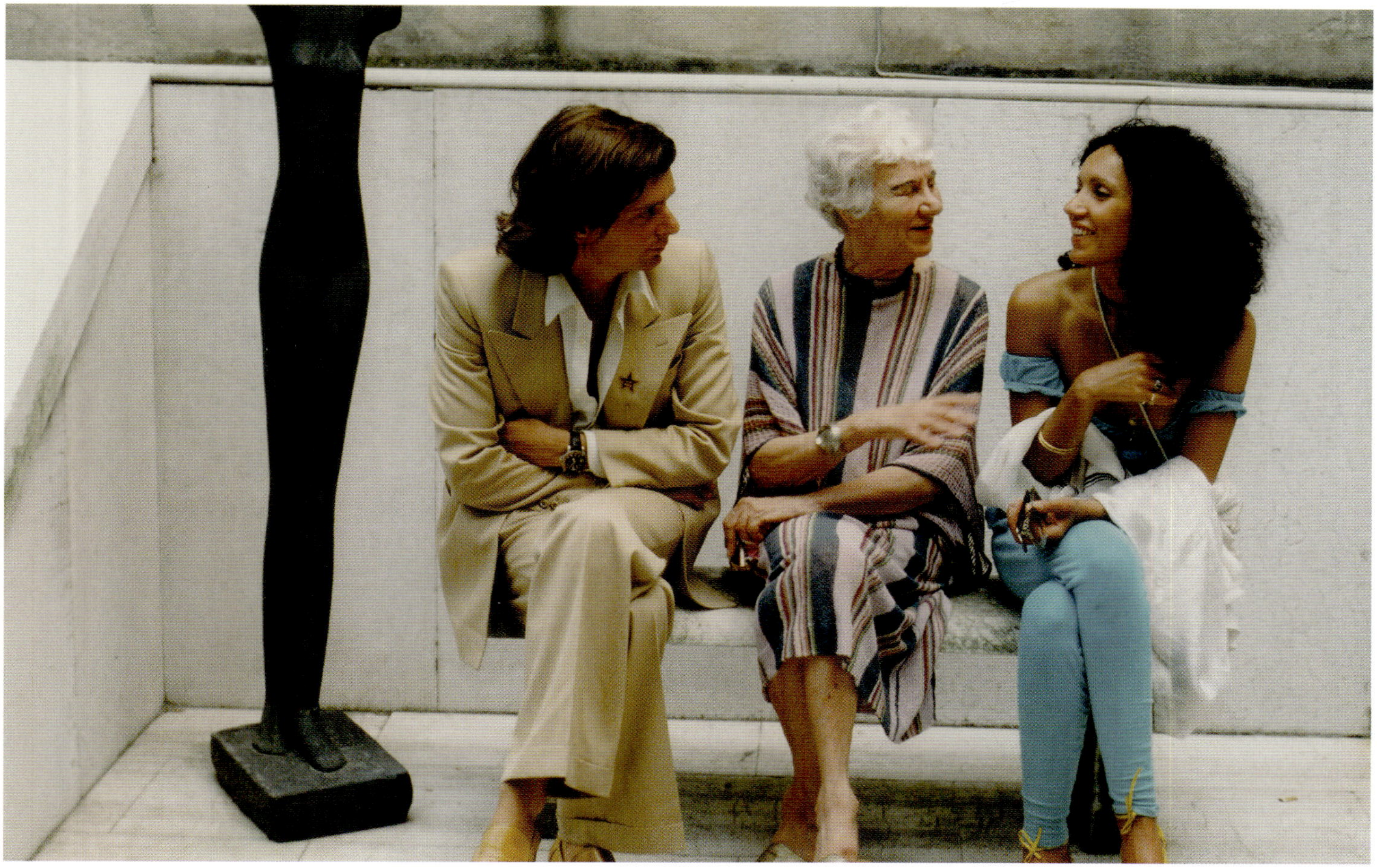

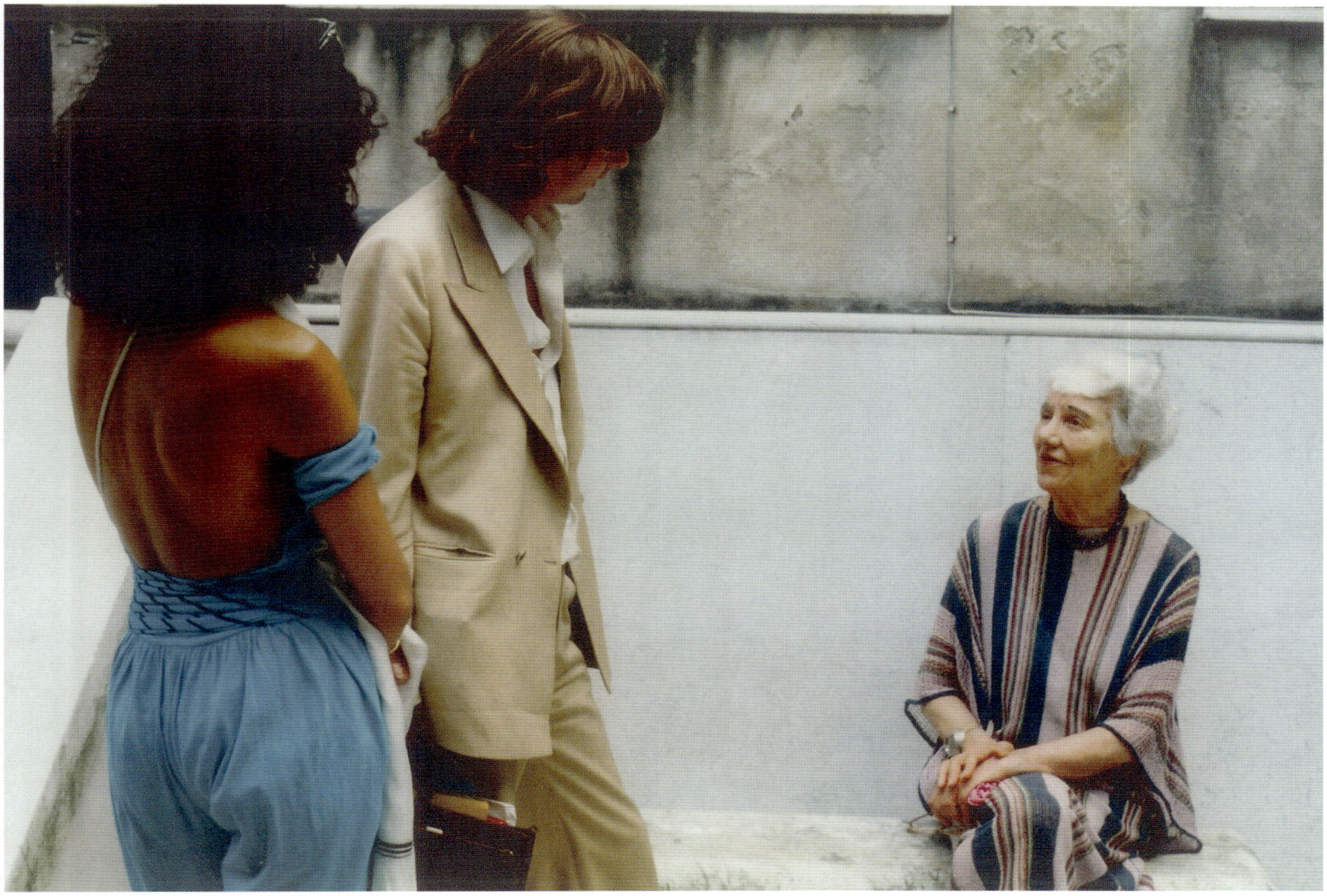

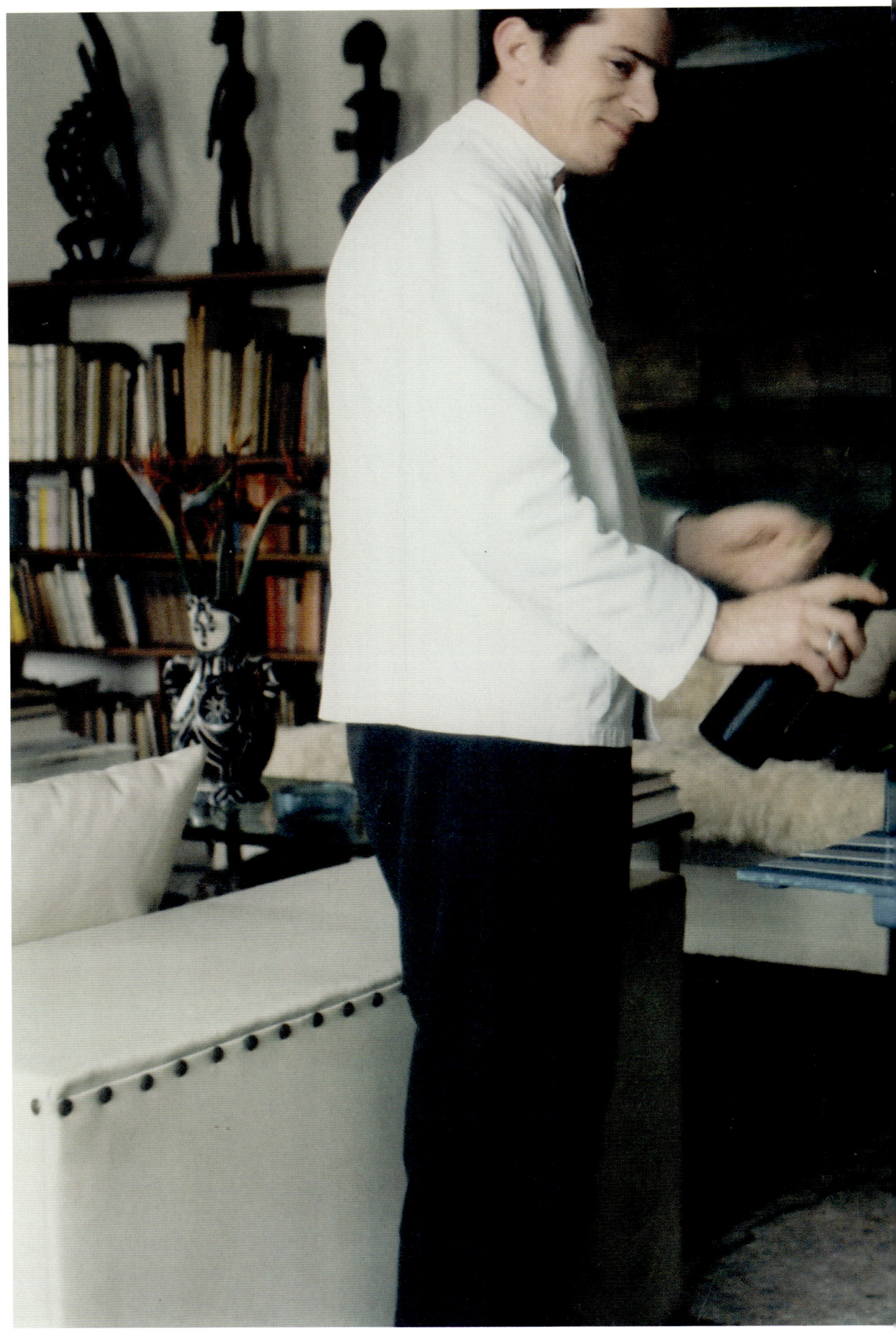

1969

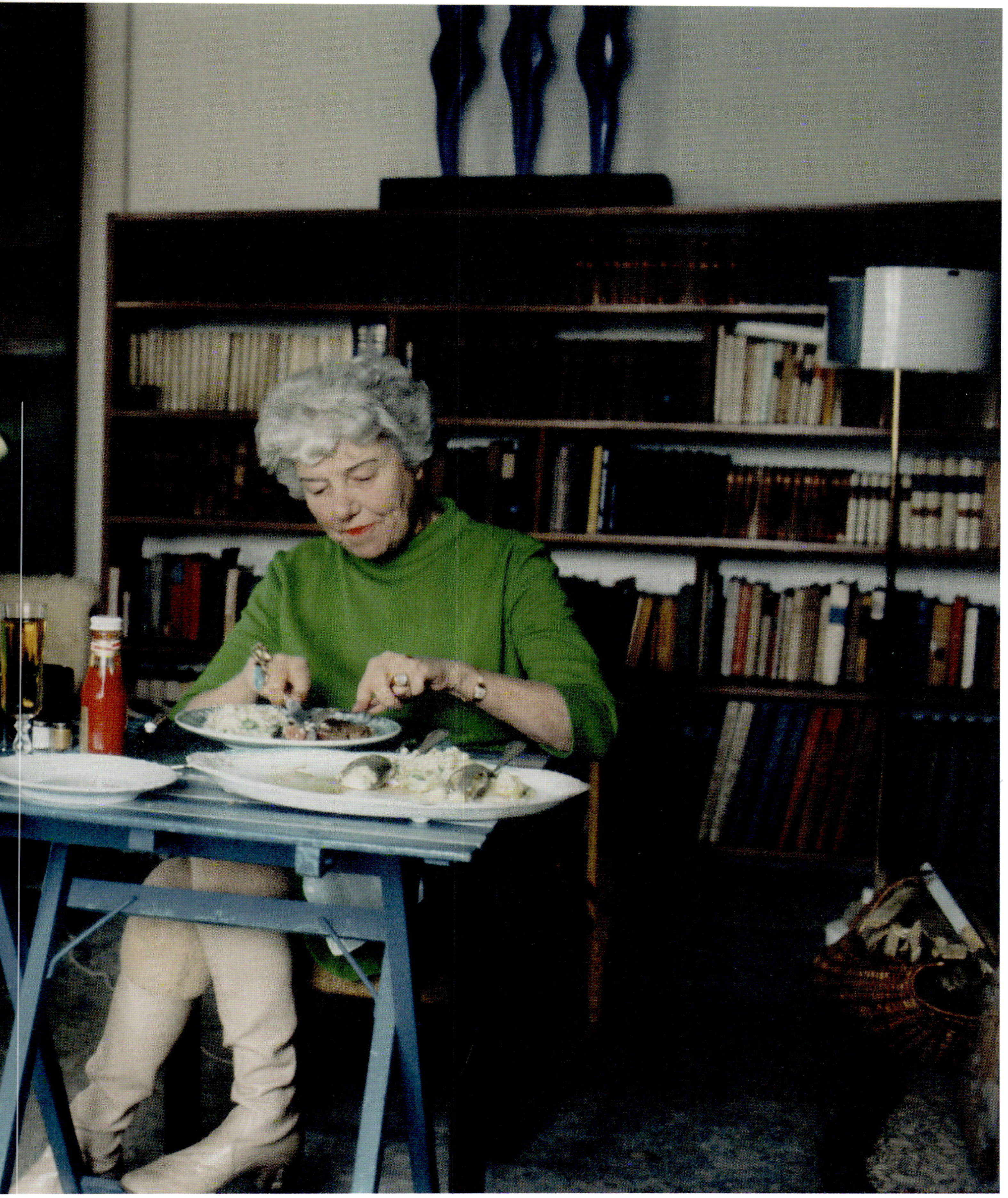

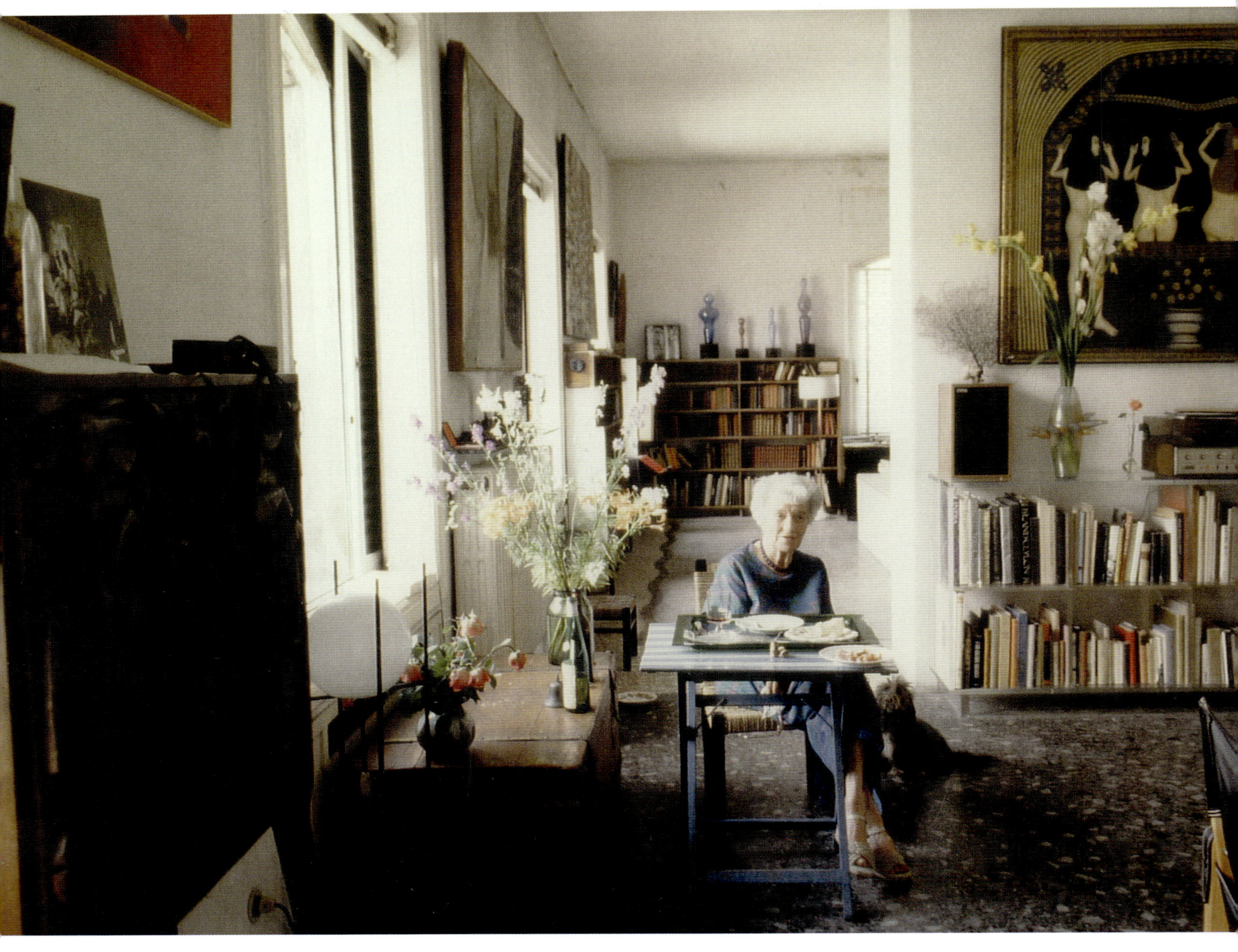



1974

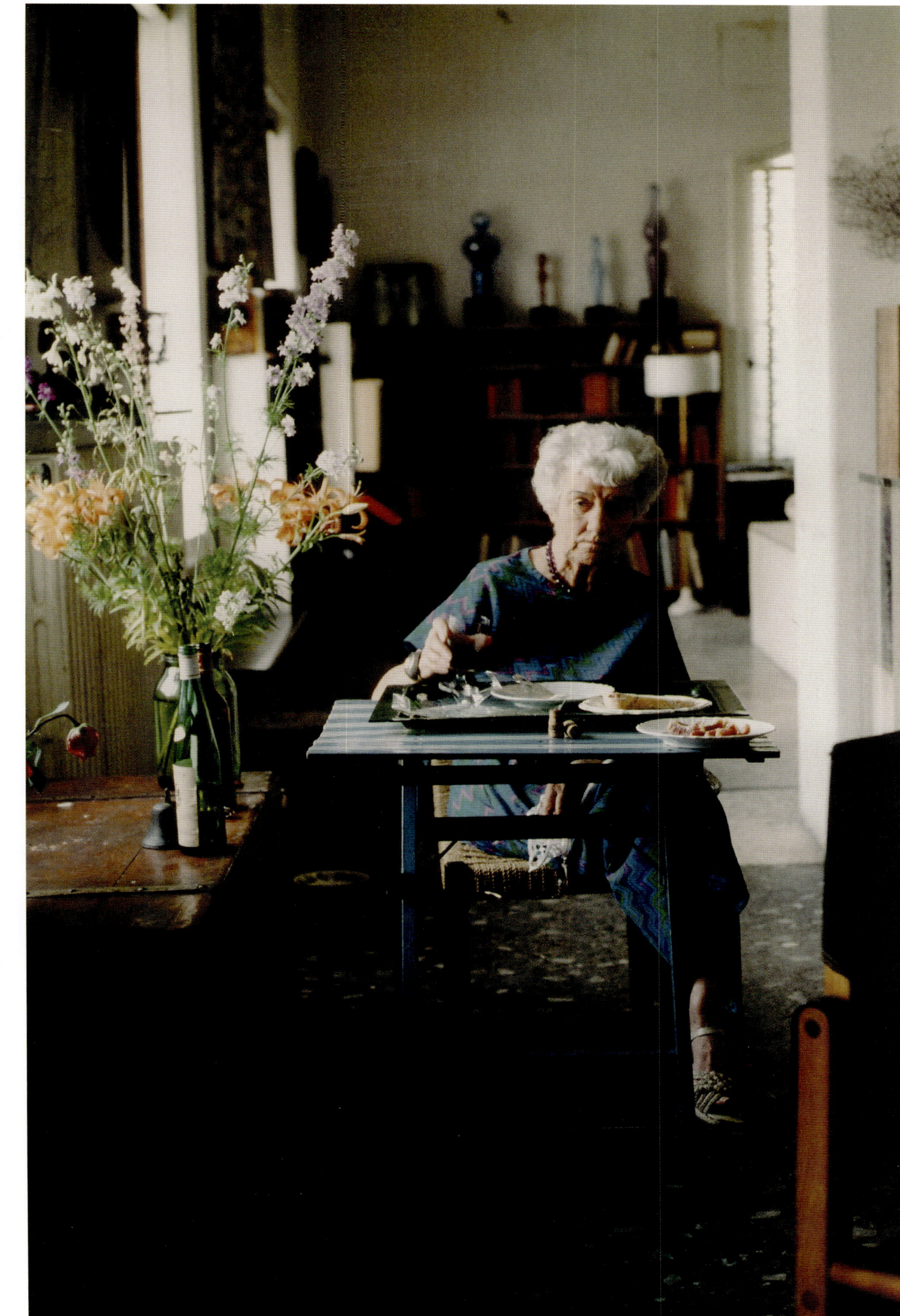

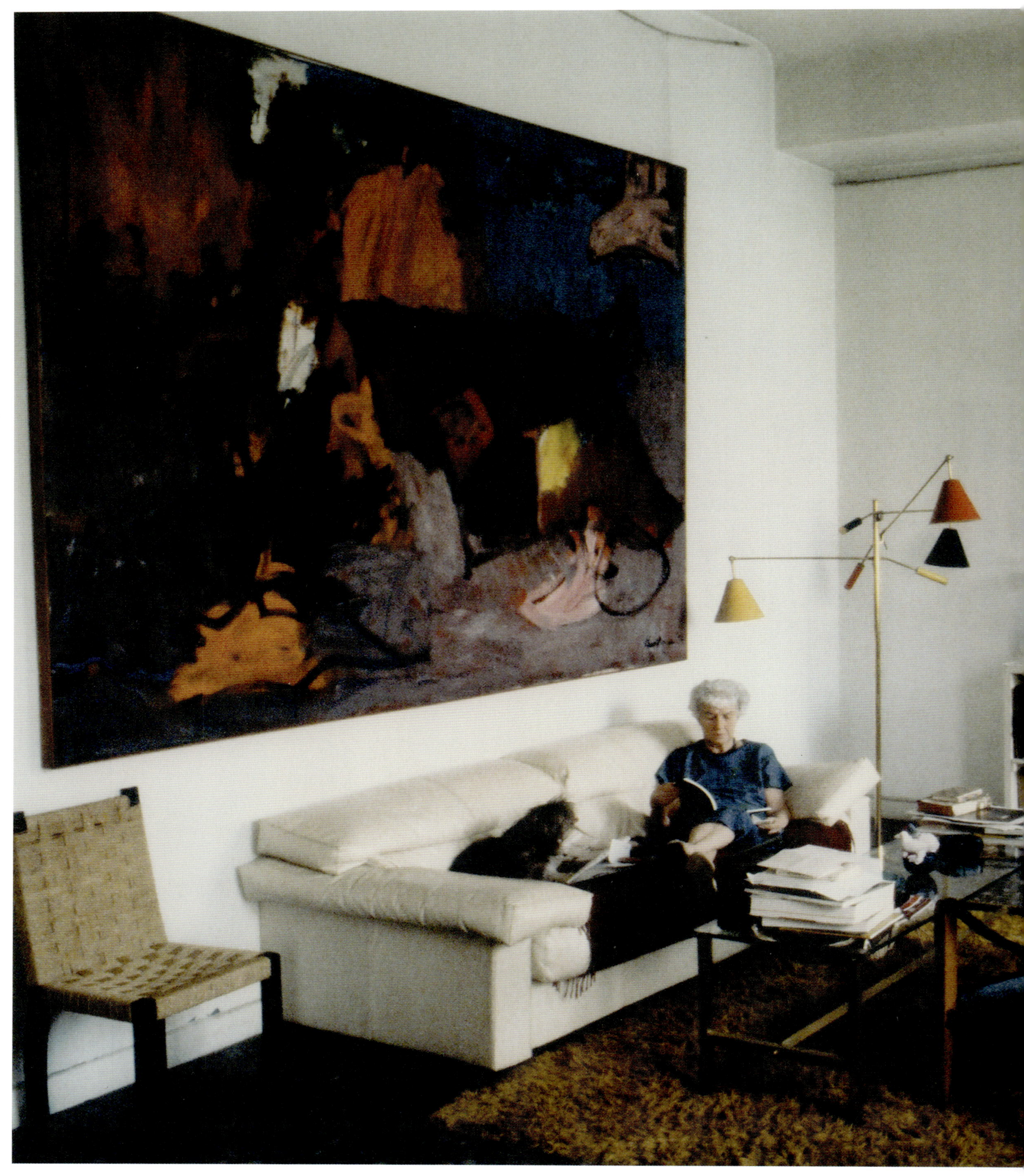

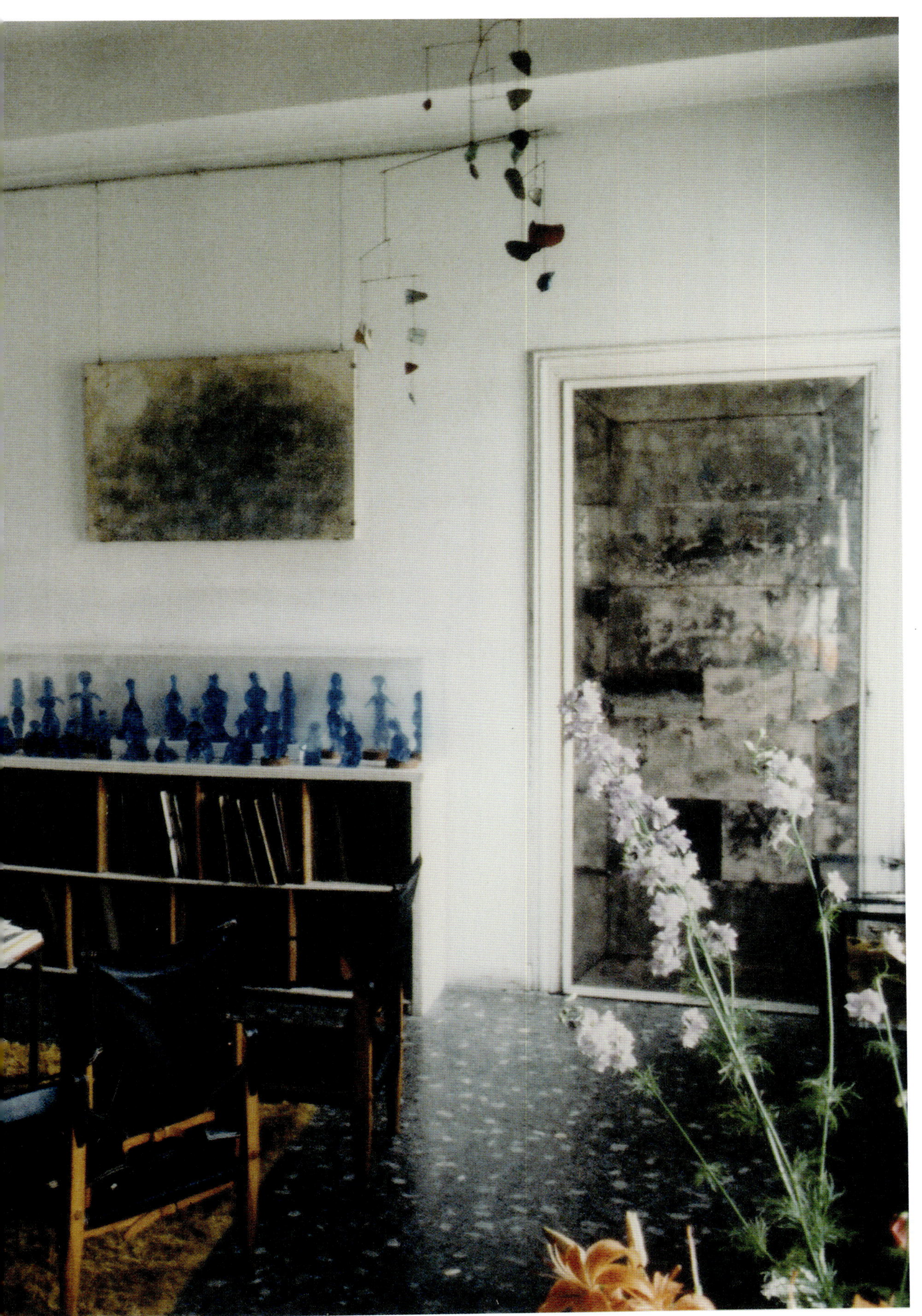

In her salon. The painting on the left is by Grace Hartigan (Ireland, 1958).
Over Egidio Costantini's blue *Glass Figures* (1964) is one of
Tancredi Parmeggiani's works on paper.

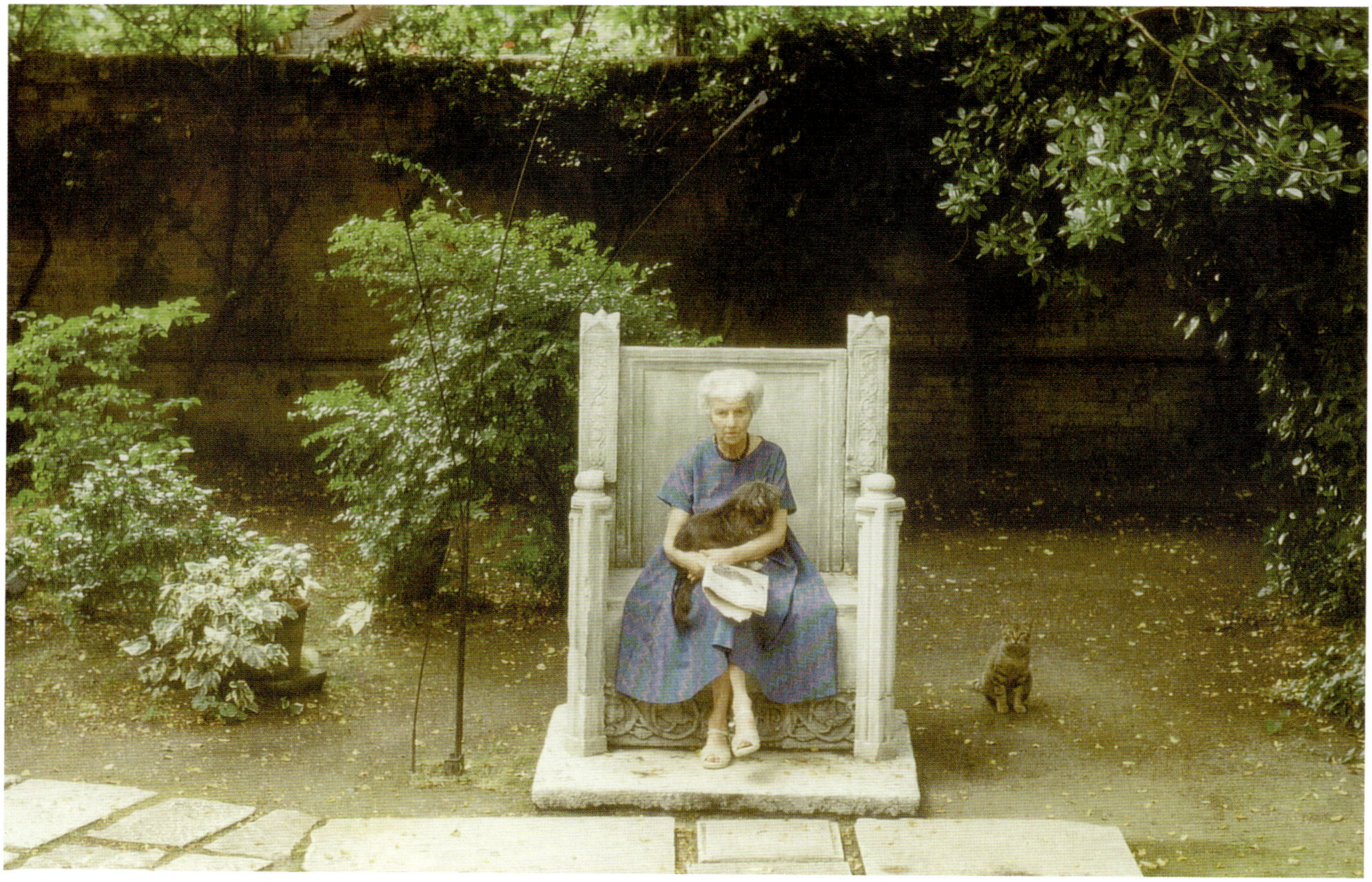

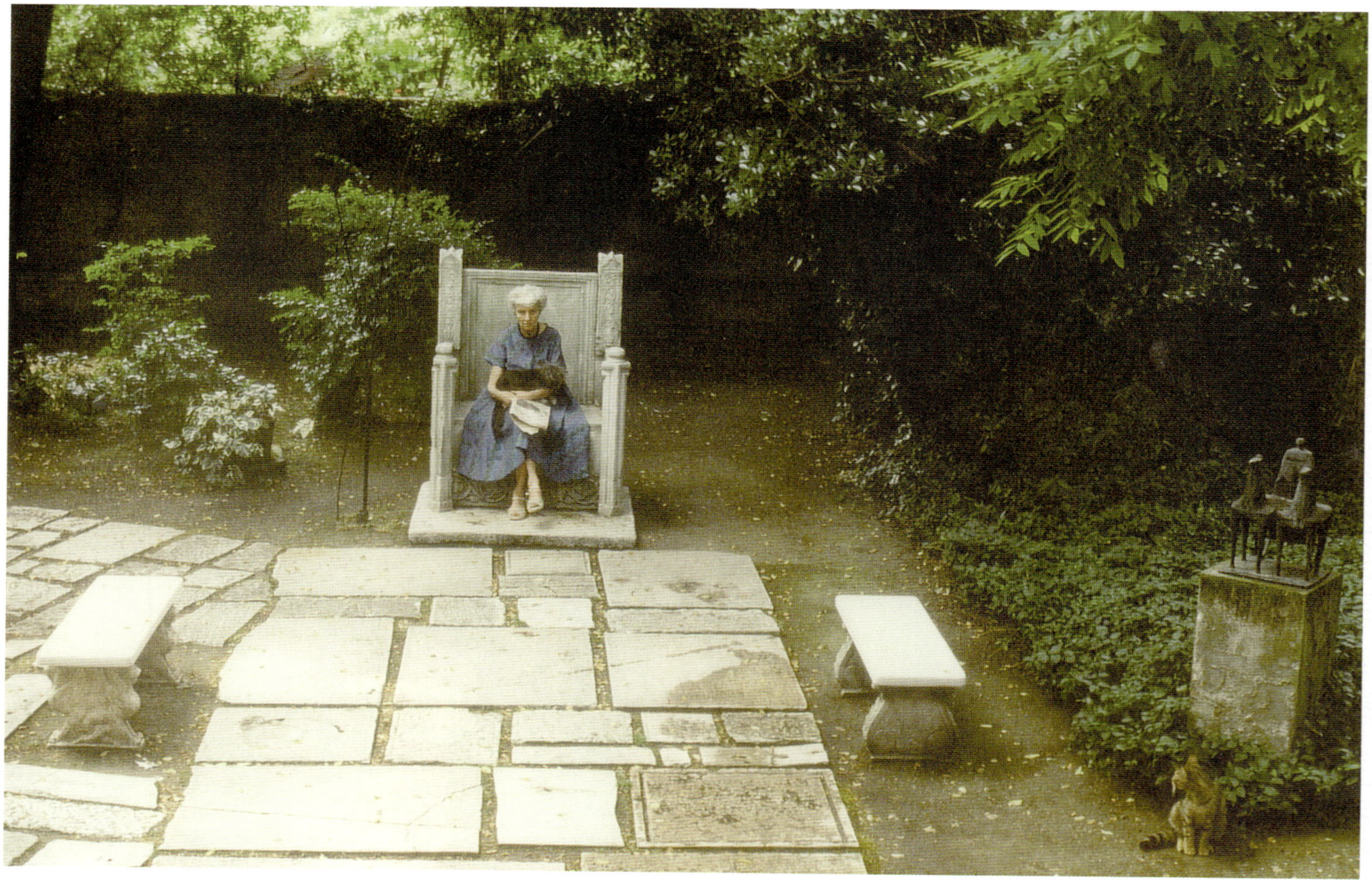

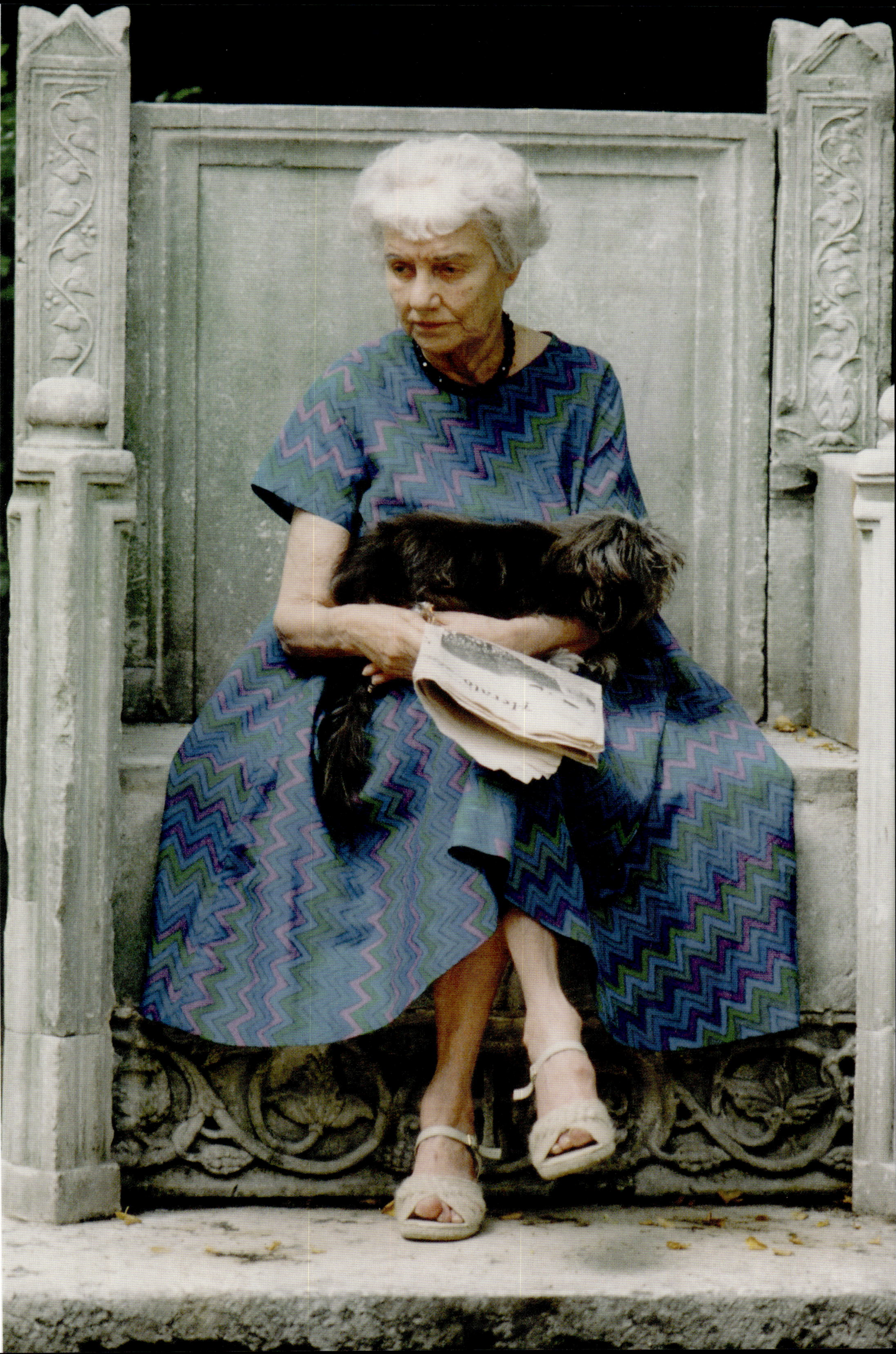

Peggy on her throne, and next to her a sculpture by Takis (Signal, 1958). Immersed in thought, with her beloved Lhasa Apsos Sir Herbert on her lap.

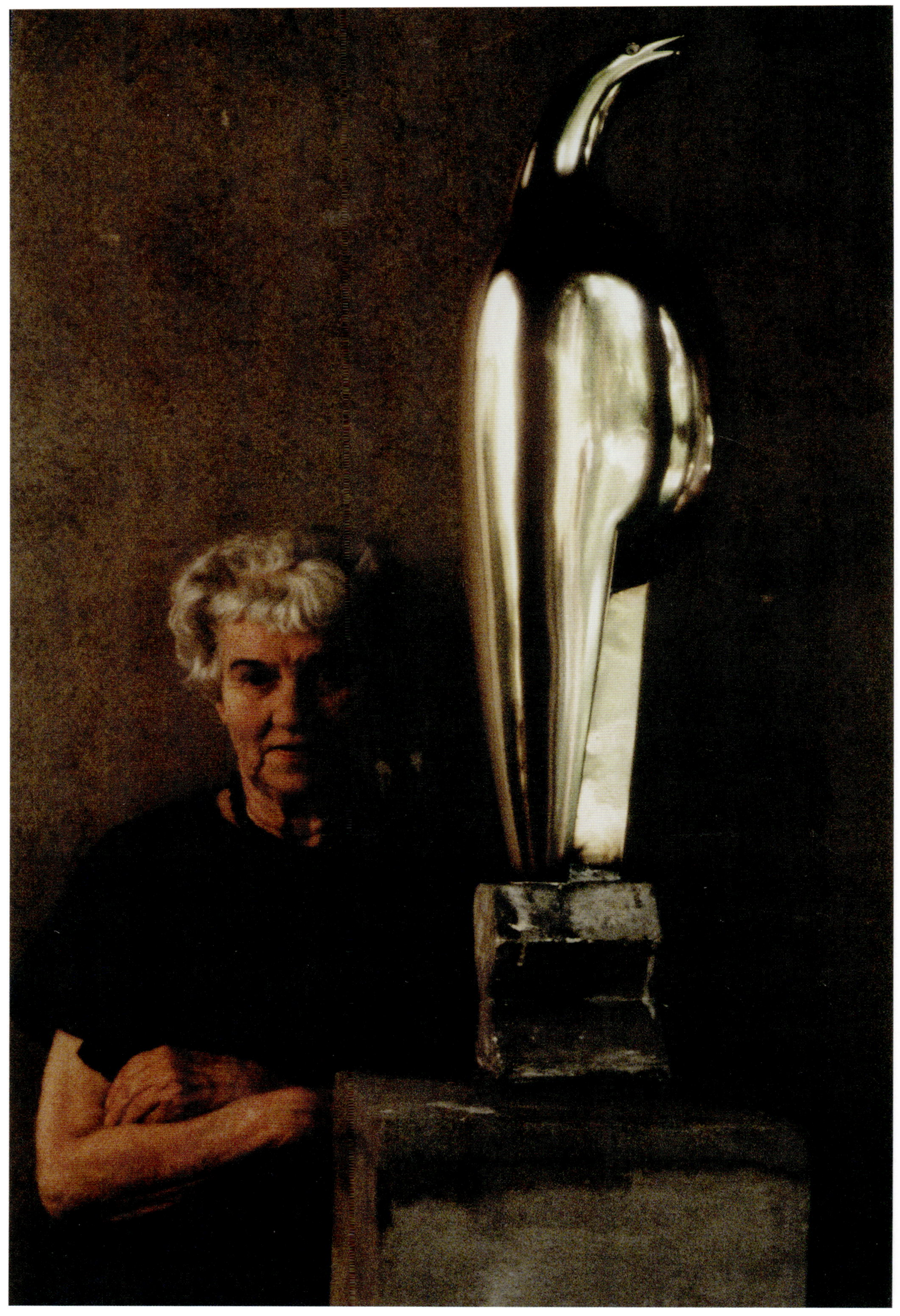

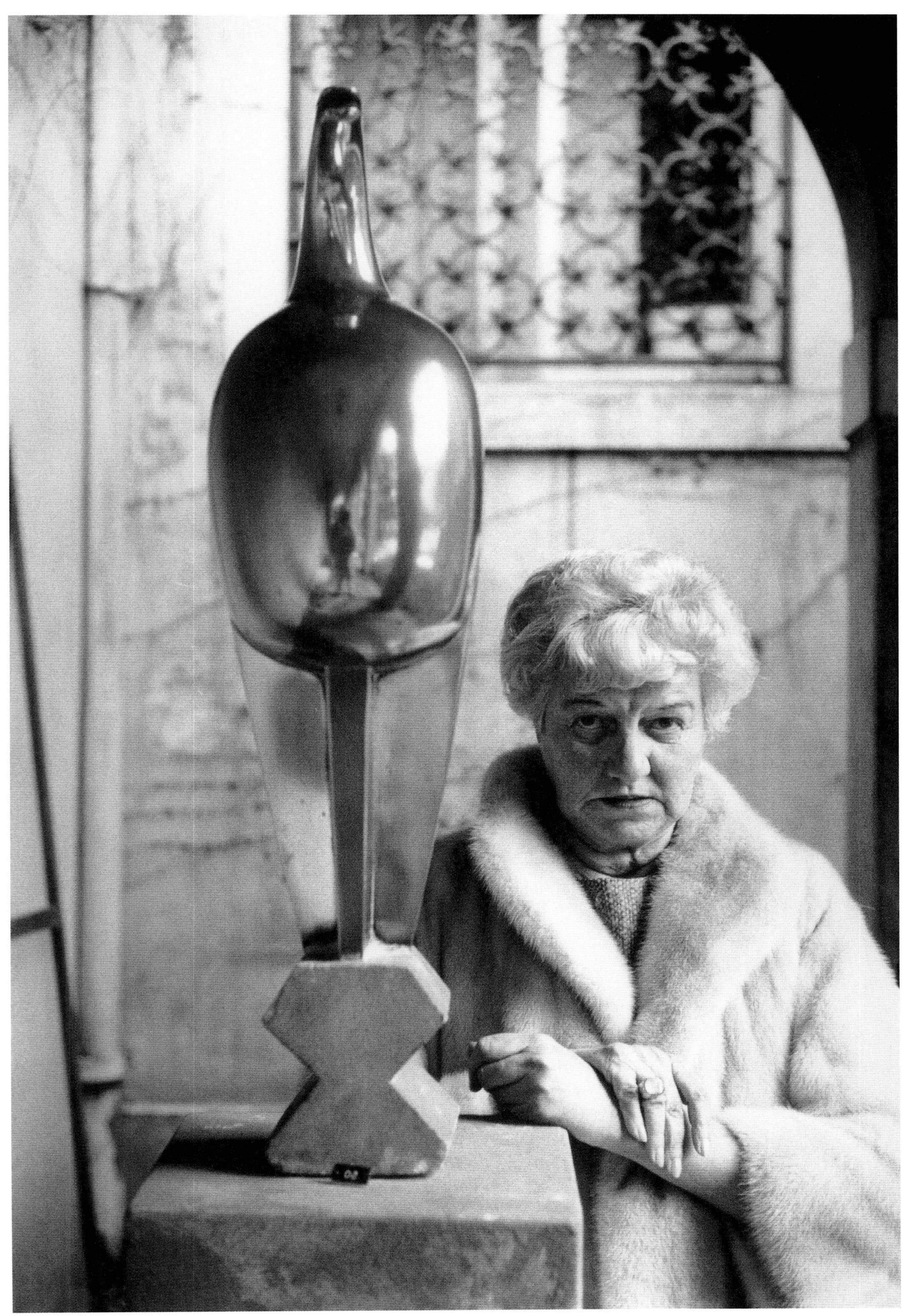

Peggy in the loggia of her barchessa next to *Maiastra* (1911) by Constantin Brâncuși.

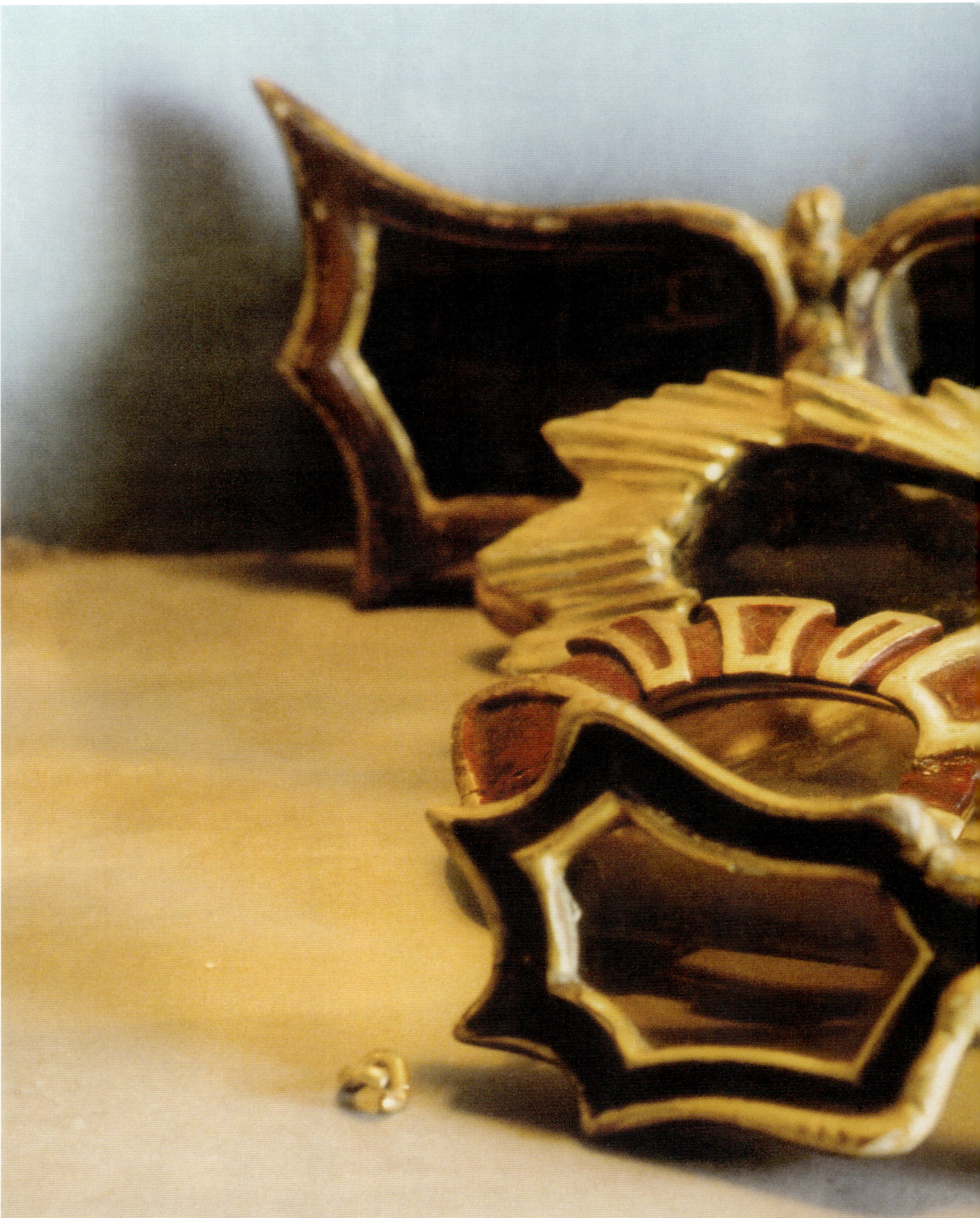

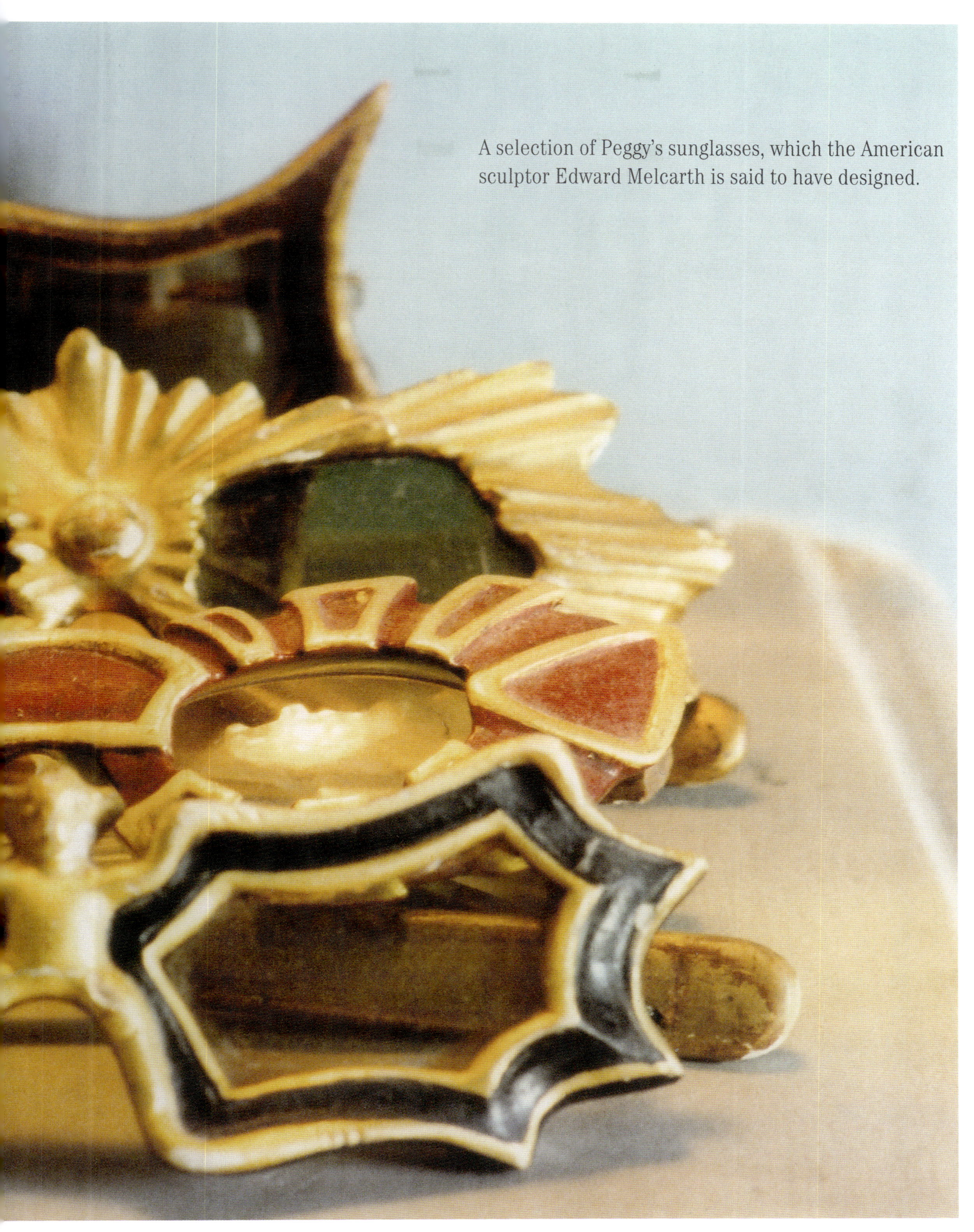

A selection of Peggy's sunglasses, which the American sculptor Edward Melcarth is said to have designed.

The publisher would like to thank the following artists, agencies, galleries and organisations for their kind permission to reproduce the photographs and artworks in this book.

© Man Ray Trust/ADAGP, Paris and DACS, London 2018.
Pages 17 left and 114.

Photo Gisèle Freund/IMEC/Fonds MCC.
Page 17 right.

© 2018 Estate of André Kertész/Higher Pictures
Page 18 left.

Berenice Abbott/Getty Images.
Page 18 right.

© The Estate of Alberto Giacometti (Fondation Annette et Alberto Giacometti, Paris and ADAGP, Paris), licensed in the UK by ACS and DACS, London 2018 / © 2018 Calder Foundation, New York/DACS London 2018.
Pages 46-47 and 128-129.

© ADAGP, Paris and DACS, London 2018.
Pages 46-47, 56-57, 61, 69, 70, 71, 84, 85, 86, 90, 91, 92, 94, 95, 96, 100, 101, 106, 107, 116-117 and 136 below.

© Succession Picasso/DACS, London 2018.
Pages 57, 58, 80, 81 and 82-83

© Günther Uecker. All rights reserved. DACS 2018.
Page 68.

© DACS 2017. 2018.
Pages 76, 77 above, 77 below, 78-79 and 108.

© 2018 Calder Foundation, New York/DACS London 2018.
Page 80.

© ARS, NY and DACS, London 2018.
Pages 93, 95 and 97.

© Successió Miró/ADAGP, Paris and DACS London 2018.
Pages 93 and 95.

© DACS 2018.
Page 94.

Chagall ® / © ADAGP, Paris and DACS, London 2018.
Page 94.

© The Pollock-Krasner Foundation ARS, NY and DACS, London 2018. Page 114.

© Succession Brancusi - All rights reserved. ADAGP, Paris and DACS, London 2018.
Pages 125, 138 and 139.

© 2018 Calder Foundation, New York/DACS London 2018.
Pages 126-127.

Grace Hartigan Ireland, 1958.  Oil on canvas. The Solomon R. Guggenheim Foundation, Peggy Guggenheim Collection, Venice, 1976.
Pages 134-5.

Every effort has been made to race the copyright holders. We apologise in advance for any unintentional omissions and would be pleased to insert the appropriate acknowledgement in any subsequent publication.

First published by © 2017 Elisabeth Sandmann Verlag GmbH, Munich
This English language edition published in 2018 by Hardie Grant Books, an imprint of Hardie Grant Publishing

Hardie Grant Books (London)
5th & 6th Floors
52–54 Southwark Street
London SE1 1UN

Hardie Grant Books (Melbourne)
Building 1, 658 Church Street
Richmond, Victoria 3121

hardiegrantbooks.com



British Library Cataloguing-in-Publication Data. A catalogue record for this book is available from the British Library.

Encounters with Peggy Guggenheim by Stefan Moses

ISBN 978-1-78488-187-0

Photography: stefan moses
Text: Thomas Elsen
Translation of text, preface and image captions: Ursula Held
Proofreading: Regina Carstensen
Design: stefan moses and Roland Hepp
Lithography, printing and binding: EBS

For the English hardback edition:

Publisher: Kate Pollard
Commissioning Editor: Kajal Mistry
Senior Editor: Molly Ahuja
Publishing Assistant: Eila Purvis
Translation: William Sleath
Typesetting: David Meikle
Editor: Lisa Pendreigh

Colour Reproduction by p2d
Printed and bound in China by 1010